Issues in Public Health

Understanding Public Health

Series editors: Nick Black and Rosalind Raine, London School of Hygiene & Tropical Medicine

Throughout the world, recognition of the importance of public health to sustainable, safe and healthy societies is growing. The achievements of public health in nineteenth-century Europe were for much of the twentieth century overshadowed by advances in personal care, in particular in hospital care. Now, with the dawning of a new century, there is increasing understanding of the inevitable limits of individual health care and of the need to complement such services with effective public health strategies. Major improvements in people's health will come from controlling communicable diseases, eradicating environmental hazards, improving people's diets and enhancing the availability and quality of effective health care. To achieve this, every country needs a cadre of knowledgeable public health practitioners with social, political and organizational skills to lead and bring about changes at international, national and local levels.

This is one of a series of 20 books that provides a foundation for those wishing to join in and contribute to the twenty-first-century regeneration of public health, helping to put the concerns and perspectives of public health at the heart of policy-making and service provision. While each book stands alone, together they provide a comprehensive account of the three main aims of public health: protecting the public from environmental hazards, improving the health of the public and ensuring high quality health services are available to all. Some of the books focus on methods, others on key topics. They have been written by staff at the London School of Hygiene & Tropical Medicine with considerable experience of teaching public health to students from low, middle and high income countries. Much of the material has been developed and tested with postgraduate students both in face-to-face teaching and through distance learning.

The books are designed for self-directed learning. Each chapter has explicit learning objectives, key terms are highlighted and the text contains many activities to enable the reader to test their own understanding of the ideas and material covered. Written in a clear and accessible style, the series will be essential reading for students taking postgraduate courses in public health and will also be of interest to public health practitioners and policy-makers.

Titles in the series

Analytical models for decision making: Colin Sanderson and Reinhold Gruen
Controlling communicable disease: Norman Noah
Economic analysis for management and policy: Stephen Jan, Lilani Kumaranayake, Jenny Roberts, Kara Hanson and Kate Archibald
Economic evaluation: Julia Fox-Rushby and John Cairns (eds)
Environmental epidemiology: Paul Wilkinson (ed)
Environment, health and sustainable development: Megan Landon
Environmental health policy: David Ball
Financial management in health services: Reinhold Gruen and Anne Howarth
Global change and health: Kelley Lee and Jeff Collin (eds)
Health care evaluation: Sarah Smith, Don Sinclair, Rosalind Raine and Barnaby Reeves
Health promotion practice: Maggie Davies, Wendy Macdowall and Chris Bonell (eds)
Health promotion theory: Maggie Davies and Wendy Macdowall (eds)
Introduction to epidemiology: Lucianne Bailey, Katerina Vardulaki, Julia Langham and Daniel Chandramohan
Introduction to health economics: David Wonderling, Reinhold Gruen and Nick Black
Issues in public health: Joceline Pomerleau and Martin McKee (eds)
Making health policy: Kent Buse, Nicholas Mays and Gill Walt
Managing health services: Nick Goodwin, Reinhold Gruen and Valerie Iles
Medical anthropology: Robert Pool and Wenzel Geissler
Principles of social research: Judith Green and John Browne (eds)
Understanding health services: Nick Black and Reinhold Gruen

Issues in Public Health

Edited by Joceline Pomerleau and Martin McKee

Open University Press

Open University Press
McGraw-Hill Education
McGraw-Hill House
Shoppenhangers Road
Maidenhead
Berkshire
England
SL6 2QL

email: enquiries@openup.co.uk
world wide web: www.openup.co.uk

and Two Penn Plaza, New York, NY 10121-2289, USA

First published 2005

A catalogue record of this book is available from the British Library

ISBN–10: 0 335 218 369
ISBN–13: 978 0335 218363

Library of Congress Cataloging-in-Publication Data
CIP data applied for

Typeset by RefineCatch Limited, Bungay, Suffolk
Printed in the UK by Bell & Bain Ltd, Glasgow

Contents

Acknowledgments

Open University Press and the London School of Hygiene and Tropical Medicine have made every effort to obtain permission from copyright holders to reproduce material in this book and to acknowledge these sources correctly. Any omissions brought to our attention will be remedied in future editions.

We would like to express our grateful thanks to the following copyright holders for granting permission to reproduce material in this book.

p. 47–49	EM Andreev, M McKee and VM Shkolinkov, 'Healthy expectancy in the Russian Federation: A new perspective on the health divide in Europe', *Bulletin of the World Health Organization*, 2003, 81(11):778–789, with permission from World Health Organization.
p. 114–116	R Beaglehole, 'Global cardiovascular disease prevention: time to get serious', *The Lancet*, 2001, 358:661–663. Reprinted with permission from Elsevier.
p. 11–13	R Beaglehole and R Bonita, 'Public health at the crossroads: which way forward?', *The Lancet*, 1998, 351:590–592. Reprinted with permission from Elsevier.
p. 99–101	R Bhopal, 'Is research into ethnicity and health racist, unsound, or important science?', *BMJ*, 1997, 317:1751, reproduced with permission from the BMJ Publishing Group
p. 19–21	S Chapman, 'Advocacy in public health: roles and challenges', *International Journal of Epidemiology*, 2001, 30:1226–32, by permission of Oxford University Press.
p. 203–205	CB Ebbeling et al, 'Childhood obesity: public-health crisis, common sense cure', *The Lancet*, 2002, 360:473–482. Reprinted with permission from Elsevier.
p. 57–58	Ezzati M et al, 'Selected major risk factors and global and regional burden or disease', *The Lancet*, 2002, 360:1347–60. Reprinted with permission from Elsevier.
p. 162–164	Farmer P, Social inequalities and emerging infectious diseases. *Emerging Infectious Diseases*, 1996. Available from http://www.cdc.gov/ncidod/eid/vol2no4/farmer.htm
p. 166–168	MR Gasner, JD Khin Lay Maw, MPH Gabriel, et al, 'The use of legal action in New York City to ensure treatment of tuberculosis', *NEJM*, 1999, 340:359–366 © 1999 Massachusetts Medical Society. All rights reserved.
p. 168–169	AK Hurtig, JDH Porter and JA Ogdent, 'Tuberculosis control and directly observed therapy from the public health/human rights perspective', *The International Journal of Tuberculosis and Lung Disease*, 3(7):553–560. Official Journal of the International Union Against Tuberculosis and Lung Disease (The Union) © The Union.
p. 175	Adapted version of figure 3.1 (p.45) from "Tobacco Control in Developing Countries" edited by Jha, P & Chaloupka, F. J. (2000). By permission of Oxford University Press.
p. 89	GA Kaplan, ER Pamuk, JW Lynch, RD Cohen and JL Balfour, 'Inequality in income and mortality in the United States: analysis of mortality and potential pathways', *BMJ*, 1996, 312:999–1003, reproduced with permission from the BMJ Publishing Group.

p. 117–122	Reprinted from *Health Policy*, vol. 46, I Koupilova, M McKee and J Holèík, 'Neonatal mortality in the Czech Republic during the transition', pp43–52, 1997, with permission from Elsevier.
p. 179	AD Lopez, NE Collishaw, T Piha, 'A descriptive model of the cigarette epidemic in developed countries', *Tobacco Control*, 1994, 3:242–247, reproduced with permission from the BMJ Publishing Group.
p. 91–94, 96–97	J Lynch, G Davey Smith, M Hillmeier et al, 'Income inequality, the psychosocial environment, and health: comparisons of wealthy nations', *The Lancet*, 2001, 358:194–200, reprinted with permission from Elsevier.
p. 50–51	CD Mathers, 'Towards valid and comparable measurement of population health', *Bulletin of the World Health Organization*, 2003, 81(11): 787–788, by permission of World Health Organization.
p. 107	T McKeown, The role of medicine: mirage or nemesis?, 1979, Blackwell Publishers, reprinted with permission from Princeton University Press.
p. 14–16	KJ Rothman, HO Adami and D Trichopoulos, 'Should the mission of epidemiology include the eradication of poverty?', *The Lancet*, 352:810–813. Reprinted with permission from Elsevier.
p. 165–166	KA Sepkowitz, 'How contagious is tuberculosis?', *Clinical Infectious Disease*, 1996, 23:954–62, © 1996 by The University of Chicago Press. All rights reserved.
p. 38	European Health for All Database website, http://www.euro.who.int/hfadb, by permission of World Health Organization.
p. 181	Tobacco or Health: A Global Status Report, 1997, World Health Organization, by permission of the World Health Organization.
p. 112–114	S Yusuf, 'Two decades of progress in preventing vascular disease', *The Lancet*, 2002, 360:2–3, reprinted with permission from Elsevier.

Overview of the book

Introduction

This book is designed for students who want to answer the question 'What is public health?'. It thus focuses on those things that societies do collectively to enhance the health of populations. This, as you will see by going through the book, includes a lot of different things, many of which you may never have thought of as public health. For one thing, it includes health care. However, you will not learn here about the interaction between the health professional and the individual patient. Instead, the book looks at how societies organize health care to make it accessible to all, and it discusses the nature of the care that is provided to ensure that the health system actually does things that will benefit people.

The book also discusses big issues. Take smoking, for example. Of course societies want to make sure that children are taught that smoking is bad for them. But it is not possible to be so naïve as to think this is enough. Much of modern public health is about tackling strong vested interests head on – in this case the transnational tobacco industries, but in other cases the food or alcohol industries. So if you want to be serious about reducing smoking, you need to know your enemy and know what it is they don't want us to do.

The book also discusses the importance of empowering people, so they can make healthy decisions. Public health actions should bring opportunities and, as importantly, hope.

Finally, the book confronts explicitly the political nature of public health. Much disease has its origins in the way that we organize our society, in deciding how much income to redistribute, how resources such as education, transport and housing should be provided, and who pays for what. Anyone who doubts the association between deprivation and ill health should read Charles Dickens' accounts of the working classes in nineteenth-century England. The political question is what to do about the situation we find ourselves in.

Why study public health?

If a society is to achieve these things, it needs skills and vision. Skills, so that it can make problems that are invisible visible, and skills to design interventions that work, not just for the average person, but also for those who are far from average, especially those who are at the bottom of the pile. Many of those who are worst off in society are effectively invisible. They are the people who clean the streets before we wake, the people who labour in sweat shops to allow us to eat low-cost junk food and to wear cheap clothes. Society does not see them, nor does it see their health needs. But even among the better off, people like us who are visible, rather like looking at the dots on an impressionist painting, health professionals may be too close to see the big picture. Unless you look at the level of a population, you may miss a large rise or fall in deaths from a particular disease.

Skills are also needed to know what works, and in what circumstances. It is important to understand the often complex determinants of disease. Take alcohol and deaths from injuries, for example. We may need to know why people drink, why they get drunk, why they injure themselves when they are drunk, why no-one helps them, and why, when they get to a health care facility, it is unable to provide them with effective care. Which of these is most important will depend on the circumstances, as will how we intervene to reduce deaths, but understanding what has gone wrong is a first, essential, step.

But skills are not enough. One also needs a vision of what the future can be. Effective public health practitioners cannot be complacent. Just because things have always been the way they are does not mean that they cannot change. This means that it is important to think laterally, understanding why things are as they are, who benefits from the status quo and who might benefit from change, what are the power structures on which our societies are based and the mechanisms by which they might change, who is really in charge and what can we do to influence them.

Public health is often seen as unexciting, even boring; in many places it is done by people who do not get out of their offices enough and who, as a consequence, are largely irrelevant to events in the real world. In some places this is a fair reflection of what happens. But it is hoped that this book will convince you that this is not the case everywhere and where public health is working it is exciting, challenging, controversial and certainly never boring!

Structure of the book

This book follows the conceptual outline of the 'Issues in Public Health' unit at the London School of Hygiene and Tropical Medicine (LSHTM). It is based on the materials presented in the lectures and seminars of the taught course, which have been adapted for distance learning.

The book is divided into two sections. The first section looks at the foundation of public health and at a series of themes that underpin public health. The second section turns to a series of specific determinants of health among the most important causes of avoidable disease globally. Inevitably, choices had to be made as it is not possible to cover everything in the time available. For example, apart from some general discussion of firearms injuries in the first session, injuries and violence are not covered. Illicit drugs, sexual health, or mental health are not covered either. All of these, and many others, are important, but it is hoped that the basic concepts that will be drawn on will provide you with the tools to understand how you might intervene to reduce the burden of disease caused by these and other factors.

The two sections, and the ten chapters within them, are shown on the book's contents page. Each chapter includes:

- an overview
- a list of learning objectives

- a list of key terms
- a range of activities
- feedback on the activities
- a summary.

It is important to point out that most examples in this book are drawn from industrialized and middle-income countries, but the principles involved apply more generally and some examples are also chosen from developing countries.

The following description of the book will give you an idea of what you will be studying.

Foundation of modern public health

This section discusses what modern public health is. The first chapter traces the historical evolution of the public health movement and at how it influences our current perception of public health and of its goals. Chapters 2 to 5 then look at a series of themes that underpin public health. These include the use of basic data on populations and mortality (Chapter 2), the methods used to estimate the burden of disease and to assess the factors that contribute to it (Chapter 3), the extent to which health care contributes, or fails to contribute, to population health (Chapter 5), and how to determine the effects on health of policies in other sectors such as transport or the environment (Chapter 6). The final theme involves looking beyond average levels of health in a population to understand how they differ within populations. Why are some people, most often the poor, less healthy than others, and what can we do about it (Chapter 4)?

Major determinants of health

The second part of the book turns to a series of specific determinants of health. Chapter 7 discusses the evolution of infectious diseases and of their control, and describes the burden of disease attributable to infectious diseases and the factors that can affect it. Tobacco use, as a major public health issue worldwide, is then explored in Chapter 8. The health impact of tobacco use and the four-stage model of the smoking epidemic are first described. Then, current debates around tobacco control policies and options for these policies are examined, as well as how globalization represents a new challenge for tobacco control. Chapter 9 discusses the historical development of thinking on nutrition and health. It examines what room for manoeuvre there is within public policy and its lever. Finally, the health and environmental impacts of waste disposal activities, including landfill and incineration, are discussed in Chapter 10, as well as the potential health effects of indoor air pollution.

A variety of activities are employed to help your understanding and learning of the topics and ideas covered. These include:

- reflection on your own knowledge and experience
- questions based on reading key articles or relevant research papers
- outlining short policy papers.

Acknowledgement

The authors would like to acknowledge the contribution of Professor Sian Griffiths, University of Oxford, for reviewing the book. They would also like to thank Deirdre Byrne for her administrative and editorial guidance.

SECTION 1

Foundation of modern public health

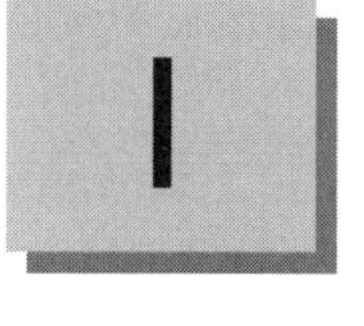

The emergence of public health and the centrality of values

Overview

In this chapter you will learn about the historical development of the public health movement. You will be introduced to some key documents that paved the way of the current public health movement and learn that public health scientists do not all share the same views about where public health should go.

Learning objectives

After completing this chapter you will be able to:

- **describe the evolution of ideas on the role of public health**
- **discuss the arguments for and against societal interventions to promote health**
- **describe the scope to use advocacy to promote health and the limitations to doing so**

Key terms

Intersectoral action for health The promotion of health through the involvement of actors in other sectors, such as transport, housing, or education.

Libertarianism Philosophical approach that favours individualism, with a free-market economic policy and non-intervention by government.

Public health The science and art of promoting health and preventing disease through the organized efforts of society.

Historical development of public health

The development of public health started in the eighteenth century with the *sanitary movement*. The concept of contagion was key to this early development, whether from disease (cholera) or ideas (communism). Then, as now, policies were often motivated as much by self-interest as by altruism. The appalling conditions in the newly industrializing cities demanded a response but there was intense debate about what to do. Many of the discussions at the time resonate with contemporary ones about the balance between the role of the individual, with the feckless poor having only themselves to blame, and that of the state in protecting them from danger and enabling them to make healthy choices. Again, the contemporary relevance of the debates will become apparent, in particular when we reflect on the concerns voiced by the employers of the time about the unfairness of the burdens being placed upon them to improve the conditions of their workers.

We then move on to the rise of what was called *preventive medicine*. This emerged in the middle of the twentieth century, coinciding with the rise of scientific medicine and optimism about its potential achievements. It was characterized by its focus on the concept of hygiene (not just in relation to infectious diseases but, in some countries in the 1930s taking a rather less innocuous form with its emphasis on genetic or racial hygiene, with profound implications for the ability to undertake collective health interventions in the countries concerned even now). Health professionals knew best and played a key role. Education (especially when undertaken by doctors or nurses) was thought sufficient to change behaviour and much disease was avoidable by means of mass activities such as screening.

Later in the twentieth century, new ideas began to emerge, rejecting the dominance of the medical model. In 1974 the Canadian Government published the 'Lalonde Report', which proposed the *health field concept* (Figure 1.1).

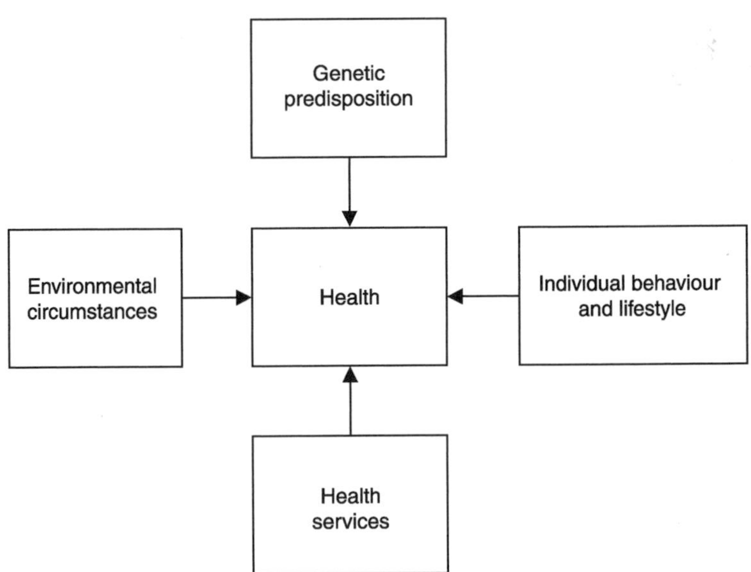

Figure 1.1 The health field concept

This report signalled the beginning of a move away from the medicalization of public health towards one that emphasized the building of *healthy public policy*. Now there was a focus on intersectoral action, working with sectors such as housing, transport, education and others, enshrined in the World Health Organization's

'Health for All by the Year 2000' (HFA) movement. These principles were then set out in the Ottawa Charter in 1986, which called for the following approaches:

- building healthy public policy
- creating supportive environments
- strengthening community actions
- developing personal skills
- reorienting health services
- demonstrating commitment to health promotion

The HFA programme emphasized intersectoral action and, somewhat controversially at the time, the importance of certain pre-requisites for health, such as peace and equity. In Europe it was developed into a set of 38 targets. However, many of these were rather vague and unquantified, and of those that were quantified, some countries had already achieved them by the time they were published, while others had little chance of reaching them before the end of the century. In addition, while all European governments signed up to the idea of HFA, few went any further to actually do anything about it. Even when they did initiate health policies, there was rarely any reference to HFA.

Yet HFA was effective in catalysing action at local level, as public health advocates used the fact that their governments had endorsed it to support initiatives such as the 'Healthy Cities' movement, in which local administrations developed wide-ranging programmes to improve health, working through policies on transport, housing and education.

By the mid-1990s, when it became clear that health for all would not be achieved by the year 2000, the World Health Organization (WHO) policy strategy was renewed, leading to 'Health 21'. It has a more limited set of targets but, like HFA, it has received relatively little attention.

At the same time, however, a new issue had emerged that was seen, by many, to link closely with issues of health. Concerns about the global environment had forced governments to come together at the Rio Earth Summit. One of the outcomes of that meeting was 'Agenda 21', a plan for sustainable development. Many people who had been working to improve health locally, implementing intersectoral responses, saw this as a process that they could link with. As a consequence, in many localities there is now a close association between those seeking to enhance health and those working for a sustainable environment.

In contrast, the commitment to improving health by national governments is less obvious. Some countries have developed health strategies but many are aspirational, providing little basis for concrete policies. We also have to take account of the fact that different countries have different models of public health that reflect their politics, the evolution of their health care systems, their economic situations, and above all their histories.

But why do we need to know all of this, you might ask? What possible relevance, at the beginning of the twenty-first century, has the historical development of public health for us? Apart from the obvious, that we can always learn from the mistakes of the past, there are two main reasons. One is that, in many countries, what is called public health has still to emerge from the model adopted in the 1950s and before, telling people what they should and should not do with little understanding of why they do things that will harm them. A second is that it helps us to understand that public health has always had an important political dimension. It is quite explicitly not value free. Its commonly used definitions talk about the organized actions of society. This assumes an acceptance that society, and not just a collection of individuals, actually exists. And it assumes that it is justifiable to

constrain the freedom of one individual to benefit the population as a whole. Indeed, a public health intervention may mean more than constraining someone's freedom to do something. It may mean actively doing something to them, such as immunizing them against disease, fortifying food with vitamins, or adding fluoride to drinking water.

Activity 1.1

Some people object to this vision of public health. Briefly describe the reasons why this might be the case.

Feedback

Some people take a very different view for various reasons. For example, Peter Skrabanek, who worked in an academic department of public health in Dublin, argued vehemently that many public health interventions were unjustified because we simply did not know enough about the determinants of disease and whether what we were proposing would work (Skrabanek and McCormick 1989). He described a whole range of activities, such as advocating a low-fat diet or cancer screening as 'gratuitous intervention'. In particular, he argued that much of our apparent understanding of risk factors for common diseases stems from an inappropriate use of epidemiology, in which we seize on chance associations between risk factors and disease as signifying that the risk factor actually causes the outcome in question.

Bruce Charlton, writing from a libertarian perspective, argued that many public health policies amounted to 'health fascism', imposing a particular lifestyle on others whether they like it or not (Charlton 2001). As noted above, this idea resonates in some countries in Europe where totalitarian regimes in the 1930s were extremely active in, for example, promoting exercise and opposing smoking. George Davey Smith has provided a detailed account of the anti-smoking policies pursued by the Nazis in pre-war Germany (Davey Smith and collaborators 1994). In the UK the concept of the 'nanny state', using the analogy of a nanny telling children what to do, is often invoked by the tabloid press to oppose public health interventions.

Another criticism is that the intersectoral approach that is now a feature of public health is a form of 'health imperialism', with 'health' being equated with 'happiness'. Criticism focuses in particular on the WHO definition of health as 'a state of complete physical, mental, and social well-being and not merely the absence of disease or infirmity' (World Health Organization 2003), which is seen as allowing public health professionals to justify their involvement in many issues where they really have no right to be.

Then there is the charge that some forms of public health intervention are patronizing and do not respect the autonomy of the individual. This is especially likely to be levelled in relation to activities such as social marketing, in which techniques traditionally associated with commercial advertising are used to promote healthy messages.

Finally, public health may on rare occasions involve depriving someone of their liberty. In the past this was much more frequent, typically in relation to psychiatric illness or contagious disease. Indeed, in some countries the threshold for detention remains low and, in others, such as the USA, the emphasis on a criminal justice rather than a health response to illicit drugs, means that very large numbers of people (predominantly young male African-Americans) are serving long periods in jail. This raises even more profound issues.

We cannot assume that everyone sees the world in the same way – indeed, some of you may have very different views. And even if we agree on an approach in broad terms we may still have many questions of detail.

Who provides the voice of society? Is it the government? What if they have been bought by powerful vested interests, such as the tobacco or oil industry? Is it our local community leaders, who may understand our concerns better than politicians who only visit us when they need our votes, showing little interest at other times?

What freedoms are we willing to give up for the collective benefit? The right to bear arms? The right to travel at speed on open roads, free from the threat of speed cameras? The right to smoke in public places? What do you think?

Activity 1.2

You will now read extracts from two papers that address some of these questions. The first is by Beaglehole and Bonita (1998) and the second by Rothman and colleagues (1998). These papers set out a quite different vision of the role of epidemiologists in public health and where public health should be going.

Read the extracts and summarize briefly the arguments of both of them. Then, decide which vision you identify with most closely and say why.

Extract from Beaglehole and Bonita (1998)

The discipline of public health

Epidemiology is flourishing, especially clinical epidemiology, but there is a shortage of epidemiologists and the workforce is not representative of the population worldwide served. Epidemiologists have collaborated with laboratory scientists to explore the mechanisms of disease and gene-environment interactions, although the danger is that such collaboration could reduce epidemiology to a mere tool of molecular biology which requires DNA samples from human populations. More importantly, epidemiology focuses on the fundamental social, economic, and cultural determinants of health status. Ecological variations are under investigation and multidisciplinary studies of the effect of the socioeconomic environment on the health of populations may yet inform social policy.

The other disciplines of public health are less well developed. For example, it is difficult to implement the powerful rhetoric of the Ottawa Charter on health promotion, and much health-promotion practice uses an outdated model of health education. Health promotion is further hampered by the privatisation of health care services and the division of 'purchaser' and 'provider' functions. This organisational model diverts attention from the powerful intersectoral determinants of health and discourages cooperation between health sectors. Only a few useful insights are available from attempts to develop intersectoral public health policy, such as work on food and nutrition.

The practice of public health

The key themes in public health practice are recurrent and must be readdressed by each new generation of public health professionals in a dialogue with the populations they serve. Most importantly, the scope and purpose of public health is unresolved. What are the current limits of public health? Should public health professionals be concerned with the fundamentals of health such as employment, housing, transport, food and nutrition, and global trade imperatives, or should attention be restricted to individual risk factors for diseases? A broad focus inevitably leads to involvement in the political process, an arena which is not emphasised in current training; the intersection between public health and democracy demands exploration.

No country has implemented the full range of public health functions. Public health in the USA was described in 1988 as being in 'disarray' in a report by the Institute of Medicine (IOM). The report stimulated programmes to link academic and practising public health communities and to upgrade public health leadership. There has also been progress in the organisation of state health agencies and the public health infrastructure, but there is still little focus on policy development at the state level. Lack of resources at the local level is the main reason for failure to implement the IOM recommendations, and public health agencies remain crippled by the need to provide last-resort medical care. In the UK, the emphasis has been on strengthening public health medicine which is increasingly concerned with the purchase of health services. The rest of the public health workforce is professionally and institutionally fragmented and there is no national focus for public health outside of communicable disease. Academic public health is dominated by public health physicians and is not integrated with operational public health services; there is also a lack of co-ordinated infrastructure for public health functions. Although the Labour government promises to target health inequalities, it will be hard to produce measurable results while continuing to stress the merits of a meagre public purse.

Public health: the way forward

The central challenge for public health practitioners is to articulate and act upon a broad definition of public health which incorporates a multidisciplinary and intersectoral approach to the underlying causes of premature death and disability. Since the value system of public health professionals tends to be egalitarian and supports collective action, it is important to affirm and make explicit these values and to seek public support for them.

A broad focus easily leads to accusations of 'woolly breadth', but this breadth is exactly what public health should be about. The challenge for public health practitioners is to justify and promote global concerns and at the same time proceed with evidence-based, public health programmes that deal with disease-specific factors and more general issues such as health inequalities. By contrast, the competing pathway, and one which increasingly characterises modern public health, is narrowly focused on health services research, evidence-based health care, and the search for new risk factors at the individual level. This activity will improve the effectiveness and efficiency of medical services, but clinical medicine is only a small part of the total public health endeavour.

An initial challenge is to improve worldwide health statistics. Sample sentinel populations are adequate to monitor trends in mortality and morbidity rates and risk factors. WHO should develop basic monitoring systems with electronic communication methods. A fundamental organisational challenge is the relationship between public health and medical-care policy. Public health is the poor cousin to medical care, both in terms of budget and status. Typically, the public health sector receives less than 5 per cent of the total health care budget and, from a policy perspective, is overshadowed by the demands of acute medical-care services and the power of the pharmaceutical industry.

Ideally, the public health sector rather than the medical care sector, should be responsible for population health status and for informing and monitoring all government policy initiatives that affect population-health status. Perhaps a more feasible option is for equality between the interests of public health and medical care through a Minister of Public Health supported by an independent Ministry. WHO is the obvious focal point for worldwide public health leadership, and for the first decades of its existence it has fulfilled this role. The question now is whether WHO can be reformed, after more than a decade of decline, to articulate a broad vision with a focused set of priorities and withstand the increasing encroachment of vested commercial interests in the guise of collaboration. As WHO's leadership has declined, other agencies, particularly the World Bank, have taken up this role often with even less explicit public health imperatives.

At the local level there is much to be gained by a closer relationship between the practitioners of public health and the society they serve. The ideology of individual responsibility and reliance on market forces must be challenged to develop strong and enduring partnerships between public health practitioners and communities, and to rekindle a commitment to sharing the benefits of national wealth. A global deregulated economy is unlikely to provide the appropriate basis for a fair and ecologically sustainable world.

There is justification for optimism. The opportunity exists for public health considerations to become central to the role of the World Trade Organisation. The revision of the health-for-all strategy includes a firm commitment to reduce poverty and its effects on health. The World Bank has recognised the need for a strong and effective state in the process of social and economic development. The next important step is to reduce Third World debt and reverse the negative effects of structural readjustment programmes. There is potential for the development of a constructive partnership between the World Bank and WHO.

Although the past 20 years have seen a stagnation in income growth in many regions, the eradication of absolute poverty, the most important priority for human development, is a feasible goal. Health professionals have a particular responsibility to exert pressure on national governments and the World Bank to support policies to reduce poverty and oppose those that increase it. Public health education for much of the world is a welcome development and public health-leadership programmes are under development. The positive impact of environmental activists on the health of communities and positive connections between academic and practical public health are promising. These developments will encourage the empowerment of local communities, a necessary step in the rejuvenation of public health. If public health becomes more broadly focused, the health outlook will be better for all.

Extract from Rothman and colleagues (1998)

Accusation 1: epidemiology is too individualistic

As with other biomedical sciences, epidemiology yields practical knowledge. Many applications can be carried out directly by individuals. For example, information about the risks of having unprotected sex can persuade people to change their sexual behaviour, and information about the risks of smoking can motivate smokers to give up their habit. These actions are, to some extent at least, personal choices, which public health programmes can influence through educational materials, as they have done through campaigns on smoking and health.

Other epidemiological knowledge, however, cannot be easily applied without actions at societal level. Thus, smallpox could not have been eradicated without a clever, global strategy to contain it, and malnutrition rooted in poverty cannot be prevented without societal interventions that ease the burden of poverty or that address malnutrition directly.

The distinction between individual and societal applications of epidemiological knowledge are at the core of the new wave of criticism. The central complaint is that epidemiologists have focused on individual risk factors to the exclusion of broader societal causes of disease.

Pearce, one of the harshest critics of epidemiologists, portrays this slant as a personal and political choice (Pearce 1996). In his view, it is not so much the lure of science as an end in itself that has swivelled epidemiologists to a biomedical orientation; rather it is a tide of political conservatism and a personal indifference to the health problems of others that account for the new direction in epidemiology. According to Pearce, epidemiologists are so self-indulgent that they prefer to study 'decontextualised individual risk factors' instead of 'upstream' causes of health problems, such as poverty . . .

Accusation 2: epidemiologists need more moral and political fibre

Critics contend that epidemiologists have a greater responsibility than merely to study the causal role in human health of factors such as poverty or tobacco consumption. In their view, epidemiologists must also strive to eradicate the upstream causes of health problems. For example, if epidemiological research indicates that poverty causes malnutrition, which in turn causes infant death, the epidemiologist's responsibility is to work towards the elimination of poverty. This activity requires the lumbering apparatus of social and political forces to be set in motion – something that most epidemiologists have been loath to attempt. Critics claim that today's epidemiologists lack the moral resolve and political fire to complete their professional mission.

In short, some critics believe that epidemiologists of today lack a firm commitment to public health. Instead, claim the critics, they fritter away their professional time by studying scientific minutiae at the expense of urgent public health problems.

Knowledge before action, or 'Ready, Fire, Aim'?

There is no denying that epidemiologists have progressively concentrated on the details of causal mechanisms. The only surprise to us is that anyone would regard this preoccupation with causal mechanisms as a problem. In past decades, epidemiologists could be criticised for studying mostly superficial relations between exposure and disease occurrence. Now the field is maturing, along with other biological sciences, and such superficiality is gradually being replaced with clearer insights into causal pathways. Whereas epidemiologists once studied factors such as dietary-fat consumption and total serum cholesterol, they have now progressed to classifying dietary fat by chemical structure – by comparison of low to high lipoprotein ratios – and are moving on to assessing the protective effect of antioxidants on fat-induced endothelial impairment.

Is the preoccupation with causal mechanisms as detrimental as critics allege? – Not if reasonable knowledge of causation is deemed a sensible antecedent to intervention. If the moral purpose of epidemiology is to alleviate the human burden of disease, the primary task of epidemiologists should be to acquire insight into the causal chain, starting from root causes and continuing up through the beginnings of the disease itself. True, we do not necessarily need to know every detail about the pathway between intervention point and outcome; we can infer the effects of interventions even with gaps in understanding. Knowledge is never perfect, and action is often indicated in the face of substantial uncertainty. Public health professionals, however, do not have a license to tinker promiscuously with society. Public health programmes may be conceived and implemented with great hope and yet turn out to be useless, or even damaging. One and a half centuries after Snow's work on cholera, the public health threat from the disease lingers, as research continues into how pathogenicity of the *Vibrio* organism depends on the El Niño Southern Oscillation, and how cholera may spread between continents through ocean currents. For cholera, as for other diseases, the more knowledge we acquire of causal pathways at all points – from the most 'fundamental' or 'ultimate' social, political, and economic determinants to the molecular and biochemical determinants most proximal to disease occurrence – the better the foundation we lay for any effective public health action.

To observe, for example, that in regions where poverty is rife, a given disease occurs at a greater rate than in areas not affected by poverty, is surely not enough. Epidemiologists have been preoccupied with methodology mainly because they understand that such comparisons are often affected by innumerable biases that can lead to false inferences. Their preoccupation with methods is the inevitable evolutionary consequence of their drive to understand the causes of disease in the natural human environment – rather than in the laboratory cage or the petri dish. The same kind of concern that makes epidemiologists wary of ecological comparisons impels them to carry out randomised trials when experiments are ethical and feasible.

When is intervention most effective?

Generally, the further upstream we move from the occurence of disease towards root causes, the less secure our inferences about the causal path to disease become. Even if our inference is correct, moreover, intervention with respect to upstream causes may be less efficient and therefore less effective than intervention closer to disease occurrence. Consider the causal path: poverty to malnutrition to infection to death. Control of infection at the level of the human individual may be the most efficient way to prevent death in this causal chain. True, if control of infection does not address the malnutrition underlying the infection, the infection is likely to recur; one might therefore reasonably look upstream to address the malnutrition problem. Nevertheless, if we attempt to combat malnutrition without also dealing with the concomitant infections, many people will die needlessly. Furthermore, there may be little that an epidemiologist can do in the short term to overcome malnutrition as a population problem. To awaken the public or political authorities to the problem of malnutrition and to redirect societal resources may eventually do the trick, but public health accomplishments mediated through social changes are won slowly. In the meantime, through their study of risk factors at the individual level and by the use of randomised trials, epidemiologists have discovered that vitamin-A supplements can prevent serious morbidity and many deaths in malnourished children. This knowledge will save lives, despite the fact that it does not alleviate gross malnutrition, does not require manipulation of any upstream cause, and is obtained from the type of epidemiological work that critics of epidemiology disparage.

What is the public health solution to the poverty problem?

The ultimate step in the preceding intervention scenario is to eliminate the poverty that causes the malnutrition. The critics urge that we take this step. It requires deep societal involvement in a laudable public health end – one that any humane person would embrace. Yet, it is only fair to ask whether epidemiologists have the means to eradicate poverty. Is poverty eradication a public health programme? How exactly should it be accomplished? Economists would seem the most likely candidates to supply the answer, which might go something like – 'Let markets be free to expand without guiding them too firmly'. But other economists might give a different answer. Do the critics of epidemiology suggest that epidemiologists should lobby against international trade barriers, or in favour of them, in the pursuit of their public health objectives? Perhaps the critics believe that epidemiologists should second-guess economists and attempt to eradicate poverty using their own epidemiological model.

All poverty is unacceptable

We agree wholeheartedly that the study of the social causes of disease is an important epidemiological goal, and that societal causes can explain much of the variation in disease occurrence. We abhor tobacco promotion and production. We would like to see the eradication of poverty, and agree that epidemiologists should be well educated with regard to their public health role.

Nevertheless, the importance of societal causes of disease does not mean that biological pathways to disease should be ignored, or that epidemiologists who choose to study causal mechanisms have been neglecting their mission. Furthermore, as with any public health professionals who share humanist values, epidemiologists do not need to establish the health effects of poverty to know that society should aim to eliminate it. Today's critics of epidemiology use health as an argument for social ends – such as the eradication of poverty – the desirability of which is obvious and quite independent of their public health consequences.

Perhaps the most valuable message in this new criticism of epidemiology is simply that those who wish to ease the burden of disease should not forget that the people of the world often bear larger burdens than those we sometimes choose to study. Nevertheless, epidemiologists cannot be expected to solve every problem, especially not those beyond our expertise.

Epidemiologists are not social engineers; they are public health scientists who have a right to specialise as they see fit. They should be free to choose the subject of their inquiries, whether it be social causes or molecular causes of disease.

It is remarkable that epidemiologists are now chastised for their scientific accomplishments, which include such victories as the elaboration of the effects of tobacco smoking on many diseases, and the effect of folic acid on neural-tube defects. Countless other fragments of useful epidemiological knowledge, such as the benefits of breast milk over infant formula, have enabled many people to improve their health even if they could not avoid poverty and repression. If an astrophysicist can study the origin of the universe without apology, should an epidemiologist have to apologise for work that is so practical?

Feedback

Summary of the arguments of both papers:

Beaglehole and Bonita argue that public health should take a multidisciplinary and intersectoral approach to dealing with health problems worldwide and that this would involve public health scientists becoming increasingly concerned with the political process. They suggest that public health measures should be global in perspective, and that epidemiology should focus on the fundamental social, economic and cultural forces affecting individual behaviour and health status. They argue that public health should proceed with evidence-based, public health programmes that deal with disease-specific factors and more general issues such as health inequalities, rather than adopting a narrow focus on activities such as health services research and evidence based health care, or – a main criticism of epidemiology – on the search for new risk factors at the individual level. They suggest that the public health sector rather than the medical-care sector should be responsible for population health, and that there should be a closer relationship between public health practitioners and the society they serve.

Although Rothman and colleagues agree that the study of the social causes of disease is an important epidemiological goal and that social inequalities should be eliminated within and between countries, they believe that the work of epidemiology in acquiring insight into the specific causes of diseases is essential to lay a good foundation for effective public health actions. They argue that epidemiologists are not social engineers or economists, but public health scientists who have the right to specialize. They also suggest that because public health accomplishments mediated through social changes are won slowly, epidemiologists help in the meantime to gain significant knowledge that can help save lives (for example, vitamin A supplementation to save the lives of malnourished children) although not resolving global upstream causes such as malnutrition or poverty.

Factors that might have influenced your choice:

There is, of course, no good or wrong answer in this exercise and various factors might have influenced your choice in deciding which vision you identify most closely with. One of them is probably the type of work that you are doing. For example, if you are involved in more methodological epidemiological work investigating disease causation, you probably identify more closely to the views of Rothman and colleagues. Conversely, if you are closely involved in public health policy and political processes, your views might then be closer to those of Beaglehole and Bonita. Undoubtedly, both visions offer advantages and are important to the future of improved public health and better health worldwide.

Gun control: a tale of two countries

Activity 1.3

You will now perform a series of activities related to gun control as a public health issue.

In March 1996 a man walked into a school in Dunblane, Scotland, armed with an assortment of high power handguns. He made his way to the gym hall and opened fire on a class full of 4- and 5-year-old children, killing 16 children and their teacher. Then he turned one of his own weapons on himself. One year later the British government imposed a comprehensive ban on the private ownership of handguns.

Also in 1996, in Port Arthur, Tasmania, a man armed with semi-automatic weapons walked into a café and killed 35 people. Soon afterwards, the Australian government introduced a ban on semi-automatic rifles and pump action shotguns, a national gun registration scheme, and a buy-back programme to reduce the number of weapons in circulation.

In April 1999 two pupils in Columbine, Colorado, walked into their school armed with a sawn-off shotgun, a semi-automatic rifle, a handgun and a selection of grenades. Within a few minutes they had killed 13 of their fellow students and teachers before shooting themselves. Although there had been four other multiple shootings in American schools in the preceding two years, the legislative response was essentially limited to additional funding for ballistics testing and media campaigns. Controls on gun ownership were seen as a non-starter.

In 1998, handguns were used to murder 51 people in New Zealand, 54 people in Australia, 19 in Japan, 54 in Great Britain, 151 in Canada, 373 in Germany and 11,215 in the United States.

Use the following resources to acquaint yourself with the background to the three events and the arguments for and against gun control in the USA.

- You can read about the Columbine shooting and the responses to it on various websites including: http://news.bbc.co.uk/hi/english/world/americas/newsid_324000/324995.stm (British Broadcasting Corporation Online Network 1999)
- Details of the Dunblane shooting and responses to it can also be found on several websites including: http://www.dvc.org.uk/~johnny/dunblane/ (Dunblane Massacre Resource Page 2005)
- You can read about the Port Arthur shooting in an internet article from Bellamy (2005) and on different websites
- For further reading on the issues surrounding gun control in the US see documents from the National Rifle Association (2005), a powerful and well financed organisation lobbying against gun control in any form, and from The Brady Campaign to Prevent Gun Violence (2005), an organization dedicated to gun control and named after Jim Brady, press secretary to President Ronald Reagan, who was shot and seriously wounded during an assassination attempt on President Reagan.
- For another perspective on advocacy in relation to gun control, you may want to view the film *Bowling for Columbine*, directed by Michael Moore (2002).

Now answer the following questions:

1. In your opinion, should gun control be a public health issue? Why do you take this view?
2. The US Centres for Disease Control (CDC) has been criticized by some American politicians for becoming involved in this issue, especially when there are much more important matters to deal with. What criteria might an organization such as CDC adopt when deciding what to focus its efforts on?

Feedback

1 This is a matter for you as an individual. The purpose of this exercise is to allow you to reflect on why to hold the view you do, and to consider why others may take a different view.

2 Criteria that might be considered include:

- the current burden of disease attributable to the issue in question (how much death and disability does easy availability of guns cause?)
- the scope for preventing this burden (will gun control be effective in reducing deaths and disability?)
- the future consequences of failing to act (this is especially relevant with infectious disease where the current burden may be small but the scope for spread great (for example, the early stages of the AIDS epidemic))
- the cost of acting (in many areas of life states decide that the cost of intervening to save a life is too high, although the implied value of a life varies widely – for example being prepared to spend enormous sums to reduce a death in a plane or train crash but much less to prevent a death on the road)
- the feasibility of acting (this is something to consider. What are the obstacles to action and what are the opportunities? Who are the stakeholders, what are their positions, and how might they be influenced?)
- where you sit in the spectrum between extreme libertarianism (the role of the state should be as small as possible) and collective action

Activity 1.4

Now read the following extract of an article by Simon Chapman (2001) which discusses how the public health community in Australia responded to the Port Arthur massacre. Do you believe that Chapman is justified in what he proposes, or should public health limit itself to identifying that a problem exists and leave others to do something about it?

Case 1: Gun control

On 26 April 1996, at Port Arthur, Tasmania, a man with no criminal or psychiatric record and using semi-automatic military style weapons killed 35 and injured 18 people, the largest death toll ever recorded in peace time involving a single gunman. Starting with the massacre, the decade before had seen 101 people killed in 11 incidents in Australia where four or more people were shot, often with rapid fire semi-automatic weapons. Following the Hungerford and Dunblane massacres in the UK, and a steady news diet of gun massacres from the US, a 'tipping point' appeared to have been reached and the Australian government moved quickly to ban private possession of semi-automatic rifles and pump action shot guns, to introduce national gun registration and require all gun owners to demonstrate legitimate purpose for owning a gun (target shooting and hunting, but not self-defence). The law reform package included a time-limited gun buy-back for semi-automatic weapons funded from levy on personal income tax that raised $A500 million (£180.9m) to compensate gun owners for the full market price of their now banned weapons. As there was no national gun registration or shooter licensing scheme, there were no national data on the number of individuals who owned the proscribed category of guns, nor on the number of guns they owned. However, the gun lobby, the police and gun control advocates all agreed that it was likely there were well over a million semi-automatic weapons in the community. In all, 640 401 guns were surrendered from an adult population of about 14.8 million leaving an unknown number of illegal guns in circulation.

Massacres and sieges generally require rapid fire weapons to effect large-scale killing and to keep police at bay. By removing this huge number of such guns from the community the hope was that such incidents would reduce. In the 63 months since the massacre, not one such incident has occurred. As each month passes, the view that the gun law reforms made Australia a safer nation gains increasing support.

In the 65 months prior to the massacre, and in the months between the incident and the implementation of the laws, huge advocacy efforts were mounted by those both promoting and opposed to the tougher gun laws. With hundreds of thousands of angered shooters marching in city streets, the gun lobby sought to frame the proposed laws as unjust and dangerous using several stock arguments. Here, I will discuss two of these: the (correct) claim that the overwhelming number of gun owners were law abiding, had not and would not represent any danger to the community; and the argument that Australia's gun death rate was insufficiently high to warrant restrictions on the liberty of these law abiding shooters. The gun lobby also argued – incorrectly – that the perpetrators of these mass shooting incidents were either mad (had records of mental illness) or bad (those with criminal records) and that both groups were incapable or unwilling to be law-abiding. In fact, the majority of perpetrators had been hitherto 'law-abiding citizens'. In summary, those resisting the gun laws argued that the probability of any gun owner running amok was infinitesimally small and that therefore the government 'gun grab' was like using a sledgehammer to crack a walnut and besmirched the character of law-abiding shooters by implying they were not to be trusted with these guns.

The gun lobby spent much energy on creatively demonstrating that gun deaths were uncommon next to dozens of other preventable causes that claimed far more lives, and that government priorities in allegedly seeking to make the community safer were therefore capricious and driven by wider political agenda bound up with notions of shooters being somehow inherently suspect citizens. 'When so many problems that claimed more lives and effected more people existed, why was the government devoting such attention to gun controls' they argued. They argued that the solution to reducing gun violence like Port Arthur lay in greater vigilance by doctors and police in identifying those at risk of future gun violence. Psychiatrists and general practitioners repeatedly denounced this as naïve folly.

While the number of gun owners and guns was not known, they were both indisputably high. Equally indisputable, was that the average (typically male) gun owner would never use his gun maliciously, and that there was very poor ability to predict those who would. Just as random breath testing and airport security checks assume that all citizens are of equal risk to the community, reducing gun violence required population-wide solutions which would inevitably involve restrictions and impositions on a large number of entirely law-abiding citizens. For many shooters, these impositions were never going to be acceptable and so gun control continues as a highly contested issue.

This case illustrates a core challenge for advocacy. The momentum for action of the advocacy campaign for gun control did not depend on any central calculus determined by multi-disciplinary teams of health economists, epidemiologists and biostatisticians showing from league tables that this was a priority issue when measured against all other health issues. As with many low probability risks, such a calculation would have relegated gun control to low priority, which gun control advocates argued would allow US style gun culture to steadily foment in the absence of far-sighted political will to prevent it developing in Australia. The preventive theme of 'not going down the American road' became the single most expressed reference point to justify the new laws. This drew on a kind of lay epidemiological understanding that a nation with a high rate of gun ownership and minimalist gun laws was more likely to have a high rate of gun violence than one where guns were less accessible. Claims that US states with 'right to carry' gun laws had lower rates of gun homicide than those which did not were dismissed by analogy that this was like arguing that wartime Rwanda was safer than Kosovo.

For gun control advocates, the principal challenge became one of framing the debate to ensure the public outrage at these massacres was maintained and translated into law reform before the community's memory faded. A principal objective became one of defining the solution to the problem as one involving gun control, rather than the gun lobby's preferred option of high-risk individual policies based on their dichotomy of 'good' and 'bad' gun owners ('Guns don't kill people. People kill people').

Much of the impetus for gun control rested with promoting the common-sense premise that citizens with malicious intent armed with rapid semi-automatic firepower could kill many people quickly. The question for society was whether it was sensible to allow virtually open access to these, or as with restrictions on civilian access to armoured vehicles, dynamite, anti-aircraft and anti-tank weapons, rapid fire weapons should be framed as antisocial. The answer to such a question will always be finally resolved by value judgements, not epidemiology. For example, the gun lobby referred to occasional massacres as the unfortunate 'blood price' that a gun-owning community needed to pay to defend its right to bear arms. The overwhelming support for the new laws by Australians showed that such a price, while rare, was deemed unacceptable. The contested nature of gun control advocacy will thus always lie beyond epidemiological resolution.

Feedback

Again, this is an issue to reflect on where you stand personally. Do you see public health as playing a major role in advocacy or do you see this as something that should be done by others.

Activity 1.5

Imagine that you are a political adviser to the health minister of a country of your choice in which guns are widely available. Your minister thinks that a stance on this issue should be taken, on grounds of public health, but his/her colleagues believe it has nothing to do with him/her. Describe the arguments that you would use in a briefing for her putting the case for this being a legitimate health concern.

Feedback

The main arguments you might make centre around the burden of disease (access to guns are as important a cause of avoidable death and disability as other risks about which it is widely agreed that public health has a role), the scope for prevention (gun control works), and that this is a legitimate area for the state to get involved (no government allows its citizens freely to purchase biological or nuclear weapons so why conventional weapons unless they have a very good reason).

Burden of disease:

- Firearms cause many premature deaths and much disability by their direct effects
- You should compare the burden from firearms with that from other causes (for example, road traffic injuries), perhaps expressing it in terms that can be visualized (for example, equivalent to x jumbo jets crashing each week)

Scope for prevention:

- Evidence that reducing access to guns reduces burden of disease
- There is evidence that the presence of a gun in a house increases the risk of the accidental death of its occupants
- Although removing guns will not necessarily reduce crime, it may reduce its consequences (it is difficult to kill 10 to 15 people at one go with a knife)

Role of the state:

You should give examples of where the state has acted in other areas to constrain individuals' rights to benefit them and society (for example, seatbelts, drink driving).

Summary

This chapter discussed the historical development of public health. It described how ideas on the role of public health have changed since the eighteenth century, and described some key international documents on the role of public health. It also discussed the arguments for and against societal interventions to promote health.

References

Beaglehole R and Bonita R (1998) Public health at the crossroads: which way forward? *The Lancet* **351**: 590–2.

Bellamy P (2005) The Port Arthur massacre: a killer among us. New York: Crime Library (available at: http://www.crimelibrary.com/notorious_murders/mass/bryant/index_1.html, last visited 2 February 2005).

Brady Campaign to Prevent Gun Violence (2005) *Fact sheets*. Washington, DC: The Brady Campaign to Prevent Gun Violence (available at http://www.bradycampaign.org/facts/factsheets, last visited 2 February 2005).

British Broadcasting Corporation Online Network (1999) World: Americas Denver killing: special report. London: British Broadcasting Corporation (available at http://news.bbc.co.uk/hi/english/world/americas/newsid_324000/324995.stm, last visited 2 February 2005).

Chapman S (2001) Advocacy in public health: roles and challenges. *Int J Epidemiol* **30**: 1226–32.

Charlton B (2001) Personal Freedom or Public Health? in M Marinker (ed.) (2001) *Medicine and Humanity*. London: King's Fund, pp. 55–69.

Davey Smith G, Strobele SA and Egger M (1994) Smoking and health promotion in Nazi Germany. *J Epidemiol Community Health* **48**: 220–3.

Dunblane massacre resource page (2005) (available at http://www.dvc.org.uk/~johnny/dunblane/, last visited 2 February 2005).

Moore M (director) (2002) *Bowling for Columbine*. Film produced by Moore M, Glynn K, Czarnecki J; Bishop C (II), Donovan M, Bishop C.

National Rifle Association (2005) *Fables, Myths and Other Tall Tales about Gun Laws, Crime and Constitutional Rights*. Fairfax, Virginia: National Rifle Association Institute for Legislative Action (available at http://www.nraila.org/media/misc/fables.htm, last visited 2 February 2005)

Pearce N (1996) Traditional epidemiology, modern epidemiology, and public health. *Am J Public Health* **86**: 678–83.

Rothman KJ, Adami HO and Trichopoulos D (1998) Should the mission of epidemiology include the eradication of poverty? *The Lancet* **352**, 810–13.

Skrabanek P and McCormick J (1989) *Follies and Fallacies in Medicine*. Glasgow: Tarragon Press.

World Health Organization (2003) WHO definition of health from the Preamble to the Constitution of the World Health Organization as adopted by the International Health Conference, New York, 19–22 June, 1946; signed on 22 July 1946 by the representatives of 61 States (Official Records of the World Health Organization, no. 2, p. 100) and entered into force on 7 April 1948. Geneva: World Health Organization.

Further reading

Marinker M (ed.) (2002) *Health Targets in Europe: Polity, Progress and Promise*. London: BMJ Publications. In this book, Marshall Marinker has brought together a group of writers from across Europe to review the experience of national and regional health strategies. Chapter 13, entitled 'Values, beliefs and implications', provides an overview of the values underpinning health systems in Europe, contrasting them with those in the USA.

2 Data on populations and mortality

Overview

This chapter discusses the building blocks of public health, that is, the data on populations and mortality. You will learn about where you can find such data and how you can combine them to describe a population's health and compare it with the health of other populations. You will also become familiar with different international sources of information on health.

Learning objectives

By the end of this chapter you should be able to:

- **describe the main sources of data on populations and mortality, and discuss their strengths and weaknesses**
- **know where to obtain data on populations and mortality**
- **interpret commonly used indicators of population health, such as age-standardized death rates and life expectancy**

Key terms

Age-standardization Way of controlling for age so that we can compare rates of deaths or disease in populations with different age structures.

Life expectancy The average number of years a person can expect to live on average in a given population.

Understanding the health of a population: data on deaths and populations

In public health, we want to understand what is happening to a population's health over time. There are several potential sources of information that can be used to do this. For example, one might think of using data on admissions to hospital, or use of health services. Unfortunately, these tell us very little about disease burden. Instead, they tell us about those who have a disease and then, for whatever reason, use health care facilities (at least those that we have information about – a problem in many health care systems with mixed systems of provision). Specifically, they tell us nothing about those people who may have disease or disability but do not seek care. For this reason, the following paragraphs will focus on the basic factors that can help one understand a population's health: deaths and population at risk.

How many people, and why are they dying?

Mortality data are a fundamental source of information on the health of a population. Because of their generally widespread availability and timeliness, they are widely used to describe and monitor major public health issues, including the progression (and decline) of chronic diseases, the emergence of recent threats to health such as HIV/AIDS, or the evaluation of public health interventions.

In order to be able to interpret mortality data you need two types of information. First, and most obviously, you need to know how many deaths have occurred, among whom, and from what. Second, and often forgotten, you need to know the composition of the population.

How many people are dying?

Vital registration of death exists in about 70 countries worldwide. In a few others, such as India and China, there are sentinel surveillance systems covering some parts of the population. Death certification is often based on a standard certificate on which the age, sex and cause of death of the deceased is recorded along with various other pieces of information (for example, gender, age, marital status, occupation, educational achievement, income, address, and so on) which vary from country to country. In some countries, the section describing the cause of death has to be completed by a doctor, or, if the death happened as a result of an accident, suicide or homicide, by the police or a coroner.

Cause of death is recorded using a classification developed by the World Health Organization, the International Classification of Disease (ICD). This classification is regularly updated to take account of changing patterns of disease, such as the emergence of AIDS. Most countries changed to the tenth revision of the ICD in the late 1990s, having used the ninth revision from about 1979. The ICD is divided into a series of chapters, such as II for 'Neoplasms' or IV for 'Endocrine, nutritional and metabolic diseases'. In the tenth revision each individual disease is given a unique alpha numeric code. For example, cancer of the stomach is C16, which can be subdivided to give more precise localization (C16.2 is cancer of the body of the stomach).

Clearly, many people die from a combination of disease processes and death certificates generally provide space for multiple causes (this is particularly important for older people who are more likely to have multiple causes of death). However, summary statistics usually report a single cause, which is selected according to standardized procedures that aim to identify the 'underlying cause of death'. In those countries where it is possible to obtain data with multiple causes of death, the scope for analysis is clearly increased.

While death registration data are generally more complete and reliable than many routine sources of morbidity data, several issues need to be taken into account when interpreting cause of death data. Diagnosis is inevitably an inexact science and comparison of causes of death certificates with those determined by autopsy often find disagreements. One reason is that, especially in patients presenting with advanced disease, it may not be considered appropriate to undertake invasive investigation just to confirm a diagnosis when there is no prospect of cure. Another issue is the effort put into attributing cause of death by the certifying doctor. Systematic differences have also been noted in the choice of diagnosis given by a physician depending on the social class of the patient or the gender of patient and doctor. A further problem arises when deaths are compared between countries, or compared over time where they may span more than one revision of the ICD. There are, however, bridging tables to inform comparisons over time.

In developing and middle-income countries, where vital registration systems are often poorly developed, it may be possible to get information from surveys. The most widely used example is the series of Demography and Health Surveys (DHS) that are conducted every few years in many countries. They are, however, limited in their coverage to childhood and maternal events.

How many people are there in the population?

Although knowing about the numbers of deaths from different causes is essential to assessing a population's health, they have very little meaning in themselves. They only become useful when divided by the number of persons in the population.

The most common method used to find out how many people there are in a population is the census. Censuses have been conducted throughout recorded history, often for military or tax purposes. However, systematic modern censuses have their origins in Western Europe in the nineteenth century. Typically undertaken every ten years, they now usually include information on age, sex, marital status, employment and a varying selection of other factors.

Carrying out a census is an enormous undertaking. For this reason, there are still many countries throughout the world where there have been no censuses, or ones covering only urban populations, for several decades. The only country never to have conducted a census is Chad. On the other hand, a few advanced industrialized countries, such as the Netherlands and Germany, have abandoned censuses. This is because they have population registers (for example, requiring everyone to register with local government when they move house). These countries are thus obtaining information on their population from the continually updated population and other registers rather than from censuses.

In an increasingly mobile world, the challenges of undertaking censuses are growing and censuses can rapidly become out of date. In some cases, certain population subgroups are especially difficult to reach. For example, in the 1991 British census it was estimated that a million people were missed. In some parts of the country, such as inner London, the figures are thought to be especially high. Censuses are also susceptible to misreporting by respondents. In particular, the elderly tend to overstate their age, divorced men tend to report that they are single (never married), and all people tend to inflate their socioeconomic status. In addition, especially at older ages, there is a tendency to give one's age to the nearest five years, causing the phenomenon known as 'heaping' (Figure 2.1). For these reasons, especially when undertaking analyses involving small populations, it is necessary to take care when interpreting results.

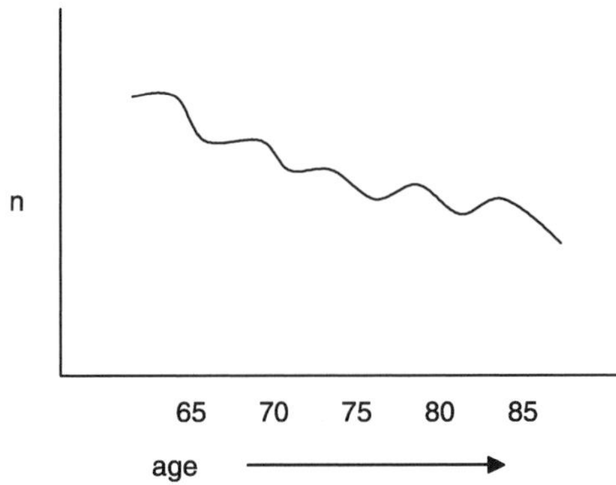

Figure 2.1 Heaping

From numbers to rates

Now, let's assume that you have gathered information on the numbers of deaths (overall and by cause) and on the population at risk. It is then possible to combine them to obtain rates. Table 2.1 gives several standard definitions used when reporting mortality data – you should become familiar with them.

Table 2.1 Standard definitions used to report mortality data

$$\text{Crude death rate} = \frac{\text{number of deaths}}{\text{mid year population}} \times 1000$$

$$\text{Cause specific mortality rate} = \frac{\text{deaths by cause x}}{\text{mid year population}} \times 1000$$

$$\text{Age specific mortality rate} = \frac{\text{deaths to persons aged x}}{\text{mid year population of persons aged x}} \times 1000$$

$$\text{Infant mortality rate} = \frac{\text{number of deaths to infants aged} < 1 \text{ year in year x}}{\text{number of live births in year x}} \times 1000$$

The infant mortality rate can also be subdivided into neonatal mortality (deaths of live born infants in the first 4 weeks) and post neonatal mortality (from 4 to 52 weeks).

$$\text{Perinatal mortality rate} = \frac{\text{stillbirths + deaths under 1 week}}{\text{stillbirths and live births}} \times 1000$$

In calculating a rate it is essential that the numerator (the top line – the events or conditions of concern) and the denominator (the bottom line – the population at risk) match. In other words, anyone who could be included in the numerator should also appear in the denominator. But this creates more problems than you might at first think. For example, death rates in a town could be inflated by deaths of people who come from surrounding areas to die in hospital, unless their death is traced back to their area of residence, where they would normally have been recorded in the last census.

The scope for analysis of death rates is almost limitless. You can analyse them for all causes combined or for specific causes, for males and females separately, for people living in different parts of a country, and for different age groups. If you are able to break down the data on population and deaths in the same way, for example by social class or ethnicity, you can explore inequalities in health (although caution is needed – see Chapter 4). Imaginative use of data, for example tracking changes in age-specific death rates, can provide many valuable insights into the health of populations (for example, the dramatic changes in mortality rates that occurred in Russia since the mid-1980s affecting predominantly young and middle-aged men and driven by deaths from injuries and cardiovascular disease).

Activity 2.1

You can find in Table 2.2 the number of deaths from cancer of the lung and bronchus that occurred in England and Wales in 2002 in individuals aged 25 to 94 years. Data are stratified by gender and 10-year age group. Table 2.3 gives the mid-year population estimates for England and Wales, as at 30 June 2002, by sex and age. Look at the data carefully and then answer the two questions that follow.

Table 2.2 Number of deaths from cancer of the lung and bronchus by sex and age in England and Wales, 2002

	Age (years)						
	25–34	35–44	45–54	55–64	65–74	75–84	85–94
Males	6	132	884	3 101	5 799	5 935	1 522
Females	14	110	668	1 753	3 367	4 116	1 249

Table 2.3 Estimated resident population (in thousands) for England and Wales, 2002

	Age (years)						
	25–34	35–44	45–54	55–64	65–74	75–84	85–94
Males	3 679.3	3 932.7	3 350.5	2 859.5	2 065.4	1 200.2	285.0
Females	3 681.8	3 994.2	3 409.0	2 939.1	2 324.0	1 783.7	727.5

1 Using data from Table 2.2, comment on the sex and age distribution of deaths from this tumour.
2 Using data from Tables 2.2 and 2.3, calculate age-specific mortality rates from lung and bronchus cancer. Comment on the sex differences in mortality rates from this tumour.

Feedback

1 In each sex, we can see that the number of lung/bronchus cancer deaths increases with age up to ages 75 to 84, decreasing at ages 85 to 94. There were more lung cancer deaths in men than in women except at ages 25 to 34. However, nothing can be said about sex and age differences in mortality from this cancer without taking into account the number of persons at risk in each sex and age group.

2 Using the formula described in Table 2.1, we can calculated sex- and age-specific death rates for cancer of the lung and bronchus. Let's calculate, for example, death rate for males aged 45 to 54 years:

Number of deaths in males aged 45–54 in 2002 = 884
Estimated population of males aged 45–54 at mid-2002 = 3350500
Death rate in males aged 45–54 = 884/3350500
= 0.00026384 per person-year
= 26,38 per 100,000 person-year

You should have obtained the following rates for each sex- and age-group (Table 2.4).

Table 2.4 Sex- and age-specific death rates (per 100,000) from cancer of the lung and bronchus in England and Wales, 2002

	Age (years)						
	25–34	35–44	45–54	55–64	65–74	75–84	85–94
Males	0.16	3.36	26.38	108.45	280.77	494.50	534.04
Females	0.38	2.75	19.60	59.64	144.88	230.76	171.68

The results confirm a general increase in risk with age. However, in males there was no decline in risk at ages 85 to 94. This means that the decline in the number of deaths in males at these ages was just a reflection of the decrease in the number of persons at risk.

Death rates were higher in males than in females in all age groups except at ages 25 to 34. The sex differences might be due to differences in survival or differences in incidence between males and females.

Age-standardized rates

Most rates such as death rates or disease rates are influenced by age. For example, the probability of death falls after the first year of life but increases again relatively steeply with increasing age, especially from middle age onwards. For many purposes, comparison of age-specific mortality rates may be appropriate. However, let's say that you were to compare total mortality between two points in time in one population or two different populations. In that case, using the crude mortality rate may be quite misleading if the underlying age structure differs in the populations being compared (for example, with one population having a higher proportion of elderly individuals). Thus, a single measure or index that takes account of such differences in age distribution will be more appropriate. This can be achieved by the process of **age-adjustment** or **age-standardization**. There are several techniques to control for age but the more common ones include *direct* and *indirect* standardization. We will describe both below.

But first, let's take an example that illustrates this problem. At the top of Figure 2.2, you can see crude mortality rates per 100,000 persons (population) for men and women. The graph suggests that rates are quite similar for the two sexes and while those for men seemed to have fallen over time, those for women remained relatively stable. At the bottom of Figure 2.2 you can see the same data, now adjusted for differences in the age structure. This shows that not only have death rates declined for both men and women but importantly, for women rates have consistently been much lower than those for men. This is because the female population has a higher proportion of elderly people than the male population and consequently a higher number of deaths.

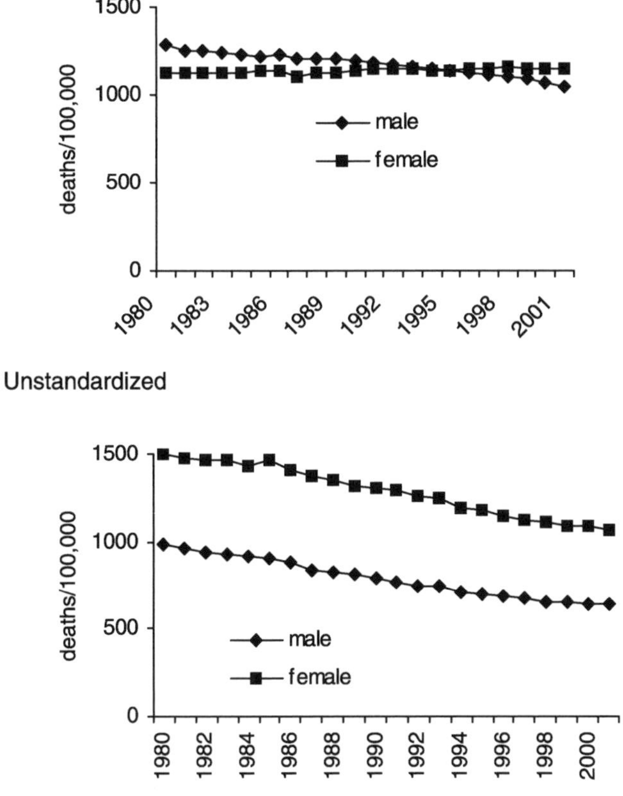

Figure 2.2 The effect of age-standardization

Direct age-standardization

For the **direct** method of age-standardization, you need two sources of information. First, you need age-specific mortality rates from the population you are interested in. Second, you need a defined standard population with a known age structure (number of persons in each age category). The direct method relates the observed age-specific mortality rates to the standard population by means of weighing the age-specific mortality rates according to the age structure of the standard population. This gives you the so-called **age-standardized mortality or death rate (SDR)**. It represents what the crude death rate would have been if the population under study had the same age distribution as the standard population. In Table 2.5 you can find an example of how the direct method of standardization can be used to compare mortality rates between two countries that have different age structures.

Table 2.5 Direct method of standardization – worked example

We have age-specific rates in two countries, Sweden and Panama, and the age structure of a defined standard population.

Age-specific rates in Sweden (per 1,000 person-years)		Age-specific rates in Panama (per 1,000 person-years)	
0–29	1.1	0–29	5.3
30–59	3.6	30–59	5.2
60+	45.7	60+	50.1

Standard population	
0–29	56,000
30–59	33,000
60+	11,000
All ages	100,000

We calculate the number of deaths expected if Sweden and Panama had the same age distribution as the standard population:

(a) Sweden		(b) Panama	
Age	Expected deaths	Age	Expected deaths
0–29	0.0011 × 56,000 = 61.6	0–29	0.0053 × 56,000 = 296.8
30–59	0.0036 × 33,000 = 118.8	30–59	0.0052 × 33,000 = 171.6
60+	0.0457 × 11,000 = 502.7	60+	0.0501 × 11,000 = 551.1
Total	683.1	Total	1,019.5

Age-adjusted rates are obtained by dividing the number of expected deaths by the total person-years at risk in the standard population (we assume one year):

Age-adjusted rate for Sweden	Age-adjusted rate for Panama
= 683.1/100,000	= 1,019.5/100,000
= 6.8 per 1,000 person-year	= 10.2 per 1,000 person-year

In international comparisons the most frequently used (hypothetical) standard populations are the Segi 'world' population and the 'European' standard population (see Table 2.6). The European standard was developed based on the experience of Scandinavian populations, which contained a relatively high proportion of elderly and was judged particularly suitable for comparison with Western Europe. The Segi was based on the experience of 46 countries to represent an intermediate

Table 2.6 Standard populations commonly used

Age group	*Segi world population*	*European standard population*	*WHO world standard**
0–4	12 000	8 000	8 860
5–9	10 000	7 000	8 690
10–14	9 000	7 000	8 600
15–19	9 000	7 000	8 470
20–24	8 000	7 000	8 220
25–29	8 000	7 000	7 930
30–34	6 000	7 000	7 610
35–39	6 000	7 000	7 150
40–44	6 000	7 000	6 590
45–49	6 000	7 000	6 040
50–54	5 000	7 000	5 370
55–59	4 000	6 000	4 550
60–64	4 000	5 000	3 720
65–69	3 000	4 000	2 960
70–74	2 000	3 000	2 210
75–79	1 000	2 000	1 520
80–84	500	1 000	910
85+	500	1 000	630
Sum	100 000	100 000	100 000

* For purposes of comparisons, the WHO world standard age group 85+ is an aggregate of the age groups 85–89, 90–94, 95–99, 100+.

Source: Ahmad and collaborators (undated)

'world' standard between the European standard and a standard with a high proportion of young people (considered appropriate for making comparisons with populations in Africa). A new WHO standard population is currently being discussed. Its age structure has been chosen to better represent the future age structure of the world's population. Mortality rates as given in the WHO Health For All database – which you will be using later in this chapter – are generally standardized to the European standard.

Indirect method of age-standardization

When there is no information on age-specific mortality rates of the population under study, we have to use the **indirect** approach, which applies the age-specific rates of a standard population to the age structure of the population under study, thus just the reverse of the direct method. This method also allows you to calculate the so-called **standardized mortality ratio (SMR)**. The SMR is the ratio (×100) of observed to expected deaths in a study population. Say, for example, you wish to compare mortality in a region with that in the entire country. The expected deaths are estimated by applying the age-specific death rates in the whole country to the population divided into age bands in the local population, and then adding together the expected deaths in each age band to get the total for the population. You can find a worked example in Table 2.7.

Table 2.7 Indirect method of standardization – worked example

A	B	C	D	D/(C× 1,000)
Age	*Deaths in study area*	*Population in study area*	*National death rate (per 1,000 person-years)*	*Expected deaths*
0–9	10	2 000	7	14
10–19	5	3 000	2	6
20–29	7	2 500	2	5
30–39	8	3 500	2	7
Etcetera	. . .	. . .	. . .	. . .
Sum	100			120
SMR = 100/120 × 100 = 88.33[1]				

[1] Allowing for the difference in age distribution in the two populations, the death rate in the study area is lower than in the country as a whole.

Activity 2.2

Table 2.8 gives population sizes (in thousands) and numbers of deaths from all causes by age group in two countries in 2000.

Table 2.8 Population sizes and number of deaths in two countries

Age group	*Country A*		*Country B*	
	Population (in 1000s)	*Deaths*	*Population (in 1000s)*	*Deaths*
0–14	10 472	22 164	9 567	
15–44	18 129	22 616	22 206	
45–54	6 481	37 131	5 756	
55–64	5 322	82 779	5 157	
65–74	3 495	135 474	4 462	
75–84	1 666	161 570	2 787	
85+	297	64 534	784	
Total	45 862	526 268	50 719	564 846

1 Calculate and compare the all-cause crude death rates for Country A and Country B.
2 Calculate a ratio to compare the observed number of deaths in Country B with the number of deaths that would be expected if the age-specific death rates of Country A were applicable. How do you interpret this ratio?

Feedback

1 Crude death rate = total number of deaths/total population in 2000

All-cause crude death rate for Country A = 11.5 per 1000 person-years (526 268/ 45 862 000)

All-cause crude death rate for Country B = 11.1 per 1000 person-years (564846/ 50719000)

The crude rates are relatively similar. However, because we have no information on the age distribution of Country B (and thus whether there are differences in the age structure in the two countries which could lead to confounding), it will be important to calculate age-standardized death rates.

2 To be able to calculate this ratio, we need the following information:

a) The total number of observed deaths in Country B (n = 564846 from above)
b) The age-specific death rates in Country A (used here as the set of standard rates) – these need to be calculated for each age group as follows:

Number of deaths in Country A (2nd column in Table 2.9) divided by estimates of the population for the selected age group in Country A (3rd column in Table 2.9).

The age-specific death rates are expressed as death rate per 1000 person-years ('py') (4th column in Table 2.9)

c) The population distribution by age groups in Country B (5th column in the table below)

As a result, the total number of expected deaths in Country B, using the age-specific death rates of Country A, is equal to the sum over all age categories (last column in Table 2.9).

Table 2.9 Calculation of the number of expected deaths in Country B using age-specific death rates in Country A as the standard rates

Age group	*Deaths in Country A*	*Population (in 1000s) Country A*	*Age-specific death rates per 1000 person-years in Country A (Standard)*[1]	*Population (in 1000s) Country B*	*Deaths expected in Country B using age-specific death rates in Country A as the standard rates*[2]
0–14	22 164	10 472	22164/ 10472 = 2.1	9 567	2.1165 × 9567 = 20249 (or 2.1165/ 1000py × 9567000)
15–44	22 616	18 129	1.2	22 206	27702
45–54	37 131	6 481	5.7	5 756	32977
55–64	82 779	5 322	15.6	5 157	80213
65–74	135 474	3 495	38.8	4 462	172957
75–84	161 570	1 666	97.0	2 787	270286
85+	64 534	297	217.3	784	170352
All ages	526 268	45 862		50 719	20249 + 27702 + 32977 + 80213 + 172957 + 270286 + 170352 = 774736

[1] Death rates included in the table are rounded to one decimal place.
[2] Results presented used 'unrounded' (4 decimal places) death rates for the calculations

The standardized mortality ratio (SMR) = observed number of deaths in Country B/ expected number of deaths in Country B when we apply the age-specific death rates of Country A as the standard = 564846 / 774736 = 0.73 or 73%.

The number of observed deaths is equal to only 73 per cent of the number of deaths that would be expected if, in Country B, the population had experienced the same mortality rates as in Country A. Unfortunately, this ratio could hide differences in age-specific death rates between the countries.

Life expectancy

Another way of looking at the health of a population is to ask how long people can expect to live. Life expectancy, usually reported as life expectancy at birth (although you may come across life expectancy at, for example, age 15 or 45) is a commonly used summary measure based on death rates at a single point in time. Life expectancy is calculated using life tables. You should become familiar with their basic principles, described below.

The basic information used in life tables are age-specific mortality rates. These are applied to a theoretical population of some multiple of 100 (typically 100,000). Starting at birth, the probability of dying in each period is applied to the number of people surviving to the beginning of the period, so that the initial figure slowly reduces to zero. Most of you will never have to calculate a life table, so we will not confuse you by explaining the mathematics involved. If you find that you do need to calculate one, then you can download from the Internet a spreadsheet that will calculate life tables (and which will also allow you to see the calculations involved) (Simple Interactive Statistical Analysis 2004).

An example of a life table is illustrated in Table 2.10. But to interpret the table you need to know certain standard notations:

l_x = number of survivors at age x
${}_nq_x$ = probability of dying between age x and x + n
${}_nD_x$ = number of deaths between age x and x + n
${}_nL_x$ = number of person-years lived between age x and x + n
T_x = total number of person-years lived after age x
e_x = life expectancy at age x.

Thus, in this example, life expectancy at birth is 69.66 years. You should also note that life expectancy at age 1 is slightly longer, at 70.5 years. This reflects the relatively high mortality in the first year of life.

Obviously, a full life table can only be calculated where comprehensive data exist. However, there are a number of model life tables that can be used to fill in gaps where data are incomplete. These are based on what has been observed in countries with different characteristics. Clearly this must be done with caution but it is a commonly used approach in developing countries.

Finally, the principles underlying life tables can also be used in any circumstances where you want to follow up outcomes over time, such as survival after a diagnosis of cancer. It is also possible to undertake more complex analysis. For example, it can be used to identify the causes of and ages at death that account for differences in life expectancy between two populations or a population at two points in time, or to ask what would happen if a particular cause of death was eliminated. But this is beyond the scope of this unit (and is covered in any of the standard demography texts).

Table 2.10 Example of a life table for a fictitious country

Age	l_x	$_nq_x$	$_nD_x$	$_nL_x$	T_x	e_x
0–1	100000	0.02623	2623.38	97638.96	6966171	69.66171
1–4	97377	0.00436	424.13	388471.6	6868532	70.53573
5–9	96952	0.00245	237.74	484120.6	6480060	66.83748
10–14	96715	0.00219	211.84	483086.5	5995939	61.99612
15–19	96503	0.00458	441.61	481565.1	5512853	57.12628
20–24	96061	0.00616	591.59	478798	5031288	52.3758
25–29	95470	0.00652	622.14	475793.2	4552490	47.68517
30–34	94848	0.00800	758.92	472416.5	4076697	42.98156
35–39	94089	0.01159	1090.91	467934.2	3604280	38.30728
40–44	92998	0.01840	1711.60	461052	3136346	33.72497
45–49	91286	0.02902	2648.86	450338.3	2675294	29.30668
50–54	88637	0.04571	4051.67	433665	2224956	25.1018
55–59	84586	0.06577	5563.01	409576.8	1791291	21.17725
60–64	79023	0.10257	8105.13	375660.7	1381714	17.48505
65–69	70917	0.14763	10469.69	329460.1	1006053	14.18625
70–74	60448	0.21472	12979.48	270439.2	676593	11.19302
75–79	47468	0.31103	14764.02	201169.6	406153.8	8.556318
80–84	32704	0.46312	15146.08	124141.6	204984.2	6.267811
85–89	17558	0.61437	10787.24	58126.06	80842.65	4.604269
90–95	6771	0.78812	5336.34	18112.55	22716.59	3.355007
95+	1435		1434.61	4604.041	4604.041	3.209264

Activity 2.3

Why is life expectancy a hypothetical measure?

Feedback

This is because, except in the rare circumstances when a cohort life table is used (which can only be done once everyone in it is dead!) this is based on *current* age-specific death rates in each age group ('period life table'). Thus, it is not a measure of how long someone born now can expect to live.

WHO: the main source of summary statistics on mortality and populations

International data

As you know, the WHO is a very important source of information on the health of populations worldwide. The numerous WHO publications (several of which are directly available from the Internet) provide health providers, researchers, public health scientists, policy makers, and members of the general population with detailed information on all aspects of health and diseases. What some of you might not know, however, is that useful comparative summary statistics are also readily available in table, graph or map formats just a 'click' away if you can access the WHO Internet web site. Indeed, if you go to the WHO website you will be able to choose a country from the list of 192 WHO member states and get various basic demographic and health statistics for that country. These include for example estimates of total population size, gross domestic product (GDP), life expectancy at birth, healthy life expectancy at birth and at age 60, child and adult death rates, and per capita health expenditure. Tables presenting data for all countries or for countries within a region are also directly available. This is particularly useful for international comparisons.

Activity 2.4

Go to the WHO website (http://www.who.int, World Health Organization 2005) and select 'Countries' (top left corner of the screen). Then find the following information:

1 Total population of Brazil, Venezuela, Panama and Saint Kitts and Nevis.
2 Life expectancy at birth in Botswana, Haiti, India, Greece and Japan.
3 Total expenditures as a proportion of national gross domestic product (GDP) in Pakistan, the Gambia and Sweden.
4 Healthy life expectancy at birth in Burkina Faso (to obtain this, click on 'Selected indicators' below the heading 'CONTEXT').

Feedback

1 By clicking in turn on the name of each of these countries you will find their total population easily. Brazil is the second most populated country (after the United States) in the WHO Region of the Americas with over 176 million inhabitants in 2002. In comparison there are only approximately 25 million persons in Venezuela, 3 million in Panama, and 42,000 in Saint Kitts and Nevis. However, as all these countries are from the same WHO Region (Americas), you could also do the following: 1) click on 'Brazil'; 2) click on the total population estimate for Brazil. This will give you a graph comparing the total population of each country of the region. Of course comparing the absolute number of deaths from a given cause among these countries (without calculating rates) would lead to many questionable conclusions!

2 By using the summary WHO data, you should have found that life expectancy at birth in 2002 was 40.4 years in Botswana, 50.1 years in Haiti, 61.0 in India, and 78.4 in Greece, and 81.9 in Japan.

3 The total expenditures on health represent 3.9 per cent of the gross domestic product (GDP) in Pakistan, 6.4 per cent in the Gambia, and 8.7 per cent in Sweden.

4 The healthy life expectancy at birth in Burkina Faso is 35.6 years. Health life expectancy is equivalent to the number of years in full health that a newborn can expect to live based on current rates of ill health and mortality. We will talk about this indicator in Chapter 3.

European data: the WHO Health for All Database

If you are more specifically looking for easy and rapid access to basic health statistics for the 52 member states of the WHO European Region, you can use the WHO Health For All (HFA) database. It was developed in the mid-1980s to support the monitoring of health trends in the region (HFA strategy). It is a key tool for international comparisons in Europe (including central Asia). It is regularly updated (twice per year) and freely available online (for direct access to the data using the Internet) or offline (to be downloaded for use on a PC). You can find both versions on the WHO Euro web site (http://www.who.dk, World Health Organization Regional Office for Europe 2005 – select 'Information Sources', then 'Data', and then 'European Health for All Database'). The offline is recommended for frequent users and also offers several different output options not available online. The database is easy to interrogate. You simply need to click on the health indicators, countries, and years you are interested in (see Figure 2.3).

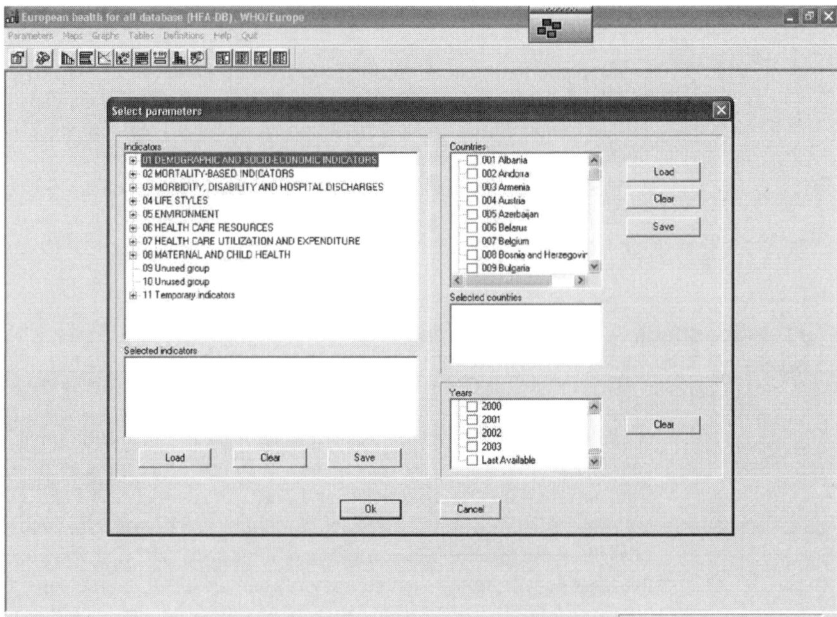

Figure 2.3 Illustration of the Health For All Database worksheet

Source: World Health Organization Regional Office for Europe (2005)

Indicators

The indicators that can be studied include demographic and socioeconomic statistics (17); mortality (60); morbidity, disability and hospital discharges (47); lifestyles (12); environment (10); health care resources (22); health care utilization and costs (27); maternal and child health (21).

Countries covered

The database covers all 52 WHO member states in the European region and allows you to select certain pre-specified groups: EUR average (52 WHO European member states); NRD average (5 Nordic countries); CARK average (5 central Asian republics); CSEC average (15 central and southeastern European countries, including Estonia, Latvia and Lithuania); CIS average (12 'Commonwealth of Independent States', the countries of the former USSR excluding Estonia, Latvia and Lithuania which are now included in the CSEC average); EU average (15 European Union member states prior to May 2004) and 25 member states since May 2004; Eur-A: 27 countries in the WHO European Region with very low child and adult mortality; Eur-B & C: 25 countries in the Region with higher levels of mortality.

Years

Data are available from 1970 to present (or latest available).

Presentation of the results

The database allows us to use several predefined table and graph formats, such as trends over time, with an option to adjust scales on both axes. You can also create scatterplots, comparing two indicators, or ranked bar charts.

Data sources

The data have been obtained from focal points for health statistics in member states, WHO technical units and collaborating centres, and other international sources, such as the Organization for Economic Cooperation and Development (OECD).

Data availability and quality

There are differences in recording practices for health data between countries, with the most complete data being for mortality-related indicators and incidence of infectious diseases.

Problems

There is incomplete registration of births and deaths in some countries, a lack of accurate populations estimates (for example, in Tajikistan, Georgia (Badurashvili and collaborators 2001), Albania, Croatia (Bozicevic and collaborators 2001), Bosnia and Herzegovina), and no mortality data in suitable detail for Andorra, Monaco, San Marino and Turkey.

Activity 2.5

You will now get information on time trends for the average life expectancy in Europe by using the HFA database. In order to do this, you simply need to follow these steps:

1 Go to the WHO Euro web site (http://www.who.dk, World Health Organization Regional Office for Europe 2005). Select 'Information Sources', then 'Data', and then 'European Health for All Database' to reach the HFA database web site.
2 Indicator group: Select 'Mortality based indicators'
3 Indicator: Select 'Life expectancy at birth in years'
4 Gender: Select 'Total'
5 Start year: Select 'First'
6 End year: Select 'Last'
7 Countries: Select 'Europe'
8 Country group: Select Russian Federation, Hungary, Sweden
9 Submit query: Click on 'Submit query'
10 Output selection screen: Select 'Line chart'
11 Click on the arrow on the right-hand side of the grey box.

Now describe the graph you have obtained.

Feedback

The graph you obtained should look like Figure 2.4.

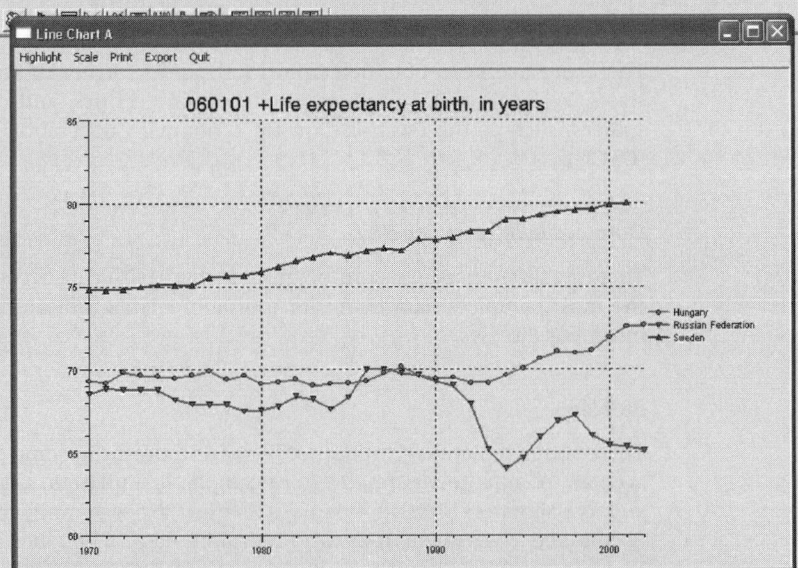

Figure 2.4 Life expectancy at birth (in years) in selected European countries
Source: World Health Organization Regional Office for Europe (2005)

This graph shows that life expectancy has been increasing steadily in Sweden since at least 1970. In contrast, it stagnated in Hungary during the 1970s and 1980s, only increasing following the early 1990s when the country introduced market reforms. In

Russia, however, life expectancy was actually falling in the 1970s and early 1980s. In the mid-1980s there was a dramatic improvement (this was at the time that Mikhail Gorbachev launched a wide-ranging anti-alcohol campaign), but it then fell back again at the end of the 1980s (when the USSR was in a period of rapid transition), accelerating after 1990. A short-lived improvement after 1994 was interrupted by a further decline after 1998, when Russia was hit by a major currency crisis.

Take some time to browse through the different health indicators, countries and group of countries and types of graphs you can get. You will see that such information can be extremely useful for international comparisons across Europe.

Summary

This chapter described the usefulness of population and mortality data in public health and discussed their strengths and weaknesses. It looked into the different sources of such data and described how they can be employed to obtain commonly used indicators of population health, such as age-standardized death rates and life expectancy. Finally, it allowed you to examine different types of basic health indicators that can be obtained from the WHO websites.

References

Ahmad OB, Boschi-Pinto C, Lopez AD, Murray CJD, Lozano R and Inoue M (undated) *Age Standardization of Rates: A New WHO Standard. GPE Discussion Series: No. 31*. EIP/GPE/EBD/ World Health Organization.

Badurashvili I, McKee M, Tsuladze G, Meslé F, Vallin J and Shkolnikov V (2001) Where there are no data: what has happened to life expectancy in Georgia since 1990? *Public Health* **115**: 394–400.

Bozicevic I, Oreskovic S, Stevanovic R, Rodin U, Nolte E and McKee M (2001) What is happening to the health of the Croatian population? *Croatian Med J* **42**: 601–5.

Simple Interactive Statistical Analysis (2004) *Life table/YPLL/SMR/CMF* (available on http://home.clara.net/sisa/spreadsh/lifexp.htm, last visited 2 February 2005).

World Health Organization (2005) *Home page*. Geneva: World Health Organization (available at http://www.who.int/, last visited 2 February 2005).

World Health Organization Regional Office for Europe (2005) *World Health Organization Regional Office for Europe website*. Copenhagen: World Health Organization Regional Office for Europe (available on http://www.who.dk, last visited 2 February 2005).

Further reading

Leon DA, Chenet L, Shkolnikov VM, Zakharov S, Shapiro J, Rakhmanova G, Vassin S and McKee M (1997) Huge variation in Russian mortality rates 1984–94: artefact, alcohol, or what? *The Lancet* **350**: 383–8. This paper discusses the dramatic changes in mortality rates that occurred in Russia since the mid–1980s.

Shkolnikov V, McKee M and Leon DA (2001) Changes in life expectancy in Russia in the mid-1990s, *The Lancet* **357**: 917–21. This is a second paper that could provide you more

details of the observed gap in life expectancy and health between Western and Eastern Europe.
World Health Organization (1993) *International Statistical Classification of Diseases and Related Health Problems, tenth revision. Volumes 1, 2, 3.* Geneva, World Health Organization. These volumes will provide you with full details of the ICD-10 classification.

3 The burden of disease and other summary measures of population health

Overview

In Chapter 2, you learned about a simple and widely used health statistic, that is, population-level mortality rates. This and various estimates of morbidity and health states are useful measures for numerous public health purposes ranging from the monitoring of new health problems to evaluating progress in reducing old ones for which disease control programmes are already in place. However, these approaches rapidly become unwieldy when several health problems and conditions are being monitored over time across numerous population sub-groups. In that case, summary measures of population health (SMPH) become useful tools that combine information on mortality and non-fatal health outcomes to represent a population health in a single number. This chapter will introduce you to SMPH, with a particular emphasis on estimates of disease burden within the context of the Global Burden of Disease (GBD) study.

Learning objectives

By the end of this chapter you should be able to:

- **describe the uses of SMPH**
- **discuss some limitations of SMPH**
- **discuss results from the GBD study**

Key terms

Burden of disease A measure of the physical, emotional, social and financial impact that a particular disease has on the health and functioning of the population.

Health expectancy Summary measure of population health that estimates the expectation of years of life lived in various health states.

Health gap Summary measure of population health that estimates the gap between the current population health and a normative goal for population health.

Summary measures of population health Indicators that combine information about mortality and health states to summarize the health of a population into a single number.

Summary measures of population health (SMPH)

Chapter 2 discussed data on mortality and populations. The use of mortality data as a fundamental component of the public policy process is related in part to their widespread availability and timeliness. Statistics on causes of death are undoubtedly useful for public health surveillance, providing overall pictures of mortality, inevitably. However, they say much less about those who are still alive. In particular, although they have formed the basis of comparisons of the health of nations for many decades, they have been criticized because they disregard the importance of widely prevalent conditions that are less likely to kill you but still create considerable disability. This has led to attempts to bring together morbidity and mortality. An ideal health metric is therefore one that simultaneously measures and contrasts both fatal and non-fatal health outcomes. Indeed, such a measure is needed to assess the benefits of health interventions, which may reduce both mortality and the period of life lived in a disabled state.

In this chapter we will discuss such indicators that combine information on mortality and non-fatal health outcomes to give information on a population's health in a single number, that is, SMPH. Interest in and work on SMPH has grown during the last decades and, although there has also been increasing debate about their application, their use has become routine in a number of settings.

SMPH fall into two broad categories: health expectancies and health gaps. Health expectancy is a generic term to describe SMPH that estimate the average time that a person could expect to live in various states of health. Health gaps quantify the difference between the actual health of a population and some stated norm or goal for population health. Both types of indicators include weights that account for time lived in health states worst than ideal health.

Activity 3.1

Think of potential uses of SMPH in the public health policy process. Give a few examples.

Feedback

There are several potential uses of SMPH in public health policy. These include:

- comparing the health of one population with that of another
- monitoring time trends in the health of a given population
- assessing overall health inequalities within populations
- providing appropriate and balanced attention to the effects of non-fatal health outcomes on overall population health
- informing debates on priorities for health service delivery and planning
- informing debates on priorities for research and development
- improving curricula for professional training in public health
- analysing the benefits of health interventions for use in cost-effectiveness analyses.

Healthy life expectancy – more than simply life and death

The most widely used example of health expectancy measures is *Health Adjusted Life Expectancy*, or HALE. Data on HALE is available for over 190 WHO member states. HALE estimates the average equivalent 'healthy' expected number of years of life for a newborn in a given population, if current disability and mortality conditions continue to apply in this population. It is calculated by subtracting from the life expectancy a figure which is the number of years lived with disability multiplied by a weighting to represent the effect of the disability. This is illustrated in Figure 3.1.

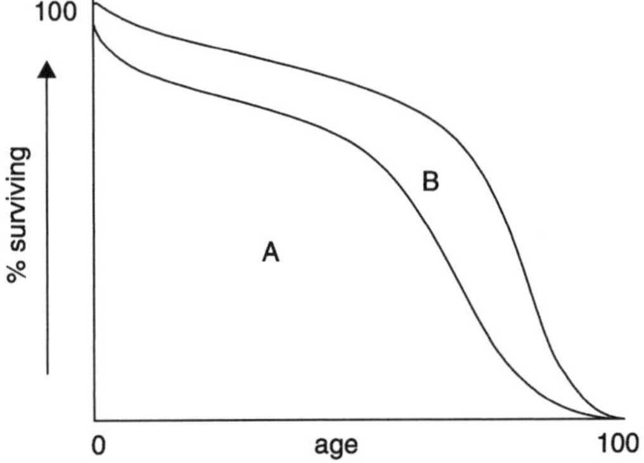

B = period with disability; life expectancy = A + B, healthy life expectancy = A + fB (where f is a weighting to reflect disability level).

Figure 3.1 Health-adjusted life expectancy

Activity 3.2

Figure 3.2 shows the probability of being healthy by age and sex in Western Europe, Eastern Europe, and the Russian Federation. Examine the figure and describe how this probability varies among regions.

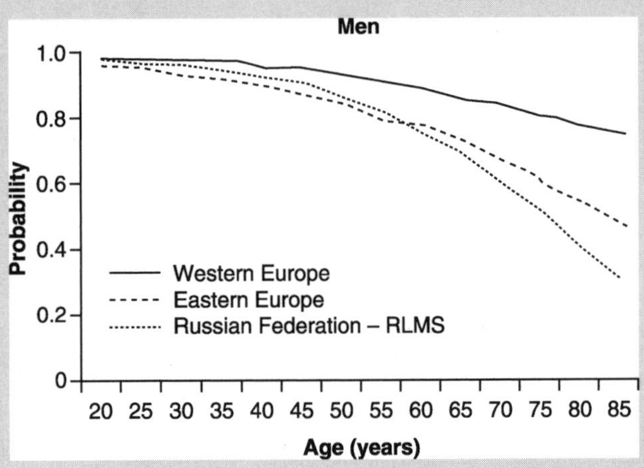

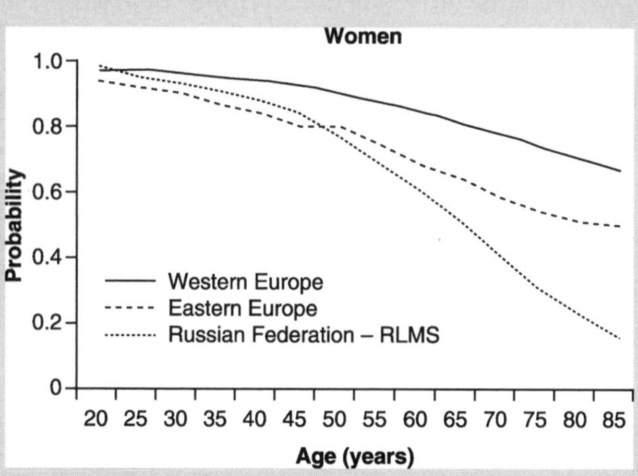

Figure 3.2 Probability of being healthy, by age and sex in Western Europe, Eastern Europe, and the Russian Federation (RLMS: Russian Longitudinal Monitoring Survey).

Source: Andreev and collaborators (2003)

Feedback

As expected, we can see that the probability of being healthy decreases with age in both genders and in all three regions. However, this decrease is steeper in Eastern Europe and the Russian Federation than in Western Europe. When comparing Eastern Europe and the Russian Federation, we can see that the probabilities are generally similar until about the age of 50 but after 50, the trends diverge with a more rapid decline in health in the Russian Federation.

Activity 3.3

Now examine Figure 3.3, in which data on health and mortality are combined to give years of healthy life expectancy by age, sex, and region, and answer the following questions.

1 How does total survival (sum of survival in good or poor health) vary among regions and genders?
2 How does survival in poor health vary among regions and gender?

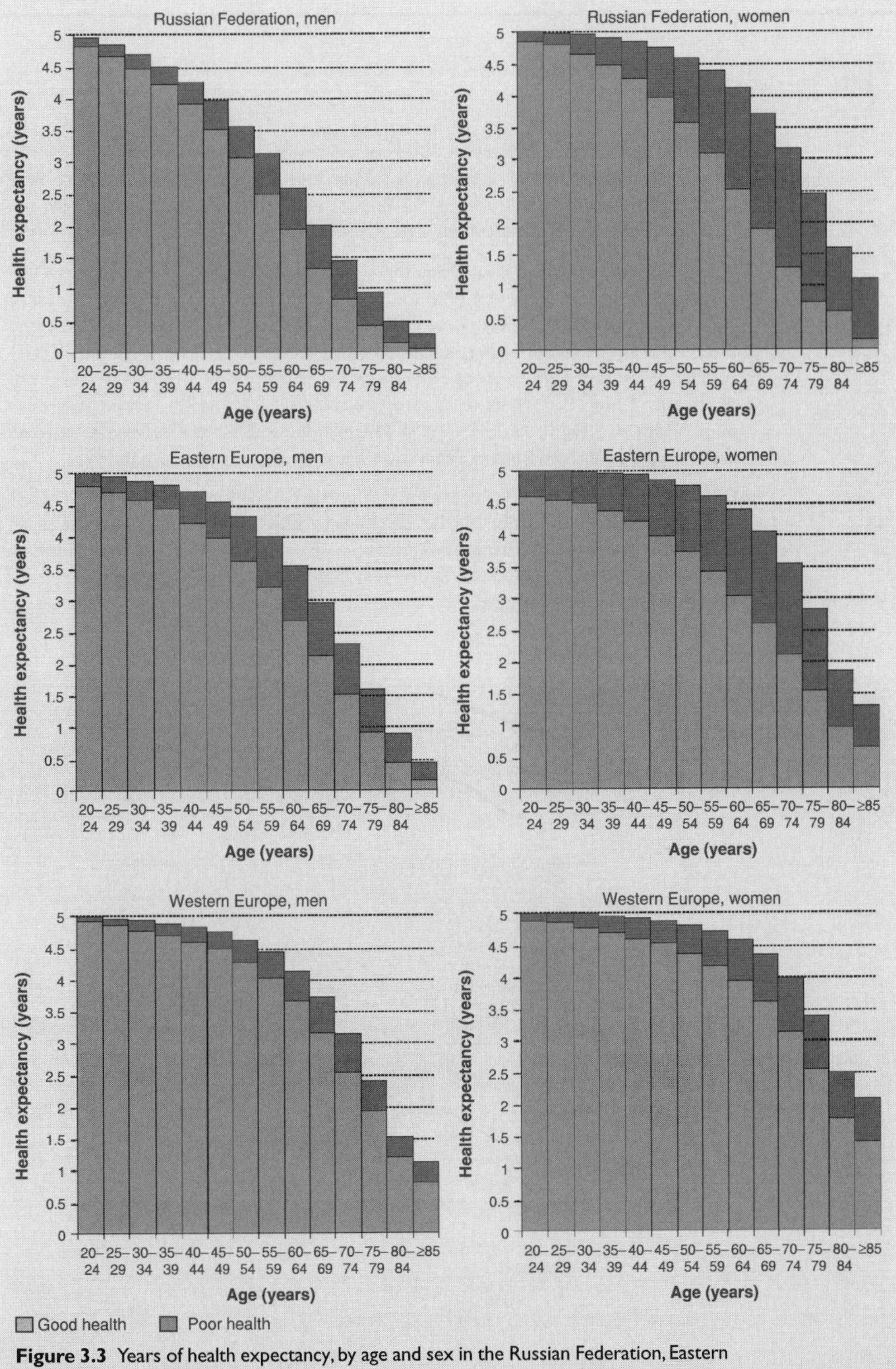

Figure 3.3 Years of health expectancy, by age and sex in the Russian Federation, Eastern Europe, and Western Europe

Source: Andreev and collaborators (2003)

Feedback

1 Survival tends to be highest in Western Europe, intermediary in Eastern Europe, and lowest in the Russian Federation. Regional differences are particularly important in men. In all regions survival is better in women than in men. The decline in survival is particularly steep in males from the Russian Federation than in females from the Russian Federation or in males from other regions.

2 In women we can see a clear gradation in the likelihood of surviving in poor health. Western European women not only are more likely to survive into old age compared with those from Eastern Europe or the Russian Federation, but they are also more likely to survive in good health (thus less likely to survive in poor health). Intermediary results are found in Eastern Europe and the worst scenario is observed in women from the Russian Federation where few appear to survive in good health. In men, survival in poor health also tends to be lowest in Western Europe but the difference between Eastern Europe and the Russian Federation is less striking than in women.

Differences in males and females are most important in the Russian Federation. Indeed, there appears to be a major burden of ill health afflicting women from the Russian Federation that is not apparent from analysing mortality data (total survival considerably higher compared to Russian Federation men). A similar but less marked pattern can be seen in Eastern Europe.

Activity 3.4

Figure 3.4 shows the contribution of ill health and increased mortality to the gap in health expectancy between the Russian Federation and Western Europe.

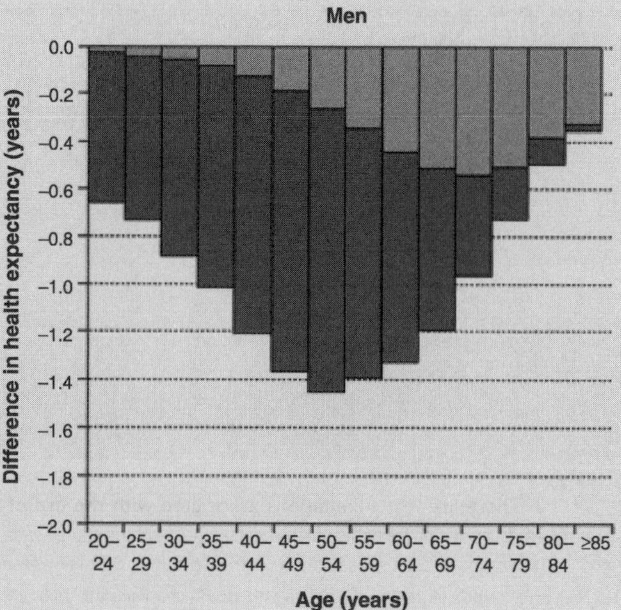

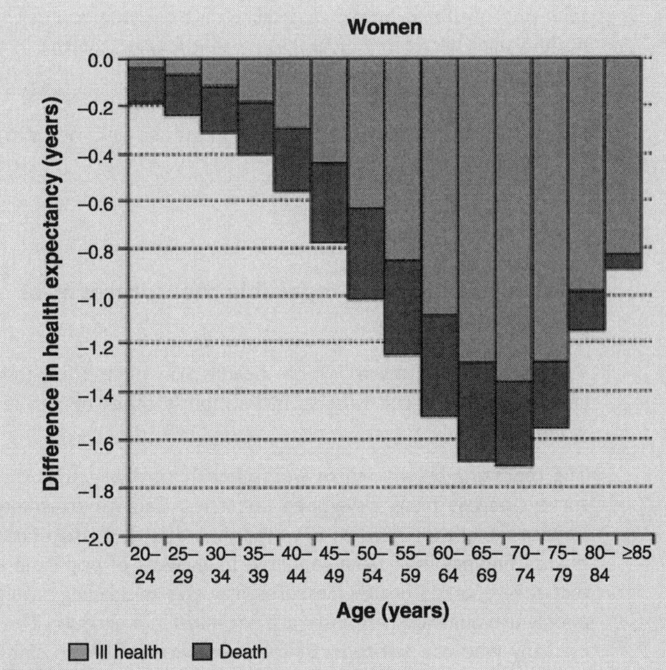

Figure 3.4 Contribution of ill health and increased deaths to the gap in health expectancy between the Russian Federation and Western Europe

Source: Andreev and collaborators (2003)

1 Find the difference in health expectancy (in years) between the Russian Federation and Western Europe, in men and women aged 50 to 54 years.
2 Describe how the contribution of ill health and death to this gap varies between genders. Try to explain the differences observed.
3 In this study, the authors used survey data on self-reported health for the calculation of healthy life expectancy. Why do you think this might be a problem?

Feedback

1 The gap in health expectancy is approximately 1.4 years in men and 1.0 years in women.

2 In men, the majority of the difference is due to death while in women it is largely due to poor health. This suggests that the responses of men and women to adversity differ, leading to premature death in men and survival in poor state of health in women.

3 There are many limitations associated with the use of self-reported health for the estimation of healthy life expectancy. For example, it is possible that self-reported health does not measure the same thing in different population sub-groups and may not be interpreted in the same way by different groups (for example, the ability of

self-rated health to predict mortality varies among countries, and the perception of health varies between genders). As well it may not be the most appropriate measure of health.

In order to learn more about this issue, read the following extract from a commentary by Mathers (2003).

Towards valid and comparable measurement of population health

Women generally report worse health than men. Thus, the large male–female gap in life expectancy in the Russian Federation is offset by worse reported health status in women.

The reporting by women of worse health, generally, than men has been seen in health surveys across many developed countries. Can we conclude that the health status of Russian Federation women is worse than that of Russian Federation men? Several paradoxical findings have been reported in analyses of population health surveys, suggesting that self-reported health measures may give misleading results if differences in the way people use question responses are not taken into account. This evidence has been ignored by many who use self-report-survey measures of health status to report on population health, health inequalities, or intervention outcomes. Indeed, there is substantial literature arguing that within-group correlations of self-reported health measures with other observed or measured health indicators, or with mortality risk, show the validity and comparability of such measures across groups.

Although there are, undoubtedly, correlations between self-reported health status measures and other health indicators, and there is no doubt that health status influences self-report, this does not ensure comparability of self-report measures across groups. Several studies have reported significant correlations between perceived health (with response categories such as excellent, good, fair, poor) and mortality risk within groups such as men and women, or groups defined by socioeconomic or ethnic characteristics, and argued that these correlations provide evidence that self-perceived health is a valid measure of health status. Similar arguments are made for within group correlations with observed or measured functional indicators, with morbidity and health service utilization.

However, it is possible to have consistent associations of perceived health with survival within groups without such associations holding across groups. This is illustrated in Fig. 3.5, where survival is lower for worse perceived health in both men and women, while at the same time the survival of women with worst perceived health is better than that of men with excellent perceived health. Suppose that a population survey found most women reporting worse health than men for a population with the associations shown in Fig. 3.5. It would clearly be fallacious to deduce that women have worse survival (or health) than men: the indicator is not comparable across groups because women are using the response categories differently to men.

Survey developers have emphasized the importance of establishing the validity of instruments and their reliability, but until recently, little attention had been paid to the

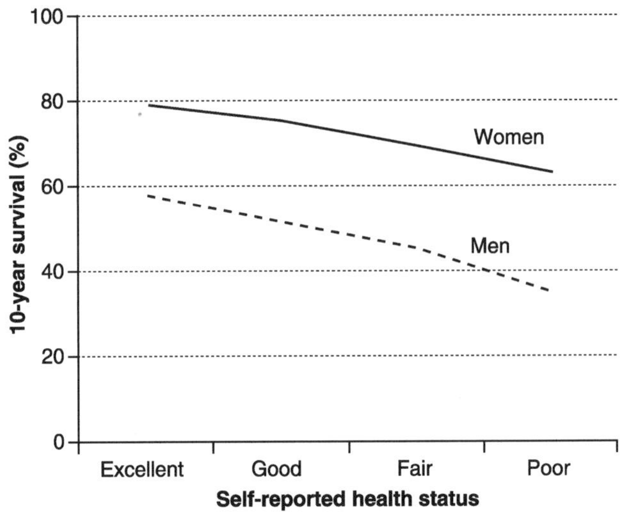

Figure 3.5 Plots showing that within group correlation of self-reported health status with other health indicators does not provide evidence for cross-group correlations

Source: Mathers (2003)

issue of cross-population comparability. The latter relates fundamentally to unmeasured differences in expectations and norms for health, so that the meaning that different populations attach to the labels used for response categories in self-reported questions, such as mild, moderate, or severe, can vary greatly. Recent developments in survey methodology using measured tests and anchoring vignettes to calibrate self-report health questions hold considerable promise in addressing this problem.

Health gaps and disease burden

Health gaps are particularly useful as they allow for the quantification of the burden of disease and injury in terms of absolute numbers of life years. The burden of disease can be seen as a measurement of the gap between the current health of a population and an ideal situation where everyone in the population lives in old age in full health. It is usually expressed in disability-adjusted life years (DALY) which represent one lost year of 'healthy' life.

Disease burden has been estimated in several countries including Australia, New Zealand, South Africa, Chile, and Andhra Pradesh (India). The GBD programme is also a major undertaking to estimate the worldwide burden of disease from major disease and injuries by geographical region. You can read more about this program on the WHO website (World Health Organization 2005). We will discuss some GBD findings later in this chapter.

Key issues in using summary measures of population health (SMPH)

Clearly the use of SMPH raise many technical and, by implication, moral complexities. The technical arguments are beyond the scope of this unit but some will be discussed below. A key issue is how to define and measure disability and then select the weights to apply to particular health states. Obviously, the choices made in respect to particular conditions will be important. There are several ways in which this can be done. Each method involves asking groups of people for their preferences. The methods used in the GBD programme will be used as an example.

In the first round of the GBD study (estimates of disease burden were for 1990), small groups of participants (medical and public health experts) were asked to make a value judgement about the severity of given health conditions and the preference for time spent in each severity level for these conditions. To a large extent, this was necessitated by the lack of population information on the severity distribution of most conditions at global and regional levels. For each condition, this assessment was based on a detailed case. For example, angina, in this exercise, was defined as reproducible chest pain when walking 50 minutes or more, that the individual would rate as a five on a subjective pain scale from zero to ten. The effect of disability weighting is that conditions which, while disabling, rarely cause death (in particular mental illness) are ranked as more important than they would be using mortality alone.

The second round of the GBD project calculated disease burden estimates for the year 2000 and subsequent years (revised versions have provided estimates for 2001 and 2002). It adopted a similar approach to health state valuation, using a standard health state description based on eight core domains of health (mobility, self care, pain and discomfort, cognition, interpersonal activities, vision, sleep and energy, affect) (Prüss-Üstün *et al.* 2003). In order to address the limitations of the methods used, WHO, in collaboration with its member states, initiated a two-tiered data-collection strategy involving general population surveys, combined with more detailed surveys among high education respondents (Ustun *et al.* 2000). The experience gained in eliciting health state valuations from general population samples was then used in designing the health status and health state valuation modules for the World Health Survey, which was carried out in 73 member states in 2003. The disability weights used in Version 3 of the GBD 2000 (examples are provided in Table 3.1) are still largely based on the GBD 1990 disability weights, but it is planned to use results from the World Health Survey to comprehensively revise the disability weights used in the GBD 2000 (Mathers *et al.* 2003; World Health Organization 2003a).

A second issue is the value placed on a life at different stages in life. This is extremely controversial. Is a year of life worth as much when it is a new born infant as it is when it is an adult responsible for a family? The authors of the GBD study decided there was a difference and placed more weight on a year of life of a young adult. The weightings they used are shown in Figure 3.6. This has the effect of reducing the burden of disease arising from deaths in childhood.

A third issue is how to obtain SMPH in countries from which data are unavailable. This is somewhat controversial and has been done using estimates. For example,

Table 3.1 Examples of disability weights in the Global Burden of Disease (GBD) 2000 (version 3)

Disease or sequelae	*Mean disability weight*
AIDS	0.505
Infertility	0.180
Diarrhoea disease, episodes	0.105
Measles episode	0.152
Tuberculosis	0.272
Trachoma, blindness	0.600
Lower respiratory tract infection, episodes	0.279
Cancers, terminal stage	0.810
Diabetes mellitus cases	0.015
Unipolar depressive disorders	0.399
Alzheimer and other dementias	0.666
Angina pectoris	0.141
Congestive heart failure	0.32
Deafness	0.234
Burns (>60%) – treated	0.441

Source: Adapted from Mathers and collaborators (2003)

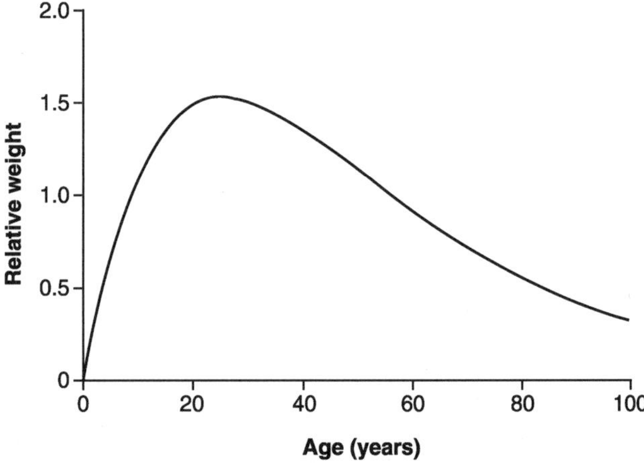

Figure 3.6 Weighting allocated to a year of life at different ages

data that exist (usually on childhood mortality) have been applied to model life tables.

Bearing in mind the limitations of SMPH, it is important to remember that their use in policy making is still debated and that further scientific developments are expected in the next decades. The book by Murray and collaborators published in 2002 provides a good description of the debates as they stood in 1999 (see list of suggested readings at the end of this chapter).

Results from the Global Burden of Disease (GBD) programme

Results from the second round of the GBD Study were published in the World Health Report 2002 (World Health Organization 2002). Revised DALY estimates can also be found in the World Health Report 2003 and 2004 (World Health Organization 2003b; World Health Organization 2004). For the presentation of results, countries were grouped into five mortality strata on the basis of combinations of child (under 5) and adult (15–59) mortality (A: very low child and adult mortality; B: low child and adult mortality; C: low child and high adult mortality; D: high child and adult mortality; E: high child and very high adult mortality). These mortality strata were then applied to the six main WHO regions (Africa, Americas, Eastern Mediterranean, Europe, South-East Asia, and Western Pacific) to produce the 14 epidemiological sub-regions.

Overall burden of disease

It is possible to estimate the contribution of different conditions to the overall disease burden. As expected, this varies greatly by gender and by region. The ten worldwide leading causes of disease burden in 2002 in males and females are described in Table 3.2.

Table 3.2 Leading causes of disease burden (DALYs) for males and females, worldwide, 2002

Males	*% DALYs*	*Females*	*% DALYs*
Perinatal conditions	6.9	Lower respiratory infections	6.3
Lower respiratory infection	6.0	Perinatal conditions	6.2
HIV/AIDS	5.5	HIV/AIDS	5.8
Ischaemic heart disease	4.4	Unipolar depressive disorders	5.7
Diarrhoeal diseases	4.2	Maternal conditions	4.7
Other unintentional injuries	3.9	Diarrhoeal diseases	4.1
Road traffic accidents	3.5	Ischaemic heart disease	3.4
Unipolar depressive disorders	3.5	Malaria	3.4
Cerebrovascular diseases	3.3	Cerebrovascular diseases	3.3
Malaria	2.9	Childhood diseases	2.9

Source: Adapted from World Health Organization (2004)

Activity 3.5

Now take a close look at Table 3.3.

1 Identify which regions bear the greatest burden of disease.
2 Describe differences in the causes of disease burden between developed and developing regions.

Table 3.3 Burden of disease in disability-adjusted life years (DALYs) by cause in WHO sub-regions, estimates for 2002[1]

	Africa		The Americas			South-East Asia		Europe			Eastern Medit.		Western Pacific	
	D	E	A	B	D	B	D	A	B	C	B	D	A	B
Population (000)	*311 273 (000)*	*360 965 (000)*	*333 580 (000)*	*445 161 (000)*	*73 810 (000)*	*298 234 (000)*	*1 292 598 (000)*	*415 323 (000)*	*222 846 (000)*	*239 717 (000)*	*142 528 (000)*	*360 296 (000)*	*155 400 (000)*	*1 562 136 (000)*
Total number of DALYs	160415139	200961340	46867930	81589086	17129512	62463254	364109648	51724683	37696931	60899991	24074148	115005189	16384021	248495239
Infectious and parasitic diseases	75966235	111482611	1227642	6718794	3943952	10597834	78355066	891022	2040402	2733602	1529017	30881071	322482	23348675
Respiratory infections	18976432	16618915	389551	1875948	1050429	1824206	31201813	689918	1524308	900964	551716	10267074	343573	8310116
Maternal and perinatal conditions	16069445	17034561	995725	6682527	1641554	4418439	46124190	668023	1962162	923831	1733153	14921441	135084	17467020
Nutritional deficiencies	4304754	5269113	493110	1056781	574529	1692676	10435081	303496	671364	729050	630503	3859902	128236	4232081
Neoplasms	2311751	2602454	5943954	4692143	769763	3279321	10791602	8733344	3324865	5386988	1108271	3075539	2855730	22295933
Diabetes mellitus and nutritional/endocrine disorders	1098645	1306258	2308940	2996524	448179	1694530	4199071	1737419	741367	690270	619506	1476174	600423	4151191
Neuropsychiatric disorders	8242336	9654700	13887758	18965529	2934104	8340235	39973543	13731640	7054951	8562405	4340106	10679638	3811928	42721969
Cardiovascular diseases	5186781	5723637	6847078	7425670	900539	6575949	36411081	8838331	8174836	17404625	2944925	9114744	2545482	29867748
Respiratory diseases	2505053	2977530	3238959	4061287	667833	2620269	13010151	3406475	1547172	1781766	842689	2877018	1066842	14468542
Digestive diseases	2377054	2726512	1589428	3309106	645354	2534411	11671231	2413933	1900100	3082243	679193	3352585	663516	9447639
Other non-communicable conditions, and congenital abnormalities	8402640	9736072	5400993	10374643	1664391	10668707	34606356	6230137	4697265	5898570	4327713	11785718	2283563	36837741
Injuries	14974014	15828977	4544793	13430133	1888884	8216677	47330463	4080945	4058139	12805678	4767358	12714285	1627163	35346584

[1] Figures are computed by WHO to assure comparibility; they are not necessarily the official statistics of Member States, which may use alternative rigorous methods.
Source: Adapted from World Health Organization (2004)

Feedback

1 A disproportionate disease burden is borne by developing sub-regions with almost two-thirds of the worldwide total burden of disease originating from South East Asia D (24 per cent), Western Pacific B (17 per cent), and the Africa D (11 per cent) and E (14 per cent) regions representing 57 per cent of the world population.

2 The results also showed marked differences in disease patterns among sub-regions. In developed sub-regions, communicable diseases and maternal, perinatal and nutritional conditions represent only low proportion of the total disease burden while in high-mortality developing regions this figure rises considerably, reaching for example more than 70 per cent in the African sub-regions. In contrast, non-communicable diseases account for a large proportion of DALYs in developed regions (for example, 84 per cent in America A and Western Pacific B, and 87 per cent in Europe A).

Underlying causes of disease burden

The next step is to look at the underlying causes of the burden of disease. This is done by combining information on the distribution of specified risk factors in the population, the relative risk of different deaths and disabilities associated with exposure to them, and the overall burden of the deaths and disabilities in question. This immediately poses a challenge because clearly very few diseases (if any) are caused by a single risk factor. For example, while smoking is clearly the immediate (or proximate) cause of the vast majority of cases of lung cancer, the risk can be modified by other factors such as diet and, almost certainly, genetics. However, there are also distal factors, which influence why people smoke. So, for example, poverty and homelessness might be considered, at this level, as another risk factor for lung cancer.

Once again, the calculations are complicated (but clearly described in the reports of the GBD for those who are interested). The first round of the GBD, which estimated disease burden in 1990, used a fairly limited set of risk factors. In the updated analysis, more risk factors were considered.

Activity 3.6

If you had been in charge of the study, what risk factors would you have selected for study?

Feedback

You probably included factors such as malnutrition, tobacco, alcohol consumption, hypertension, unsafe sex, air pollution, and so on. But have you also thought about indoor smoke from solid fuels (you will read about this in Chapter 10), physical workload in the working environment that could lead to low back pain, noise, childhood sexual abuse, or lead? In the second round of the GBD, a total of 26 risk factors covering a wide range of physiological, behavioural, environmental, and socio-economic factors were examined. You will be introduced to these in the following activity.

Activity 3.7

Read the following extract from a paper by Ezzati and collaborators (2002). It will give you an overview of the methods used to estimate the contributions of the 26 risk factors to global and regional burden of disease in the GBD study, and the main results found. Then answer the following questions:

1. List the main limitations of the methods used to obtain the results presented in the paper.
2. Using data from Figure 3.9, describe what the authors mean by 'cross-sectional risk-factor transition'.
3. Some say that nutritional diseases create a dual burden. What does this mean?

Selected major risk factors and global and regional burden of disease

. . . The Comparative Risk Assessment module of the global burden of disease (GBD) 2000 study has been set up as a systematic assessment of the changes in population health, which would result from modifying the population distribution of exposure to a risk factor or a group of risk factors. This unified framework for describing population exposure to risk factors and their consequences for population health is an important step in linking the growing interest in the causal determinants of health across various public health disciplines from natural, physical, and medical sciences to the social sciences and humanities.

Our aim was to develop such a framework by selecting risk factors in various levels of causality. Although gaps in epidemiological research on multiple layers of causality and risk-factor interactions would not allow inclusion of all inherently inter-related risk factors of interest, this selected group serves to emphasise the potential for disease prevention as a public health tool.

Methods

Mathers and colleagues describe two models for causal attribution of health outcomes or states: categorical attribution and counterfactual analysis. In categorical attribution, an event such as death is attributed to a single cause (such as a disease or risk factor) or group of causes, according to a defined set of rules – eg, the International Classification of Disease (ICD) system for attribution of causes of death. In counterfactual analysis, the contribution of one or a group of risk factors to disease or mortality is estimated by comparison of the current or future disease burden with the magnitude that would be expected in some alternative hypothetical scenario (referred to as the counterfactual), including the absence of, or reduction in, the disease(s) or risk factor(s) of interest. In theory, causal attribution of the burden of disease to risk factors can be done with both categorical and counterfactual approaches. For instance, categorical attribution has been used in attribution of diseases and injuries to occupational risk factors in occupational health registries and attribution of motor vehicle accidents to alcohol consumption. Categorical attribution to risk factors, however, overlooks the fact that many diseases have multiple causes. In the Comparative Risk Assessment project, the estimates of burden of disease and injuries due to risk factors are based on a counterfactual exposure distribution that would result in the lowest population risk, irrespective of whether currently attainable in practice, referred to as the theoretical minimum exposure distribution. Use of theoretical minimum exposure distribution as the counterfactual has the advantage of providing a vision of potential gains in population health by risk reduction from all degrees of suboptimum exposure in a consistent way across risk factors.

Table 3.4 shows the selected group of risk factors included in the project. The criteria for selection of risk factors included: likely to be among the leading global or regional causes of disease burden; not too specific – eg, every one of the thousands of occupational chemicals – or too broad – eg, environment or food; high likelihood of causality based on scientific knowledge from different disciplines; availability of reasonably complete data on exposure and risk levels or methods for extrapolation when needed; potentially modifiable. For each risk factor, an expert working group did a comprehensive review of published work and other sources (government reports, international databases, etc.) to obtain data on the prevalence of risk-factor exposure and hazard size (relative risk or absolute hazard size when appropriate; table 3.4). This review included collection of primary data, several re-analyses of original data, systematic reviews, and meta-analyses.

Each expert working group compiled data separately for men and women, eight age groups (0–4, 5–14, 15–29, 30–44, 45–59, 60–69, 70–79, ≥80 years), and 14 epidemiological subregions of GBD 2000, which are based on a combination of WHO regions and child and adult mortality rates, as summarised in figure 3.7.

The contribution of a risk factor to disease or mortality (expressed as the fraction of disease or death, *AF*, attributable to risk factor in a population) is provided by the generalised potential impact fraction (or its discrete version when exposure variable was categorical).

Population attributable fractions obtained in this way estimate the percentage reduction in disease or death that would take place if exposure to the risk factor were reduced to the counterfactual distribution, with all other factors remaining the same. Because most diseases are caused by multiple factors, and because some risk factors act through other, more proximal factors, population attributable fractions for multiple risk factors for the same disease can add to more than 100 per cent. For example, some deaths from childhood pneumonia might have been prevented by removal of exposure to indoor smoke from solid fuels, childhood underweight, and zinc deficiency (which itself affects weight-for-age); or some of the cardiovascular disease events might be due to a combination of smoking, physical inactivity, and inadequate intake of fruits and vegetables (both acting partly through obesity, cholesterol, and blood pressure). Such instances would be attributed to all these risk factors. Although lack of additivity can initially seem problematic, multicausality offers opportunities to tailor prevention based on availability and cost of interventions. For each risk factor-disease pair, population attributable fractions (*AF*) for each of the 224 age, sex, subregion groups were calculated, separately for mortality (*AFM*) and incidence (*AFI*) when the relative risks for mortality and incidence were different. For each of these 224 groups, the estimates of mortality (*AMij*) and burden of disease (*ABij*) from disease *j* attributable to risk factor *i* were obtained. Burden of disease was expressed in disability-adjusted-life-years (DALY) . . .

Table 3.4 Risk factors, exposure variables, theoretical minima, disease and injury outcome, and data sources for the risk factors assessed

Risk factor	*Exposure variable*	*Theoretical minimum*	*Outcomes**	*Sources for exposure estimates*	*Sources for hazard estimates*
Childhood and maternal undernutrition					
Under-weight	Children <–1 SD weight-for-age compared with international reference group in 1 SD increments; maternal BMI <20 kg/m^2; children aged <5 years	Same fraction of children <–1 SD weight-for-age as international reference group; all women of childbearing age with BMI ≥20 kg/m^2	Mortality and acute morbidity from diarrhoea, malaria, measles, pneumonia, and selected other group I diseases; perinatal conditions from maternal underweight: *long-term morbidity from undernutrition*	WHO Global Database on Child Growth and Malnutrition – based on systematic analysis of raw data from 310 nationally representative nutritional (anthropometry) surveys in 112 countries	Childhood underweight: re-analysis of 10 cohort studies for mortality to obtain hazard in 1 SD increments, and systematic review and new meta-analysis of existing cohort studies for morbidity; maternal underweight: systematic review and meta-analysis of existing cohort studies
Iron deficiency	Haemoglobin concentrations (g/dL) estimated from prevalence of anaemia	Haemoglobin distributions that halve anaemia prevalence, estimated to occur if all Iron deficiency were eliminated†	Anaemia and its sequelae (including cognitive impairment), maternal and perinatal mortality	WHO anaemia database from population-based studies of haemoglobin concentration	Systematic review and new meta-analysis of cohort studies
Vitamin A deficiency	Prevalence of vitamin A deficiency, estimated as low serum retinol concentrations (<0·70 mmol/L) among children aged <5 years and among pregnant women (aged 15–44 years)	No vitamin A deficiency	Mortality due to diarrhoea, measles, malaria, and miscellaneous infectious causes of disease (children <5), morbidity due to malaria (children <5), maternal mortality (pregnant women), vitamin A deficiency and its sequelae (all age groups); *maternal morbidity, low birthweight, and other perinatal conditions*	Comprehensive review of data from multiple sources, including WHO and Micronutrient Initiative summary reports, journal articles, published and unpublished survey reports (data available for 66 countries for children and 34 for pregnant women; for more than 90 other countries prevalence was zero or negligible based on indirect data)	Systematic review and new meta-analysis as well as re-analysis of randomised trials for childhood and maternal outcomes

Table 3.4 *continued*

Risk factor	*Exposure variable*	*Theoretical minimum*	*Outcomes**	*Sources for exposure estimates*	*Sources for hazard estimates*
Zinc deficiency	Less than the US recommended dietary allowances for zinc	Entire population consuming sufficient dietary zinc to meet physiological needs, taking into account routine and illness-related losses and bioavailability	Diarrhoea, pneumonia, malaria in children aged <5 years; *adult and pregnancy outcomes*	International Zinc Nutrition Consultative Group (IZiNCG) method for estimating the prevalence of inadequate zinc intakes based on the presence and bioavailability of zinc in each country's food supply (from UN-FAO food balance sheets)	Systematic review and new meta-analysis as well as re-analysis of randomised trials
Other nutrition-related risk factors and physical activity					
High blood pressure	Level of systolic blood pressure	115 (SD 6) mm Hg	Ischaemic heart disease (IHD), stroke, hypertensive heart disease and other cardiovascular disease; *renal failure*	Systematic review of almost 200 studies with over 450 000 participants	Meta-analysis of 37 cohort studies with 425 000 individuals and 23 randomised trials of blood pressure lowering with 70 000 participants
High cholesterol	Concentration of total blood cholesterol	3·8 (SD 1) mmol/L	IHD, stroke; *other cardiovascular disease*	Review of 150 surveys with more than 630 000 participants	Meta-analysis of 10 cohorts with 490 000 North American and European participants, 29 cohorts with 350 000 participants from the Asia Pacific region, and 49 trials of cholesterol lowering
High BMI (overweight and obesity)	BMI (kg/m^2)	21 (SD 1) kg/m^2	IHD, stroke, hypertensive heart disease, diabetes, osteoarthritis, endo-metrial and colon cancers, post-menopausal breast cancer; *gallbladder cancer, kidney cancer, breathlessness, back pain, dermatitis, menstrual disorders and infertility, gallstones*	Full or part (ie, some age-sex groups) data from more than 66 countries on mean BMI or prevalence of overweight and obesity from published work, WHO and other reports, and unpublished data	Meta-analysis of 33 cohorts with 310 000 participants for vascular risks, 27 cohorts for cancer risks, and systematic review of other cohort studies for diabetes risks

Low fruit and vegetable intake	Fruit and vegetable intake per day	600 g (SD 50 g) intake per day for adults	IHD, stroke, colorectal cancer, gastric cancer, lung cancer, oesophageal cancer	Country-based food surveys for 26 countries in 9 subregions; for regions without food surveys, UN-FAO food balance sheet data combined with survey information from other regions on the age and sex distribution	Systematic review and new meta-analysis of published cohort studies
Physical inactivity	Three categories of inactive, insufficiently active (<2·5 h per week of moderate-intensity activity, or <4000 KJ per week), and sufficiently active. Activity in discretionary-time, work, and transport considered	All having at least 2·5 h per week of moderate-intensity activity or equivalent (4000 KJ per week)	IHD, breast cancer, colon cancer, diabetes; *falls and osteoporosis, ostearthitris, lower back pain, prostate and rectal cancer*	Systematic review of published work, contacts with national government and non-governmental agencies and cardiovascular disease electronic list-servers to identify data on physical activity levels in three domains (occupation [8 countries], transportation [14 countries], leisure [50 countries]) plus an ecological model for prediction of the activity in the three domains in countries without data (model data from World Bank)	Systematic review of published literature and new meta-analysis of cohort studies
Sexual and reproductive health					
Unsafe sex	Sex with an infected partner without any measure to prevent infection (represented as parameters of an HIV model)	No unsafe sex	HIV/AIDS, sexually transmitted infections, and cervical cancer	UNAID Reference Group Epidemic Projection Model, fit to data from antenatal clinics for high-HIV prevalence regions; sexual mixing model with surveys of high risk groups for low-HIV prevalence regions; by definition 100% of other STI was attributable to this risk factor	

Table 3.4 *continued*

Risk factor	*Exposure variable*	*Theoretical minimum*	*Outcomes**	*Sources for exposure estimates*	*Sources for hazard estimates*
Lack of contra-ception	Prevalence of traditional methods or non-use of contraception	Use of modern contraceptives for all women who want to space or limit future pregnancies	Maternal mortality and morbidity; *increased perinatal and child mortality*	Demographic and health survey (DHS) nationally representative surveys in 58 countries	DHS surveys for contraceptive failure rates and systematic review of published work for conception probabilities among non-users; WHO abortion database
Addictive substances					
Tobacco	Current degree of smoking impact ratio (indirect indicator of accumulated smoking risk based on excess lung cancer mortality); prevalence of oral tobacco use	No tobacco use	Lung cancer, upper aerodigestive cancer, all other cancers, chronic obstructive pulmonary disease (COPD), other respiratory diseases, all vascular diseases, and other medical causes in adults >30; *fire injuries, maternal outcomes and perinatal conditions*	WHO GBD lung cancer mortality database based on complete (about 70 countries) or partial (about 40 countries) vital registration and IARD estimates	ACS-CPS II prospective study of risk factors for mortality in more than one million Americans and retrospective proportional mortality study of one million deaths in 24 urban centres and 74 rural areas of China
Alcohol	Current alcohol consumption volumes and patterns	No alcohol use‡	IHD, stroke, hypertensive heart disease, diabetes, liver cancer, mouth and oropharynx cancer, breast cancer, oesophagus cancer, selected other cancers, liver-cirrhosis, epilepsy, alcohol use disorders, depression, intentional and unintentional injuries; *selected other cardiovascular diseases and cancers, social consequences*	WHO Global Status Report (including production and trade data) on average alcohol consumption; systematic review of country surveys on abstinence and levels of alcohol consumption, including contacting researchers for unpublished data; systematic review of published work and multiple regional expert consultation for unrecorded consumption; primary key informant questionnaires on patterns of drinking	Published systematic reviews and meta-analyses of health effects plus modelling for role of patterns on IHD and injuries

Illicit drugs	Use of amphetamine, cocaine, heroin, or other opioids and intravenous drug use	No illicit drug use	HIV/AIDS, overdose, drug use disorder, suicide, and trauma; *other neuro-psychological diseases, social consequences, hepatitis B and hepatitis C*	Systematic review of published work and databases of United Nations Drug Control Program and European Monitoring Centre for Drugs and Drug Addiction	Updated systematic review of published work on cause-specific and all-cause standardised mortality ratio; UNAIDS estimates for HIV incidence among drug users (based on prevalence surveys among high-risk groups)
Environmental risks					
Unsafe water, sanitation, and hygiene	6 scenarios, ranging from regulated water and sanitation with hygiene through to no improved water supply and no improved sanitation	Absence of transmission of diarrhoeal disease through water, sanitation, and hygiene	Diarrhoea	Global Water Supply and Sanitation Assessment 2000, based on Demographic Health Surveys (DHS), UNICEF Multiple Indicator Cluster Surveys (MICS), national census reports, other national sample household surveys, together covering countries with 89% of global population	Systematic reviews of multi-country randomised controlled trials and observational studies
Urban outdoor air pollution	Estimated annual average particulate matter concentration for particles with aerodynamic diameters <2·5 microns ($PM_{2.5}$) or 10 microns (PM_{10})	7·5 μg/m^3 for $PM_{2.5}$, 15 μg/m^3 for PM_{10}	Mortality from combined respiratory and selected cardiovascular causes in adults >30, lung cancer, acute respiratory infection mortality in children <5; *cardiovascular and respiratory morbidity*	PM_{10} estimated for 3211 cities with population larger than 100 000 and national capitals based on measured annual average concentrations of PM_{10} and total suspended particulates in 304 cities, with a combined population of 559 million with an econometric model of the scale and composition of economic activity, and geoclimatic factors	ACS-CPS II prospective study of risk factors for mortality in more than one million Americans for adult estimates; systematic review and new meta-analysis of time-series studies of mortality in children <5 years

Table 3.4 *continued*

Risk factor	*Exposure variable*	*Theoretical minimum*	*Outcomes**	*Sources for exposure estimates*	*Sources for hazard estimates*
Indoor smoke from solid fuels	Household use of solid fuels and ventilation	No household solid fuel use	Acute lower respiratory infections in children <5, COPD, lung cancer (coal); *cataracts, tuberculosis, asthma, lung cancer from biomass*	National censuses, DHS, World Bank Living Standard Measurement Surveys, other surveys and reports by ministries of energy in 52 countries; estimated for other countries from an economic-energy model	Systematic review and new meta-analysis of cross-sectional, cohort and case-control studies
Lead	Current blood lead concentrations	0.016 μg/dL §	Cardiovascular diseases, mild mental retardation; *anaemia, gastrointestinal effects; nervous and reproductive system effects; social consequences of IQ loss*	Systematic review (more than 700 published sources) on blood lead levels plus data on leaded gasoline use and outphasing	Published systematic reviews and meta-analysis
Global climate change	Climate scenarios based on various carbon emissions and concentrations	1961–1990 concentrations	Diarrhoea, flood injury, malaria, malnutrition; *dengue fever, cardiovascular mortality, effects arising from population movement*	Climate projection models used by the Intergovernmental Panel on Climate Change (IPCC)	Models for effects of meteorological variables on the incidence of vector-borne and diarrhoeal disease, on flood risk and food production
Occupational risks					
Risk factors for injuries	Current proportions of workers exposed to injury risk factors	Exposure corresponding to lowest rate of work-related fatalities observed: 1 per million per year for 16–17-year-olds employed as service workers in the USA	Unintentional injuries: *Intentional injuries*	International Labour Organization (ILO) Yearbook of Labor Statistics and databases, World Bank World Development Indicators, regional and national databases to estimate employment in various sectors and occupations; exposures assigned based on occupation and sector with review of existing data in a few countries	Occupational mortality statistics from social security, insurance, and other sources from several countries plus correction for under-reporting based on independent studies

Carcinogens	Proportions of workers exposed to background, low, and high concentration of workplace carcinogens	No work-related exposure above background to chemical or physical carcinogens	Leukemia, lung cancer, mesothelioma; *cancers of multiple other sites*	Same as occupational risk factors for injuries plus European Carcinogen Exposure (CAREX) database	Reviews of published work
Airborne particulates	Proportions of workers with background, low and high levels of exposure	No work-related exposure above background	COPD and asthma; *pneumoconiosis, silicosis, asbestosis*	Same as occupational risk factors for injuries	Review of published literature
Ergonomic stressors	High, moderate, and low exposure based on occupational categories	Physical workload at the level of managers and professionals (low)	Lower back pain	Same as occupational risk factors for injuries	Review of observational studies and published reviews of literature
Noise	High and moderate exposure categories (>95 dBA and 85–90 dBA)	Less than 85 dBA on average 8 h work	Hearing loss	Same as occupational risk factors for injuries	Published reviews of observational studies
Other selected risks					
Unsafe health care injections	Exposure $\geqslant 1$ contaminated injection	No contaminated injections	Acute infection with HBV, HCV and HIV, cirrhosis and liver cancer; *selected other infectious diseases*	Systematic review of published work, WHO reports, Expanded Programme of Immunization reviews, unpublished reports made available through the Safe Injection Global Network (SIGN) for number of injections and re-use of syringes	Mass action model of infection with hazard modelled on background prevalence of infections (GBD database) and the risk of infection with HBV, HCV, and HIV after a needlestick exposure from an infected source-patient (review of published work)
Childhood sexual abuse	Prevalence of non-contact abuse, contact abuse, and intercourse	No abuse	Depression, panic disorder, alcohol misuse/dependence, drug misuse/dependence, post-traumatic stress disorder and suicide in adulthood; *non-mental health outcomes, such as sexually transmitted diseases, unwanted pregnancies, and injuries*	Systematic review of 136 published studies in 30 countries	Systematic reviews and new meta-analysis of 48 observational studies from 12 countries

* Outcomes in italic are those that are likely to be causal but not quantified because of lack of sufficient evidence on prevalence or hazard size, or both. †The resulting haemoglobin concentrations vary across regions and age-sex groups (from 11·66 g/dL in children younger than 5 in SEAR-D to >14·5 g/dL in adult men in developed countries) because the other risks for anaemia (eg. malaria) vary. ‡Theoretical minimum for alcohol is zero, the global theoretical minimum. Specific subgroups might have a non-zero theoretical minimum. §Theoretical minimum for lead is the blood lead concentration expected at background exposure levels. Health effects were qualified for blood lead concentrations above 5 μg/dL where epidemiological studies have quantified hazards.

Source: Ezzati and co-workers (2002)

WHO region	Mortality stratum	Countries
AFR	D	Algeria, Angola, Benin, Burkina Faso, Cameroon, Cape Verde, Chad, Comoros, Equatorial Guinea, Gabon, Gambia, Ghana, Guinea, Guinea-Bissau, Liberia, Madagascar, Mali, Mauritania, Mauritius, Niger, Nigeria, Sao Tome and Principe, Senegal, Seychelles, Sierra Leone, Togo
	E	Botswana, Burundi, Central African Republic, Congo, Côte d'Ivoire, Democratic Republic of the Congo, Eritrea, Ethiopia, Kenya, Lesotho, Malawi, Mozambique, Namibia, Rwanda, South Africa, Swaziland, Uganda, United Republic of Tanzania, Zambia, Zimbabwe
AMR	A	Canada, Cuba, United States of America
	B	Antigua and Barbuda, Argentina, Bahamas, Barbados, Belize, Brazil, Chile, Colombia, Costa Rica, Dominica, Dominican Republic, El Salvador, Grenada, Guyana, Honduras, Jamaica, Mexico, Panama, Paraguay, Saint Kitts and Nevis, Saint Lucia, Saint Vincent and the Grenadines, Suriname, Trinidad and Tobago, Uruguay, Venezuela
	D	Bolivia, Ecuador, Guatemala, Haiti, Nicaragua, Peru
EMR	B	Bahrain, Cyprus, Iran (Islamic Republic of), Jordan, Kuwait, Lebanon, Libyan Arab Jamahiriya, Oman, Qatar, Saudi Arabia, Syrian Arab Republic, Tunisia, United Arab Emirates
	D	Afghanistan, Djibouti, Egypt, Iraq, Morocco, Pakistan, Somalia, Sudan, Yemen
EUR	A	Andorra, Austria, Belgium, Croatia, Czech Republic, Denmark, Finland, France, Germany, Greece, Iceland, Ireland, Israel, Italy, Luxembourg, Malta, Monaco, Netherlands, Norway, Portugal, San Marino, Slovenia, Spain, Sweden, Switzerland, United Kingdom
	B	Albania, Armenia, Azerbaijan, Bosnia and Herzegovina, Bulgaria, Georgia, Kyrgyzstan, Poland, Romania, Slovakia, Tajikistan, The Former Yugoslav Republic of Macedonia, Turkey, Turkmenistan, Uzbekistan, Yugoslavia
	C	Belarus, Estonia, Hungary, Kazakhstan, Latvia, Lithuania, Republic of Moldova, Russian Federation, Ukraine
SEAR	B	Indonesia, Sri Lanka, Thailand
	D	Bangladesh, Bhutan, Democratic People's Republic of Korea, India, Maldives, Myanmar, Nepal
WPR	A	Australia, Brunei Darussalam, Japan, New Zealand, Singapore
	B	Cambodia, China, Cook Islands, Fiji, Kiribati, Lao People's Democratic Republic, Malaysia, Marshall Islands, Micronesia (Federated States of), Mongolia, Nauru, Niue, Palau, Papua New Guinea, Philippines, Republic of Korea, Samoa, Solomon Islands, Tonga, Tuvalu, Vanuatu, Viet Nam

A = very low child mortality and very low adult mortality; B = low child mortality and low adult mortality; C = low child mortality and high adult mortality; D = high child mortality and high adult mortality; E = high child mortality and very high adult mortality. AFR = Africa. AMR = The Americas. EMR = Eastern Mediterranean. EUR = Europe. SEAR = Southeast Asia. WPR = Western Pacific Region.

Figure 3.7 GBD 2000 subregions

Source: Ezzati and co-workers (2002)

For risk factors for which a relative risk model was not appropriate – eg, occupational or alcohol-caused injuries or effects of lead exposure on blood pressure – disease, injury, or mortality was estimated with existing registers and corresponding hazard relations.

The theoretical minimum exposure distribution was zero in most instances, since zero exposure indicated minimum risk – eg, no smoking. For some risk factors, zero exposure was an inappropriate choice, either because it was physiologically impossible – eg, body-mass index (BMI) and cholesterol – or because there existed physical lower limits to exposure reduction – eg, ambient particulate matter concentration or occupational noise. For these risk factors, the lowest levels observed in specific populations and epidemiological studies were used to choose the theoretical minimum. For example, a theoretical minimum of 115 mm Hg for systolic blood pressure and 3·8 mmol/L for total cholesterol (each with a small SD), are the lowest concentrations at which the dose-response relations have been characterised in meta-analyses of cohort studies. Alcohol has benefits as well as harms for different diseases, depending on the disease and pattern of alcohol consumption. A theoretical minimum of zero was chosen for alcohol, because, despite benefits for vascular diseases in some populations, the global and regional burden of disease due to alcohol was dominated by its effects on neuropsychological diseases and injuries, which are considerably larger than the benefits to vascular diseases. Finally, for factors with protective effects – ie, fruit and vegetable intake and physical activity – a counterfactual exposure distribution was chosen based on high-intake populations and the level to which the benefits could continue in view of current scientific evidence. The theoretical minimum for the risk factors are reported in table 3.4. With theoretical minimum as the baseline, this work is distinct from intervention analysis, the purpose of which is to estimate the benefits of a particular intervention or group of interventions. In addition to information on risk exposure, interventional analysis would require data on effectiveness of interventions.

Results

The mortality and burden of disease for men and women attributable to risk factors included in the Comparative Risk Assessment project in the 14 GBD subregions are presented in tables 3.5 and 3.6. Figure 3.8 shows the contribution of the 20 leading global risk factors to mortality and burden of disease for the world and for three broad combinations of regions – demographically and economically developed, lower-mortality developing, and high-mortality developing. Figure 3.9 presents the burden of disease due to the leading ten risk factors for each of these regional groups, also showing the disease composition, divided into broad groups of disease and injury. The different ordering of risk factors in their contributions to mortality and disease burden reflect the age profile of mortality – eg, mortality from underweight results in larger loss of healthy life years because it is concentrated in children aged younger than 5 – and the non-fatal effects – eg, neuropsychological outcomes of alcohol.

Despite disaggregation into underweight and micronutrient deficiency (which are not additive) and methodological changes, undernutrition has remained the single leading global cause of health loss (figure 3.8), with comparable contributions in 1990 (220 million DALY, 16 per cent for malnutrition) and 2000 (140 million DALY, 9·5 per cent, for underweight; 2·4 per cent, 1·8 per cent, and 1·9 per cent for iron, vitamin A, and zinc deficiency, respectively; 0·1 per cent for iodine-deficiency disorders). This pattern exists because although prevalence of underweight has decreased in most regions of the world in the past decade, it has increased in sub-Saharan Africa, where its effects are disproportionately large because of simultaneous exposure to other childhood disease risk factors. A part of the decrease in the burden of disease due to poor water, sanitation, and

Table 3.5 Mortality (thousands of deaths) by sex due to risk factors in 14 GBD subregions

	Africa		*The Americas*			*Eastern Meditterrean*		*Europe*			*Southeast Asia*		*Western Pacific*		*World*	
	High child, high adult	High child, very high adult	Very low child, very low adult	Low child, low adult	High child, high adult	Low child, low adult	High child, high adult	Very low child, very low adult	Low child, low adult	Low child, high adult	Low child, low adult	High child, high adult	Very low child, very low adult	Low child, low adult		
	M/F	M/F	M/F	M/F	M/F	M/F	M/F	M/F	M/F	M/F	M/F	M/F	M/F	M/F	M/F	Total
Total population	147 133/ 146 945	171 600/ 173 915	160 494/ 164 689	213 309/ 217 623	35 471/ 35 759	72 156/ 66 903	174 275/ 168 301	201 514/ 210 376	108 182/ 110 277	114 051/ 129 133	147 173/ 146 646	639 087/ 602 719	75 796/ 78 558	785 055/ 747 878	3 045 295/ 2 999 722	6 045 017
Total mortality	2206/2050	3154/3001	1342/1392	1459/1120	290/237	409/287	1750/1602	2020/2054	1034/916	1878/1721	1234/1022	6358/5764	616/519	5483/4944	29 232/26 629	55 861
Childhood and maternal undernutrition																
Underweight	438/402	487/441	0/0	14/11	14/11	8/8	223/229	0/0	9/8	0/0	40/29	573/614	0/0	95/94	1900/1848	3748
Iron deficiency	59/67	65/80	2/3	13/13	3/4	3/4	36/44	2/3	3/3	2/2	15/19	139/185	0/0	34/39	375/466	841
Vitamin A deficiency	90/112	120/151	0/0	2/3	2/2	0/0	34/53	0/0	0/0	0/0	10/13	68/101	0/0	7/9	333/445	778
Zinc deficiency	74/68	128/116	0/0	3/2	5/4	2/2	44/45	0/0	2/2	0/0	5/4	132/141	0/0	6/6	400/389	789
Other nutrition related risks and physical inactivity																
High blood pressure	87/128	79/116	179/191	170/162	20/20	76/57	164/171	325/354	281/289	514/671	133/139	668/519	85/76	711/758	3491/3649	7141
High cholesterol	34/52	36/53	161/189	88/79	10/9	51/31	114/101	265/282	144/136	387/518	72/40	488/507	39/39	222/265	2112/2303	4415
High BMI	14/19	21/35	135/137	117/144	15/18	36/28	58/67	183/197	117/141	202/265	44/58	42/110	21/20	163/184	1168/1423	2591
Low fruit and vegetable intake	21/31	33/41	92/79	81/58	7/7	27/15	51/48	95/75	80/67	234/247	55/48	378/311	26/19	269/232	1449/1277	2726
Physical inactivity	20/25	21/27	74/81	52/55	6/6	21/13	47/43	103/103	64/62	147/175	34/34	218/185	23/19	132/134	961/961	1922
Sexual and reproductive health risks																
Unsafe sex	198/234	805/923	8/8	22/27	17/11	0/4	33/39	3/9	1/8	3/13	30/25	231/177	0/3	18/36	1370/1516	2886
Lack of contraception	··/16	··/33	··/0	··/5	··/4	··/1	··/23	··/0	··/0	··/0	··/7	··/56	··/0	··/3	··/149	149

Addictive substances																
Tobacco	43/7	84/26	352/294	163/58	5/1	43/10	114/19	531/145	255/53	548/73	181/12	785/132	128/49	661/137	3893/1014	4907
Alcohol	53/15	125/30	27/–22	207/39	22/6	6/1	8/1	65/–85	100/25	338/88	51/9	148/21	23/–28	465/66	1638/166	1804
Illicit drugs	5/1	1/0	10/7	7/4	1/0	5/1	18/4	11/6	3/1	18/5	13/1	40/8	2/1	28/2	163/41	204
Environmental risks																
Unsafe water, sanitation, and hygiene	129/103	207/169	0/1	16/15	13/10	9/9	117/135	0/1	8/7	1/1	25/21	326/327	0/0	42/35	895/835	1730
Urban outdoor air pollution	11/11	5/5	14/14	16/14	3/2	5/3	28/23	12/11	20/18	22/24	17/15	72/60	10/8	176/179	411/388	799
Indoor smoke from solid fuels	93/80	118/101	0/0	7/9	5/5	1/1	56/60	0/0	8/9	1/3	15/22	218/304	0/0	137/366	658/961	1619
Lead	5/4	4/3	2/1	14/7	2/1	5/2	12/6	4/2	15/8	26/13	6/3	38/19	0/0	21/10	155/79	234
Global climate change	9/9	18/18	0/0	0/0	0/0	0/0	10/11	0/0	0/0	0/0	1/0	35/38	0/0	2/1	76/78	154
Occupational risks																
Risk factors for injuries	14/1	18/1	3/0	17/1	2/0	8/0	27/2	4/0	5/0	15/1	19/1	79/5	2/0	78/5	291/19	310
Carcinogens	1/0	1/0	7/2	4/1	0/0	1/0	2/0	12/2	6/1	13/2	4/0	13/2	4/1	30/9	98/20	118
Airborne particulates	5/2	7/3	12/2	9/1	1/0	1/0	9/2	17/2	7/2	15/3	10/3	54/17	4/1	113/54	264/92	356
Ergonomic stressors	0/0	0/0	0/0	0/0	0/0	0/0	0/0	0/0	0/0	0/0	0/0	0/0	0/0	0/0	0/0	0
Noise	0/0	0/0	0/0	0/0	0/0	0/0	0/0	0/0	0/0	0/0	0/0	0/0	0/0	0/0	0/0	0
Other selected risks to health																
Unsafe health-care injections	10/7	27/23	0/0	1/0	1/1	0/0	24/20	0/0	1/0	6/4	19/9	92/62	0/0	137/58	317/184	501
Childhood sexual abuse	0/0	2/1	1/1	1/0	0/0	0/0	1/1	1/1	1/1	3/2	1/0	16/18	1/1	10/14	38/41	79

The table shows the estimated mortality for each risk factor considered individually. These risks act in part through other risks and act jointly with other risks. Consequently, the mortality due to groups of risk factors will usually be less than the sum of individual risks.

Source: Ezzati and co-workers (2002)

Table 3.6 Burden of disease (thousands of DALYs) by sex due to risk factors in 14 GBD subregions

	Africa		*The Americas*			*Eastern Meditterrean*		*Europe mortality*			*Southeast Asia*		*Western Pacific*		*World*	
	High child, high adult	High child, very high adult	Very low child, very low adult	Low child, low adult	High child, high adult	Low child, low adult	High child, high adult	Very low child, very low adult	Low child, low adult	Low child, high adult	Low child, low adult	High child, high adult	Very low child, very low adult	Low child, low adult		
	M/F	M/F	M/F	M/F	M/F	M/F	M/F	M/F	M/F	M/F	M/F	M/F	M/F	M/F	M/F	Total
Total population	147 133/ 146 945	171 600/ 173 915	160 494/ 164 689	213 309/ 217 623	35 471/ 35 759	72 156/ 66 903	174 275/ 168 301	201 514/ 210 376	108 182/ 110 277	114 051/ 129 133	147 173/ 146 646	639 087/ 602 719	75 796/ 78 558	785 055/ 747 878	3 045 295/ 2 999 722	6 045 017
Total DALY	73 650/ 70 695	103 191/ 101 977	24 480/ 21 804	45 372/ 35 065	9158/7895	12 590/ 10 131	55 790/ 54 140	28 006/ 25 314	21 304/ 17 689	35 099/ 24 144	33 585/ 29 302	178 923/ 177 345	8780/7591	131 634/ 110 818	761 562/ 693 911	1 455 473
Childhood and maternal undernutrition																
Underweight	15 530/ 14 375	17 189/ 15 710	12/11	570/498	512/410	324/312	8203/8407	10/9	367/324	32/29	1634/1239	21 297/ 22 766	6/6	4048/3972	69 733/ 68 067	137 801
Iron deficiency	2263/2521	2451/2905	223/255	446/465	121/217	239/277	1449/1746	87/211	166/271	110/161	681/847	5614/6883	31/81	1876/2462	15 756/ 19 301	35 057
Vitamin A deficiency	3178/3856	4208/5167	0/0	79/103	53/68	9/8	1159/1758	0/0	1/1	0/0	347/406	2321/3368	0/0	241/306	11 596/ 15 042	26 638
Zinc deficiency	2625/2414	4563/4150	1/1	115/99	174/138	66/63	1547/1574	0/0	65/56	5/4	197/152	4635/4961	0/0	208/219	14 201/ 13 833	28 034
Other nutrition related risks and physical inactivity																
High blood pressure	980/1295	984/1177	1642/1141	1807/1438	208/178	840/570	1781/1698	2624/1828	2699/2180	5386/4632	1394/1402	7010/5316	781/451	6783/6044	34 920/ 29 350	64 270
High cholesterol	395/563	456/578	1451/1012	1070/803	109/87	605/320	1273/1051	2062/1317	1461/996	4109/3211	828/412	5562/5528	380/227	2376/2195	22 136/ 18 301	40 437
High BMI	246/318	341/546	1825/1654	1505/1918	189/234	534/456	882/1027	1922/1735	1420/1445	2578/2684	650/818	686/1939	334/295	2430/2804	15 543/ 17 872	33 415
Low fruit and vegetable intake	253/354	434/471	833/536	896/581	72/67	322/172	607/550	785/413	777/511	2431/1684	614/524	4139/3521	237/118	2718/2042	15 117/ 11 544	26 662
Physical inactivity	225/280	262/309	691/576	582/585	61/68	265/164	559/492	852/654	636/494	1461/1236	414/409	2489/2186	228/160	1436/1318	10 159/ 8933	19 092
Sexual and reproductive health risks																
Unsafe sex	6205/7753	24 059/ 29 664	281/235	843/912	521/310	30/162	1125/1508	114/202	50/240	134/295	1009/925	7413/6004	12/65	804/995	42 600/ 49 200	91 869
Lack of contraception	··/997	··/1732	··/2	··/375	··/203	··/119	··/1210	··/3	··/83	··/47	··/397	··/3354	··/1	··/290	··/8814	8814

Addictive substances																
Tobacco	591/97	1311/367	3567/2606	2190/813	51/14	593/197	1780/379	4991/1464	3381/715	7230/832	2712/180	10 474/ 1621	994/325	8313/1296	48 177/ 10 904	59 081
Alcohol	1441/393	3621/785	2925/702	7854/1443	789/170	162/22	328/36	3103/416	2183/446	7543/1570	1793/284	4927/675	708/43	12 020/ 1941	49 397/ 8926	58 323
Illicit drugs	543/156	495/163	808/379	791/310	200/71	449/78	620/153	786/344	181/81	762/223	406/121	1386/282	231/101	1110/259	8769/2719	11 488
Environmental risks																
Unsafe water, sanitation, and hygiene	3797/3119	6365/5355	31/30	686/603	436/320	314/315	3797/4506	33/33	287/262	64/57	734/506	8762/9725	14/13	2112/1879	27 432/ 26 726	54 158
Urban outdoor air pollution	153/132	80/67	87/65	133/99	24/20	47/30	305/253	73/44	170/118	191/129	154/128	718/594	53/31	1343/1161	3533/2871	6404
Indoor smoke from solid fuels	3036/2358	3865/3059	2/4	193/251	175/154	32/32	1817/1691	0/0	233/244	18/49	458/532	6641/7596	0/0	2569/3528	19 040/ 19 499	38 539
Lead	512/488	460/433	68/49	907/789	140/125	238/187	606/504	75/43	304/189	424/211	379/337	1489/1198	15/10	1496/1251	7112/5814	12 926
Global climate change	321/305	631/636	1/2	35/36	13/10	10/10	357/391	1/2	5/5	2/2	19/15	1213/1325	–/1	92/77	2700/2816	5517
Occupational risks																
Risk factors for injuries	662/55	773/68	116/14	745/74	92/9	287/25	1224/96	180/22	243/19	495/41	715/63	3517/258	85/10	2939/301	12 071/ 1054	13 125
Carcinogens	11/4	16/6	58/16	42/9	4/1	13/2	21/4	97/14	66/9	134/19	38/7	134/22	25/4	303/103	962/220	1183
Airborne particulates	106/37	141/69	184/36	213/44	21/4	37/4	148/39	216/43	105/32	167/43	135/47	862/315	68/18	1726/493	4130/1224	5354
Ergonomic stressors	21/16	25/20	17/10	32/15	4/2	9/3	25/16	21/11	18/12	21/14	26/19	111/78	9/5	146/110	485/333	818
Noise	109/49	127/60	92/31	122/43	15/6	60/21	142/88	117/47	92/50	136/92	219/185	799/303	26/22	735/365	2788/1362	4151
Other selected risks to health																
Unsafe health-care injections	244/187	804/742	0/0	13/5	20/12	0/0	437/390	0/0	8/5	106/59	356/156	2341/1759	0/0	2028/791	6356/4105	10 461
Childhood sexual abuse	49/102	167/238	98/320	147/118	46/27	41/83	85/225	61/175	72/158	132/205	42/56	1079/2340	29/96	888/1158	2934/5302	8235

The table shows the estimated disease burden for each risk factor considered individually. These risks act in part through other risks and act jointly with other risks. Consequently, the burden due to groups of risk factors will usually be less than the sum of individual risks.

Source: Ezzati and co-workers (2002)

hygiene (from 6·8 per cent in 1990 to 3·7 per cent in 2000) is due to a decline in mortality associated with global diarrhoeal disease (from 2·9 million deaths in 1990 to 2·1 million in 2000); a result of improved case-management interventions, particularly oral rehydration therapy.

Leading causes of burden of disease in all high-mortality, developing regions were childhood and maternal undernutrition – including underweight (14·9 per cent), micronutrient deficiencies (3·1 per cent for iron deficiency, 3·0 per cent for vitamin A deficiency, and 3·2 per cent for zinc deficiency) – unsafe sex (10·2 per cent), poor water, sanitation, and hygiene (5·5 per cent), and indoor smoke from solid fuels (3·6 per cent).

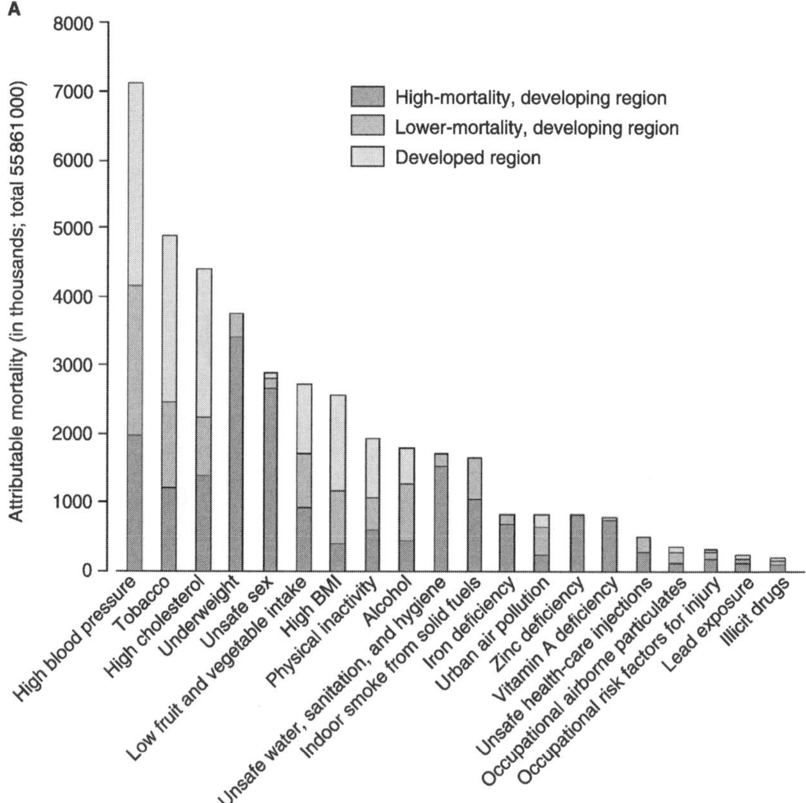

Figure 3.8 Mortality (A) and burden of disease (B) due to leading global risk factors. High-mortality, developing regions = subregions in D and E mortality strata. Lower-mortality, developing regions = AMR-B, EMR-B, SEAR-B, and WPR-B subregions. Developed regions = AMR-A, EUR, and WPR-A. The figure shows the estimated mortality and disease burden for each risk factor considered individually. These risks act in part through other risks and act jointly with other risks. Consequently, the burden due to groups of risk factors will usually be less than the sum of individual risks.

Source: Ezzati and co-workers (2002)

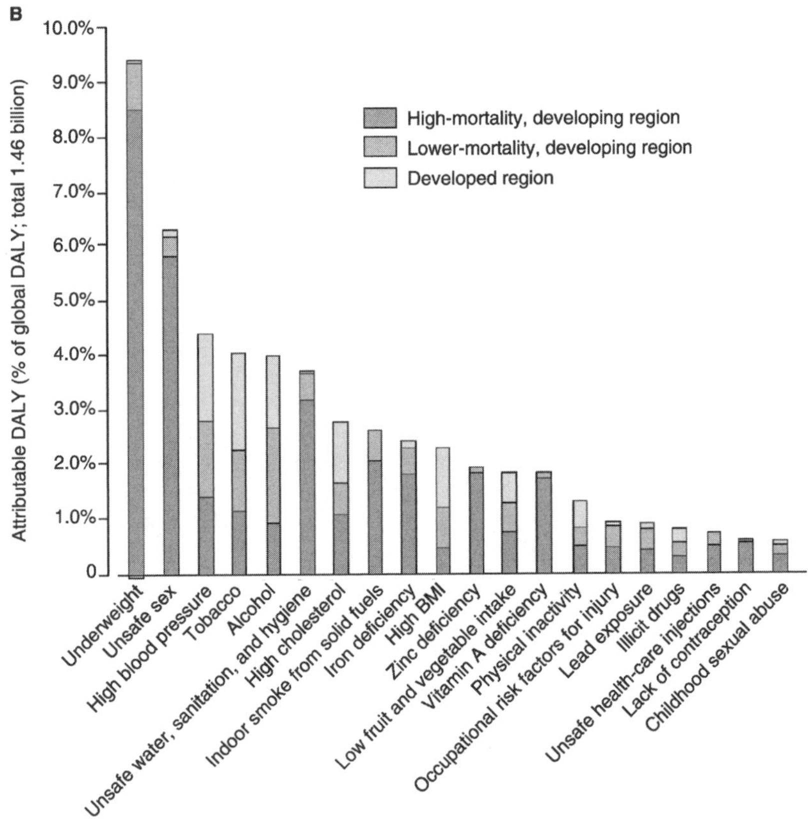

The relative contribution of unsafe sex was disproportionately large (26·2 per cent) in GBD subregion AFR-E (figure 3.7), where prevalence of HIV-1 is the highest, making it a leading cause of burden of disease in this region. The outcomes of these risk factors were mostly communicable, maternal, perinatal, and nutritional conditions (figure 3.9), which dominate the disease burden in high-mortality developing regions. Despite the large contribution of these diseases and their underlying risk factors, tobacco, blood pressure, and cholesterol already resulted in significant loss of healthy life years in these regions. For example, in GBD subregion SEAR-D (figure 3.7; dominated by India in terms of population) the burden of disease attributable to tobacco, blood pressure, and cholesterol had comparable magnitude to micronutrient deficiencies and is only marginally

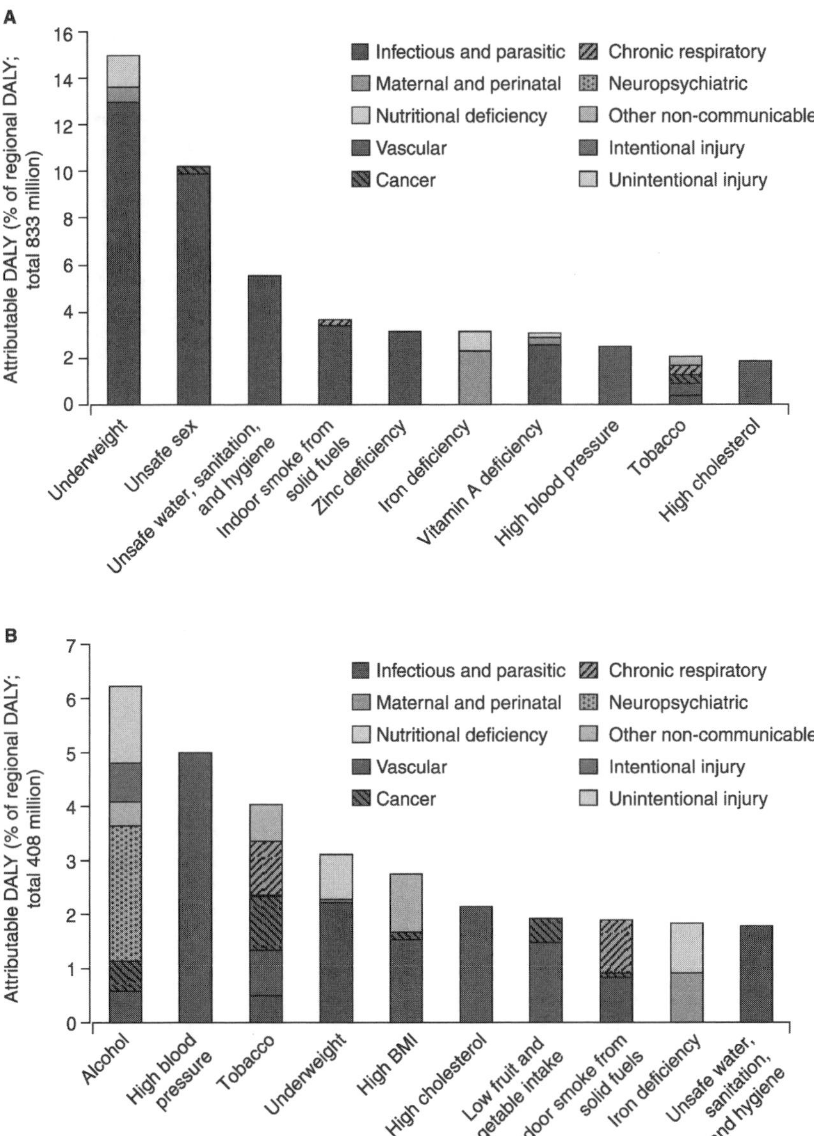

Figure 3.9 Burden of disease due to leading regional risk factors divided by disease type in high-mortality developing regions (A), lower-mortality developing regions (B), and developed regions (C)

Attribution of disease burden to specific disease categories (versus risk factors) is an example of categorical attribution, according to the *International Classification of Disease* (ICD) system.

Source: Ezzati and co-workers (2002)

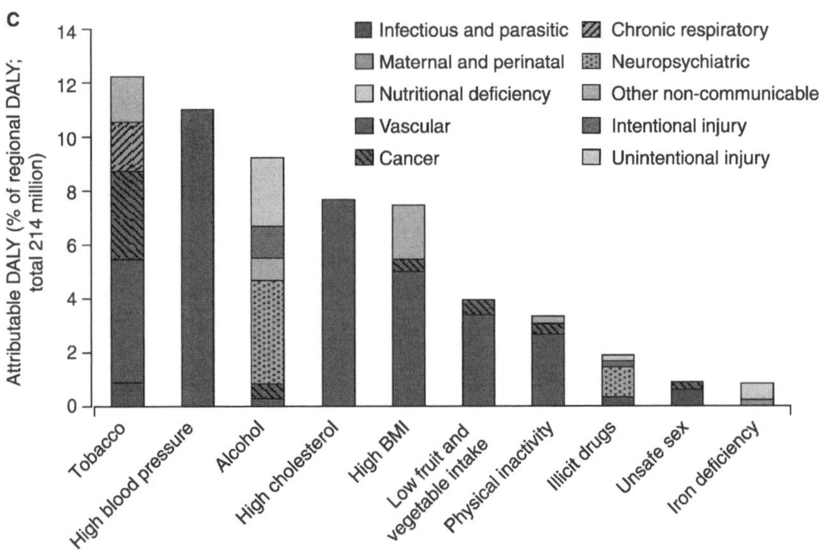

smaller than that attributable to indoor smoke from solid fuels and poor water, sanitation, and hygiene.

In addition to their relative magnitude within these regions, the absolute size of the loss of healthy life years attributed to risk factors in high mortality, developing regions is enormous. Childhood and maternal underweight and unsafe sex in these regions alone (with 38 per cent of global population) contribute as much (>200 million DALY) to loss of healthy life as do all diseases and injuries combined in developed countries (with 22 per cent of global population).

Across developed regions, tobacco (12·2 per cent), high blood pressure (10·9 per cent), alcohol (9·2 per cent), high cholesterol (7·6 per cent), and high BMI (7·4 per cent) were consistently the leading causes of loss of healthy life, contributing mainly to noncommunicable diseases and injuries. Tobacco was the leading cause of disease burden in all developed-country regions, except EUR-C (figure 3.7; dominated by Russia) where alcohol resulted in a slightly larger loss of healthy life. The increase in the disease burden due to high blood pressure compared with 1990 (from 3·9 per cent in the established market economies and 5·9 per cent in the formerly-socialist economies) mainly reflects new evidence on hazard size after correction for regression dilution bias. The contributions of these risk factors to disease burden are consistently larger than those of leading diseases in these regions – eg, ischaemic heart disease (9·1 per cent), unipolar depressive disorders (7·1 per cent), cerebrovasular disease (6·2 per cent) – emphasising the potential health gains by risk reduction.

The lower-mortality, developing regions present possibly the most striking mixture of leading risk factors and diseases. The leading risk factors in these regions (40 per cent of global population) include those from both developed regions and high-mortality, developing regions with comparable magnitudes – eg, underweight (3·1 per cent) and high BMI (2·7 per cent) had comparable contributions to the burden of disease. Furthermore, the decline in the share of burden of disease due to the risk factors – eg, the ratio of 1st and 10th leading risk factors – in lower-mortality, developing regions was slower than those in the other two groups of countries – ie, less clustering of risk factor burden – further emphasising the role of a more extended and mixed group of risk factors.

Alcohol led the causes of burden of diseases in lower-mortality, developing regions as a whole (6·2 per cent) and in GBD subregions AMR-B and WPR-B (table 3.6), but had relatively low contribution to the burden of disease in GBD subregion EMR-B (table 3.6). In general, regions AMR-B and EMR-B had risk-factor profiles similar to the developed regions (tobacco, blood pressure, cholesterol, BMI, and alcohol) whereas regions SEAR-B and WPR-B (table 3.6) had a more mixed risk-factor profile (with the leading five of these selected risks being underweight, blood pressure, tobacco, unsafe sex, and alcohol in SEAR-B; and alcohol, blood pressure, tobacco, underweight, and indoor smoke from solid fuels in WPR-B).

An important finding of this analysis is the key role of nutrition in health worldwide. About 15 per cent of the global disease burden can be attributed to the joint effects of childhood and maternal underweight or micronutrient deficiencies. Additionally, almost as much can be attributed to risk factors that have substantial dietary determinants – high blood pressure, high cholesterol, high BMI, and low fruit and vegetable intake. These patterns are not uniform within regions and in some countries nutritional transition has been healthier than in others. Furthermore, the major nutritional and related risk factors show inter-regional heterogeneity – eg, the relative contributions of blood pressure, cholesterol, and BMI were different in regions AMR-A, SEAR-D, and WPR-B. This heterogeneity further indicates the importance of concurrent and comparable quantification of distal and proximal risk factors to provide a more complete picture of the role of various distal and proximal risk factors.

The analysis also provides quantitative evidence on the public health importance of several previously unquantified risk factors, including indoor smoke from solid fuels (2·6 per cent of global disease burden), high BMI (2·3 per cent), and zinc deficiency (1·9 per cent). The burden of disease due to other risks – eg, physical inactivity – was lower than expected if methodology and results from the limited number of industrialised countries had been extrapolated. The finding that the contribution of physical inactivity to burden of disease is less than expected could arise partly because of difficulties in measuring exposure to this risk factor, which resulted in the use of a categorical exposure variable with a conservative baseline of sufficient (versus vigorous) activity. But this finding also reflects the inclusion of occupational and transportation domains of activity (that are common among rural populations of developing countries) in addition to usual leisure-time activity, which is more relevant to developed countries and urban populations.

For those risk factors that solely or primarily affected children (except childhood sexual abuse), there was little difference in health loss between the sexes. By contrast, the risk factors that affect adults, generally differed between the sexes. Unsafe sex, lack of contraception, and iron and vitamin A deficiency, which affect maternal conditions, and childhood sexual abuse contributed to larger burden of disease among women. The effects of diet and exercise are comparable in magnitude, although in general slightly larger for men. The burden of disease due to smoking, alcohol, and illicit drugs was much greater among men, especially in developing countries, indicating the social and economic forces that have so far made addictive substances more accessible to men. The burden of disease due to occupational risks was also concentrated more among men than women, partly because of the inclusion of only formal employment in the analysis, and partly because of differences in jobs held by men and women, with men having a greater presence in heavy industrial jobs and formal agriculture.

Discussion

Quantitative risk assessment is always affected by uncertainty of exposure, and of both the existence and magnitude of hazard. In one classification, risk assessment uncertainty can be divided into parameter uncertainty and model uncertainty. Parameter uncertainty is often quantifiable with random-variable methods – eg, uncertainty due to sample size or measurement error. Model uncertainty is due to gaps in scientific theory, measurement technology, and data. It includes uncertainty in causal relations or the form of the exposure-response relation (threshold versus continuous, linear versus non-linear, etc), the degree of bias in measurement, etc. Defined broadly, model uncertainty also includes extrapolation of exposure or hazard from one population to another. Uncertainty in international risk assessment is dominated by the model uncertainty, which is a result of lack of and difficulty of direct studies on exposure, hazard, and background disease burden. This difficulty has motivated innovative assumptions and extrapolations even in the best-studied risk factors in a limited number of countries.

Uncertainty in disease causation in practice was secondary to uncertainty on hazard size, because when causality was uncertain, estimates of hazard needed for risk assessment were also unknown or uncertain. For example, whether climate change or inequality would increase disease, or whether the relations between occupational factors or physical inactivity and lower back pain are causal, each have equivalent questions on hazard magnitude. The collectivity of scientific knowledge from a diverse group of scientific disciplines would confirm the possibility of a causal relation in the above instances, but would shift the debate to hazard size. As a result, for some risk factors, only the contribution to a subset of disease outcomes could be quantified in our analysis, because epidemiological studies did not provide enough information for hazard quantification for all risk factor-disease pairs, even when the causal relation is believed or suspected (table 3.4).

In this analysis, estimates of hazard size in individual studies were as much as possible adjusted for confounding. Extrapolation of hazard from a limited number of studies to other populations has, however, received less attention in epidemiological research. Although the robustness of relative measures risk has been confirmed for more proximal factors in studies across populations, their extrapolation is an important source of uncertainty for more distal risks – eg, childhood sexual abuse – or for those whose effects are heterogenous – eg, alcohol and injuries versus alcohol and cancer. Because multiple risks and disease are often correlated – eg, concentrated among certain socioeconomic groups – estimating population attributable fraction would require stratified – eg, by other risk factors – prevalence and disease data. Lack of stratified data is another source of uncertainty, leading to underestimation of effects in the presence of positive risk factor correlation.

Direct exposure data for many risk factors were limited because of difficulties in their measurement and because of underinvestment in risk-factor surveillance, especially in developing countries. To allow maximum use of available data, such risk factors were represented with indirect or aggregate indicators – eg, smoking impact ratio for accumulated hazards of smoking, weight-for-age for childhood undernutrition, and use of solid fuels for indoor air pollution. Furthermore, for some risks, multiple data sources allowed limiting the range of exposure estimates. For example, in the absence of alcohol surveys, total alcohol production, trade, and unrecorded consumption, provided upper bounds on the fraction of the population that would be in the highest consumption category. Finally, some of the risk factors in table 3.4 are represented with continuous exposure variables – eg, high blood pressure. Others have used categorical variables – eg, indoor smoke from solid fuels, underweight, and physical inactivity – even though the health effects occur along a continuum. This choice reflected the availability of exposure data and hazard estimates in categories. In such instances, the contribution to disease within the baseline category would not be captured.

Feedback

1 The main limitations include:

- Lack of data on exposure levels (risk factors) in the population, and limitations of the data available (for example, due to difficulties in measurement and/or lack of risk factor surveillance).
- Lack of data on hazard (estimates of relative risks for the exposure-disease relationships examined) and limitations of the data available (for example, due to remaining uncertainty in disease causation for some risk factor-disease relationships, limitations of the studies performed to obtain hazard estimates (for example, case-control or cohort studies), possibility of residual confounding, and so on).
- The need to extrapolate information on exposure levels or hazard from one population (with data available) to another (without data available).
- Lack of data stratified to show potential correlations among risk factors.
- Uncertainty around the methods used to estimate disease burden.

2 Several differences among the three mortality groups suggest such that demographic changes and a better economic environment are accompanied by a reduction in the relative importance of communicable disease risk factors and an increase in non-communicable disease risk factors. We can see, for example, a gradation in the relative importance of factors such as underweight, unsafe water/sanitation/hygiene, iron deficiency, indoor smoke from solid fuels, these being most important in high mortality developing countries, least important in developed countries, and of intermediary importance in low mortality developing countries. A reverse trend is observed for factors generally related to non-communicable diseases, including blood pressure, cholesterol, smoking, overweight, low fruit and vegetable intake.

3 The dual burden of nutritional diseases includes the problems caused by malnutrition and micronutrient deficiencies and the chronic, non-communicable diseases of adults. The rapidity of the nutritional transition means that many low- and middle-income countries (for example, in the low mortality developing countries) must now respond to both sets of diseases.

Summary

This chapter discussed SMPH with an emphasis on the burden of disease. You should now be able to describe the different uses of SMPH, as well as their advantages and limitations. You should also be more familiar with the GBD study, including its methods used and main results.

References

Andreev EM, McKee M and Shkolnikov VM (2003) Health expectancy in the Russian Federation: a new perspective on the health divide in Europe. *Bull WHO* **81**: 778–85.

Ezzati M, Lopez AD, Rodgers A, Vander Hoorn S, Murray CJL, Comparative Risk Assessment Collaborating Group (2002) Selected major risk factors and global and regional burden of disease. *The Lancet* **360**: 1347–60.

Mathers CD (2003) Towards valid and comparable measurement of population health. *Bull WHO* **81**: 787–8.

Mathers CD, Bernard C, Moesgaard Iburg K, Inoue M, Ma Fat D, Shibuya K, Stein C, Tomijima N and Xu H (2003) *Global Burden of Disease in 2002: Data Sources, Methods and Results. Global Programme on Evidence for Health Policy Discussion Paper No. 54*. Geneva: World Health Organization.

Prüss-Üstün A, Mathers C, Corvalán C and Woodward A (2003) *Introduction and Methods: Assessing the Environmental Burden of Disease at National and Local Levels. Environmental Burden of Disease Series No. 1*. Geneva: World Health Organization.

Ustun TB, Chatterji S, Villanueva M, Bendib L, Celik C, Sadana R *et al.* (2000) *WHO Multi-country Survey Study on Health and Responsiveness 2000–2001. GPE Discussion Paper No. 37*. Geneva: World Health Organization.

World Health Organization (2002) *World Health Report 2002. Reducing Risks to Health, Promoting Healthy Life*. Geneva: World Health Organization.

World Health Organization (2003a) *WHO World Health Survey*. Geneva: World Health Organization (available on http://www3.who.int/whs/ last visited 7 January 2005).

World Health Organization (2003b) *World Health Report 2003. Shaping the Future*. Geneva: World Health Organization.

World Health Organization (2004) *World Health Report 2004. Changing History*. Geneva: World Health Organization.

World Health Organization (2005) *Home page*. Geneva: World Health Organization (available at http://www.who.int/, last visited 2 February 2005)

Further reading

Mathers CD, Sadana R, Salomon JA, Murray CJ and Lopez AD (2001) Healthy life expectancy in 191 countries, 1999. *The Lancet* **357**: 1685–91.

Morrow RH, Hyder AA, Murray CJ and Lopez AD (1998) Measuring the burden of disease. *The Lancet* **352**: 1859–61.

Murray CJ and Lopez AD (1999) On the comparable quantification of health risks: lessons from the Global Burden of Disease Study. *Epidemiology* **10**: 594–605.

Murray CJL, Salomon JA, Mathers CD and Lopez AD (eds) (2002) *Summary Measures of Population Health: Concepts, Ethics, Measurement and Applications*. Geneva: World Health Organization.

Inequalities in health

Overview

In Chapters 2 and 3 you learned about ways of measuring the average level of health of a population and why these are important for public health planners. In this chapter we will go beyond average measures of health to discuss how health can vary within a population, thus leading to health inequalities. You will learn about why these inequalities take place and what can be done about them. Health inequalities are now prominent on the policy agenda. They are recognized as one of the greatest challenges facing the world today as failure to address this problem could have dramatic consequences for global economy, social order and justice, and for civilization as a whole.

Learning objectives

By the end of this chapter you should be able to:

- **describe the main developments in the debate about inequalities in health over the past 150 years**
- **discuss the evidence for and against the explanations proposed for the persistence of health inequalities in the UK in the 1970s**
- **apply a framework for action on health inequalities to the development of a health strategy**

Key terms

Discrimination (based on the definitions of the European Union) Direct discrimination occurs where one person is treated less favourably than another is, has been, or would be treated in a comparable situation on grounds of race, ethnic origin or other factor; indirect discrimination occurs where an apparently neutral provision, criterion or practice would put persons with a given trait (for example racial or ethnic origin) at a particular disadvantage compared with other persons, unless that provision, criterion or practice is objectively justified by a legitimate aim and the means of achieving that aim are appropriate and necessary.

Health inequalities Differences in health experience and health status between countries, regions and socioeconomic groups.

Life course epidemiology Study of the long-term effects on later health or disease risk of physical or social exposures during gestation, childhood, adolescence, young adulthood or later adult life (Kuh and Ben-Shlomo 2004).

Regeneration Reviving run-down or deprived areas, for example by providing employment and training schemes, improving housing, developing transport links, offering local health services, landscaping and creating green spaces from derelict areas etc. (Public Health Electronic Library 2005).

Health inequalities and inequities – working definitions

Improving the health of the poor and reducing health inequalities has become the central goals of many international organizations including the World Bank and World Health Organization (WHO), and of several national governments within the context of their domestic policies and development assistance programmes. Using a common terminology is thus crucial when discussing this major public health concern.

The expression '**health inequalities**' is used to refer to a broad range of differences between different population groups (for example, countries, regions, socio-economic groups, ethnic groups, genders). It generally reflects population differences in circumstances and behaviours that are in most case socially determined (Leon and collaborators 2001). The expression '**health inequities**' represents unfair inequalities that, at least in theory, could be remediable. The term is often used to describe unjust access to health services, a major concern in developing countries and countries in transition (if access to health care was the same for everyone in a region or country, then access inequities would not exist). Although the same terms are used in many countries, it is important to note that health inequalities and inequities within countries are not understood in the same way everywhere. Do Activity 4.1 to see what they mean in your country.

Activity 4.1

Think about what inequalities in health mean in your country and discuss with some of your colleagues. Write down some examples of these inequalities.

Feedback

In general terms, you might have said, for example, something like:

- mortality rates are higher in poorer people compared with richer people
- individuals living in a certain region more often suffer from a certain type of cancer
- people from a certain ethnic background have a higher risk of dying from cardio-vascular diseases
- poor people suffering from chronic diseases cannot afford seeing a doctor regularly

Your answers will vary according to where you live. Indeed, the way we perceive health inequalities often vary among countries. Some believe that looking at inequalities in health status is what counts. Others prefer focusing on health services as the determinant of health status health professionals can most easily influence. For example, in some rich countries of Western Europe such as the United Kingdom (UK) or Sweden, health inequalities often focus on socioeconomic gradients in ill health and mortality as access to health services is relatively universal. However, in some developing countries and countries in transition, the problem is often seen as being related to access to health care with poorer population sub-groups having a lower probability of obtaining health care when they need it. The constraints that prevent the poor from taking advantage of the available health services thus need to be examined.

Changing concepts of health inequalities – historical background

Research on inequalities in health has a long history but much of the early work was undertaken in the UK. Indeed, until the latter part of the twentieth century, there was relatively little research, and few explicit policy responses, in many other parts of Europe. There were several reasons for this. One was that the UK was the first country to go through the Industrial Revolution. This was due in large part to its rich resources of coal and iron ore. It was thus the first country to have to confront the health problems arising in the rapidly expanding, industrializing cities (these conditions have been described graphically by Frederick Engels in his classic book on the *Condition of the Working Class in England*. Across Europe, 1848 had been a year of revolution, except in England. As a consequence, those in authority fell under less pressure to develop systems of social solidarity to prevent the worst consequences of the growing inequality between rich and poor.

By 1860 William Farr was using mortality data to document differences in mortality between localities. He argued that we needed to understand the differences in the environments in which different classes worked. However, a major step in our understanding of inequalities came in 1911 when the British government introduced into the census questions on occupation (rather than simply what industry someone worked in). In 1913, T. H. C. Stevenson, a medical statistician in the General Register Office, used this classification by occupation to generate a set of tables of mortality according to what was described as 'social grades', later referred to as 'social classes'.

Until then, social class had been thought of simply in terms of upper, middle and working classes. However, Stevenson produced an eight-fold classification, with intermediate classes between the upper and middle and between the middle and working classes and by adding three industrial groups for those working in mining, textiles and agriculture.

In 1921 this system was revised. The industrial classes re-allocated to the other classes to create the new five class scheme used since then in the UK. The scheme is as follows:

I Professional occupations
II Managerial and technical occupations
III Skilled occupations
(N) Non-manual
(M) Manual
IV Partly skilled occupations
V Unskilled occupations

In a paper given to the Royal Statistical Society in 1928, Stevenson argued that 'culture' was more important than material factors in explaining the lower mortality of the 'wealthier classes'. 'Culture', in which Stevenson included knowledge of health and hygiene, was more closely linked to occupation than to income or wealth. He conceded that the allocation of occupations to classes was largely a matter of judgement but he argued that the system was validated by the emergence of a uniform increase in mortality moving down the scale, although there is also some evidence that the allocation process was designed to show this.

For much of the twentieth century, the UK was unique in publishing mortality data by social class, although other measures were used elsewhere. For example, mortality data were disaggregated by ethnicity in the USA, showing a large gap in life expectancy (Levine and collaborators 2001).

By the early 1970s there was a widespread sense of optimism in much of Europe. Economies were booming and welfare states were in place. It was widely assumed that the combination of economic growth and social protection would ensure that health inequalities would soon be a thing of the past (this was, of course, before the economic shock caused by the 1974 oil crisis). Consequently it came as a surprise to many people when a report on patterns of mortality in the UK showed that the gap was as large as ever. The **1970–72 Decennial Supplement of Occupational Mortality** took advantage of the fact that, at the time of a census, it was known with considerable precision both how many people in each social class had died (that was always known) but also how many had been alive. By putting the two together it was possible to specify with some accuracy the scale of any inequality. The report showed that men in social class V (unskilled) were 2.5 times as likely to die before age 65 than those in social class I (managerial and professional) and that children in social class V families were twice as likely to die as those in social class I.

Partly stimulated by these findings, a large research effort began in other countries to determine the scale and nature of health inequalities. To many people's surprise it soon became apparent that inequalities could be found almost anywhere one looked. For example: a study in Australia found that children with no parent in paid work were 25 per cent more likely than those with one working parent to have serious chronic illness; a study in Norway found that the proportion of unskilled men reporting a chronic illness was 1.4 times that of professionals; in the USA the age-adjusted mortality of men with lowest level of education was 2.5 times that of those with the highest education; in France men in low status jobs had 5 times the death rate of those in high status jobs. The precise relationship varied among countries but the general pattern was clear.

In the face of this evidence the then UK Labour government commissioned a report into the causes of inequalities in health. The 1992 **Black Report**, named after its chair, Sir Douglas Black, was completed just after the election that brought Margaret Thatcher to power in 1979. It was immensely controversial. The new government was determined to minimize its impact so it cancelled the planned press conference and made available only a few poorly reproduced photocopies. However this plan backfired and an unofficial press conference attracted major interest. The text was subsequently published commercially, rapidly becoming a best seller.

The Black Report confirmed that health inequalities were not narrowing in the UK.

It proposed four possible mechanisms to explain the increasing gap: artefact, selection, behavioural, and materialist. These are now considered in turn:

1. Artefact

This is based on the possibility that biases could arise in the Decennial Supplement as the numerator derived from death certificates and the denominator derived from census. It is possible that an individual may not be described in the same way in the two sources. However this would tend to reduce the scale of inequalities as more deaths would be recorded in the higher classes as people posthumously promoted their departed relatives.

Another possibility was that inequality appeared to be widening simply because social class V was shrinking, with fewer people who were completely unskilled. As a result, the average level of health in social class V moved further from that in social class I (Figure 4.1).

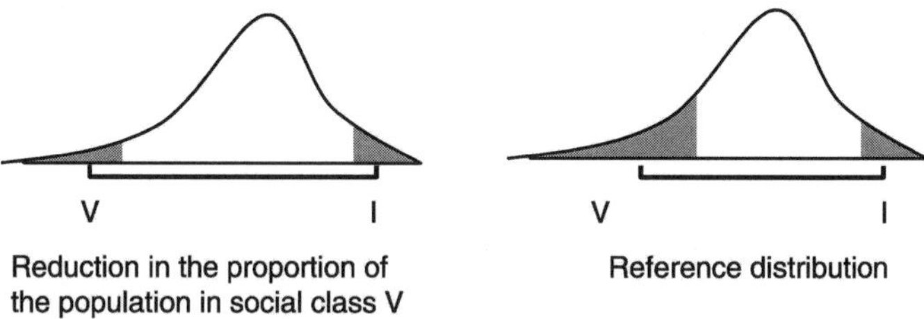

Figure 4.1 The impact of a reduction in the size of social class V

Other possible factors included the changing meaning of social class over time, as old jobs disappear and new ones emerge. For these reasons it was argued that we really could not be sure what the data were showing.

2. Social selection

This was based on the idea that healthy individuals tend to be promoted whereas unhealthy ones loose their jobs. In other words, it is not that low social class makes you unhealthy but rather that poor health causes you to move down the social scale. Evidence in favour of this mechanism included the finding that tall women (by implication who were healthier) marry into higher social classes than their fathers. But it was also known that health inequalities were as great in the retired (and who could not move down the scale as their classification was based on their last employment) as in those of working age.

3. Behaviour

This theory held that the poorest people have the worst health because they indulge in health damaging behaviour. Evidence in favour of this is that smoking is more common in lower socioeconomic groups. However, there was also considerable evidence that behavioural factors and the traditional risk factors that go with them can only explain some of the variation in health. Two other points were also noted: (a) behaviour is determined, in part, by social position, for example when smoking is used as a coping strategy in adversity; and (b) patterns of behaviour by social class, again using the example of smoking, have changed considerably over time and are influenced by government policies.

4. Material circumstances

This saw poverty as the principle cause, with many studies linking levels of deprivation at area level with poor health. To many it was obvious that poverty would lead to poor health.

At the time the Black Report was published it was not possible to determine with certainty which of these theories was correct. However several research projects in the UK were underway that would soon provide important new insights. One of the most important of these was the Office of Population, Censuses and Surveys (OPCS) Longitudinal Survey. Undertaken in England and Wales, it involved identifying a 1 per cent sample of the 1971 census and following them up until death. It had several advantages over previous studies. In particular it avoided posthumous promotion and it was able to detect any selection from downward mobility. It confirmed the existence of large inequalities in health, with little evidence that selection was taking place and it identified the importance of factors that had previously not been considered as important, and which led to gradations within the existing social class system, such as housing tenure or car ownership.

Another landmark study also involved following up people over many years (a cohort study). This was the Whitehall Study of British civil servants which begun in 1967. Even though it only looked at males who were in employment in the British civil service, hardly a complete cross-section of the population, it still found marked inequalities in health and mortality according to employment grade. Unlike the OPCS study it collected detailed information on risk factors, such as weight, cholesterol, smoking, and blood pressure. It showed that, even when all of these were taken into account, they could only explain about one third of the variation observed. The Whitehall II Prospective Study, which started in 1985, is now continuing this line of research among London based male and female office staff aged 35 to 55 years working in 20 civil service departments.

Later in the 1980s a large number of other studies emerged, looking at other measures of health. For example, the Health and Lifestyle Survey, which was a survey of self assessed and objective measures of health undertaken in 1985–86 on 9,000 subjects. Its results showed that a wide range of health measures varied with social class (for example, self perceived health, body mass index and lung function).

This research, as well as a growing amount that was by now emerging from other countries, showed that many aspects of health are determined by social class. The explanations based on artefact and social selection had been dismissed and the emerging consensus, which remains, is that health inequalities can be explained largely by a combination of materialist and behavioural factors. Of course, life is never quite so simple . . .

Activity 4.2

Assuming that health inequalities would come from differences in material circumstances (third theory above), describe a few possible ways in which poverty could lead to poor health.

Feedback

There are numerous ways in which poverty could lead to poor health. The following description sums it up well.

> . . . damp housing leading to increased amounts of respiratory infection; household overcrowding facilitating the spread of infection; inadequate diet associated with low incomes . . . failure to perceive the seriousness of childhood illnesses by poorly educated and informed parents; stresses leading to child abuse; a generally poor environment increasing the risks of child accidents; together with the everyday strain of coping with a demanding young family in inadequate circumstances in areas suffering from multiple deprivation.
>
> Source: Robinson and Pinch (1987)

Emerging potential mechanisms to explain health inequalities

There are two other themes that are increasingly recognized as important. One is the evidence that it is not just one's circumstances now that determine one's health but instead the accumulated experience throughout life (and in some cases in-utero). This idea is sometimes referred to as the Barker hypothesis, after David Barker. This researcher found that poor intrauterine growth (identified from surviving birth records from the 1930s) was associated with disease in adulthood, especially cardiovascular disease and stroke. This has led to a mass of research in what has become known as **life course epidemiology**. There is now compelling evidence to link conditions in early childhood and before birth with a wide range of common (and less common) diseases. The mechanisms vary. For example, cardiovascular disease and cancers may be due to a phenomenon known as programming, in which certain physiological responses are determined in early life, or by exposure to specific agents, such as helicobacter pylori infection which leads to later stomach cancer. The policy implication is that interventions should primarily focus on circumstances of children and those with young families.

A second theme is the importance of **psychosocial factors**. Research has shown that people working in conditions described as 'non-learning' or monotonous have higher mortality from cardiovascular disease after adjustment for social class or that increased mortality is associated with poor social integration. This highlights the need to look beyond the more obvious material factors to include broader measures of well-being.

During the 1980s and most of the 1990s health inequalities were off the political agenda in the UK, although eventually the conservative government accepted that it was permissible to speak (quietly) of 'variations' in health. When the labour party returned to power in 1997, however, they commissioned a new report, essentially updating the Black report. The **Acheson Report** (not to be confused with the earlier report of the same name on the public health function) noted that the number of people living below the poverty line had increased considerably in the UK during the 1980s and that the gains in health among the highest social class had not been shared by those in the lowest class. The Acheson Report summarized the evidence on the causes of and responses to inequalities available at the time and made 123 recommendations for action (only a few were directed at the health service, however). This has been criticized for being somewhat of a shopping list, as it neither prioritized nor costed these recommendations. Nevertheless, it does provide a useful and reasonably up to date summary of the evidence on health inequalities. A major theme, drawing on the work on life course epidemiology, was the need to focus attention on children and families.

Potential actions to tackle health inequalities

So what can be done to reduce health inequalities? Goran Dahlgren and Margaret Whitehead have developed a framework for action that includes four broad areas: strengthening individuals; strengthening communities; improving access to essential facilities and services; encouraging macroeconomic and cultural change. We will look at each of these in turn.

Strengthening individuals involves giving people the ability to make health choices. It recognized that giving people 'Knowledge' does not necessarily lead to changes in either their 'Attitudes' or 'Practices' (the 'KAP' model). It includes, for example, advice on smoking cessation, healthy nutrition and the benefits of exercise. However it understands that this will be less effective with disadvantaged individuals, although it is not ineffective. It also understands that the poor face major barriers to changing their behaviours. For example, in the early 1990s it was shown that families with children in the UK living on social security benefits did not have enough money to meet the basic necessities for life. As a consequence there is a growing focus on empowerment of individuals (this is a major focus of the 2004 English White Paper: 'Choosing health: making healthier choices easier', for example). This links with the second strategy.

Strengthening communities can take two forms. One is **community development**, in which local groups identify what are problems to them and develop local alliances to address them. The second is **community regeneration**. This involves integrated action to improve social conditions, with an emphasis on economic regeneration. This is especially challenging as it is often a top-down initiative and faces problems gaining local ownership. There is, however, a growing body of research on what works and what does not. Thus, success is associated with: strong citizen groups; integrated programmes; priority given to employment and alleviating poverty; a sense of partnership; a long-term commitment; and adequate, protected resources. Failure is most likely where there is mainly physical refurbishment, a short timescale, and no locally managed infrastructure in place.

Improving access to services. This recognizes that the poor face many barriers to services (not only health services but also all types of social services), such as the time involved, the cost of getting there, distance (big supermarkets see little point in investing in poor areas), and knowledge of what is available (increasingly important with the growing use of the internet and the creation of a digital divide). It invokes a concept originally proposed by a Welsh general practitioner, Julian Tudor Hart, who argued that 'the availability of good medical care tends to vary inversely with the need for it in the population served', in other words, those who need health care most are least likely to have access to it (the inverse care law).

The neo-liberal agenda, with privatization of services and commercial consolidation in some countries, has often exacerbated this situation. In many countries, health care and social reforms may make access more difficult. For example, the growth of supermarkets has led to closures of small shops and in the UK rural bus services collapsed following privatization. Consequently, in some parts of the UK, such as the run-down suburbs of some large cities, it is almost impossible to obtain fresh fruit and vegetables at affordable prices.

There are, however, ways to overcome these problems, including development of local co-operatives, making available finance for small enterprises, and outreach activities by health services.

Encouraging macroeconomic and social change. This addresses the big political issues, specifically to what extent should we redistribute resources within society? The argument can be made on two grounds. One is simply fairness: it is unfair to concentrate ever more resources in the hands of the already rich. However a second argument is attracting more attention from some political commentators. It stipulates that countries with large income inequalities tend to experience lower rates of economic growth. There is growing evidence that this can be accounted for by the tendency of such countries to under invest in the less well off in their population, and not just in housing and health but also in the skills that are ever more important to compete in a knowledge based economy.

In the UK, where health inequalities are widening, a framework for action has been developed. In 1998–99, for example, the 'Health Action Zones' was commissioned by the Department of Health. Health Action Zones are multi-agency partnerships between the National Health System, local authorities (including social services), the voluntary and business sectors and local communities. Their aim is to tackle inequalities in health in the most deprived areas of the country through health and social care modernization programmes. As well as dealing with key health priorities (for example cardiovascular diseases, cancer and mental health, teenage pregnancy, drug (misuse) prevention, and smoking), they are addressing other interdependent and wider determinants of health, such as housing, education and employment, and linking with other initiatives. In 1999, the Government published a public health strategy for England in its White Paper entitled 'Saving Lives: Our Healthier Nation'. The strategy identifies the reduction of health inequalities as a key aim (along with the improvement of health) of its strategy and a shared priority for health and social services. It concurrently developed a 'Programme for Action' with the goal of reducing the gap in infant mortality across social groups, and raise life expectancy in the most disadvantaged areas faster than elsewhere. The Programme recognizes the need for a better coordination of activities across traditional boundaries, and work in partnership with front-line staff, voluntary, community and business sectors, as well as service users. More recently, the English White Paper: 'Choosing health: making healthier choices easier' highlighted the importance of supporting people from all sections of the population to make healthier choices in order to help reduce health inequalities.

One of the most controversial issues in recent years in the area of health inequalities has been whether societies that have less equal income distributions have worse health. This was originally proposed by Richard Wilkinson. This researcher showed that death rates among a group of industrialized countries, from which there were data on income distribution, were higher in those with more unequal income distributions. Subsequent research in the USA, at the level of individual states (Kaplan and collaborators 1996), seemed to support this view. You can see in Figure 4.2 the relation (statistically significant) between the proportion of total household income received by the less well off 50 per cent of the population in each state in 1990 and mortalities adjusted for age.

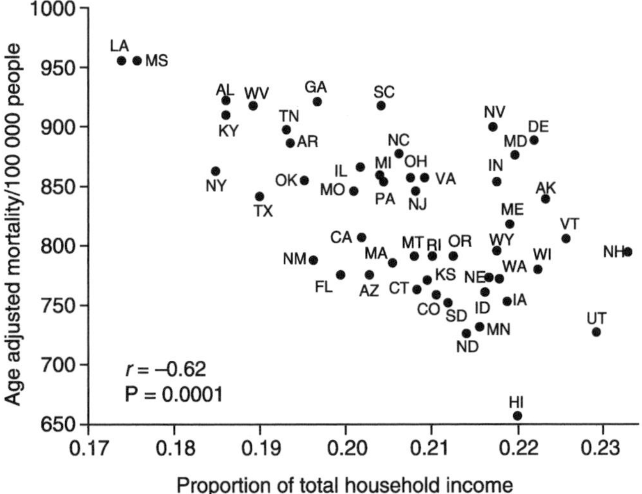

Figure 4.2 Inequality in income in the United States, 1990

Source: Kaplan and collaborators (1996)

This research was highly controversial, not least because the idea that inequality may be more important than absolute income challenged the neo-liberal belief in the 'trickle down theory'. This theory suggested that as the wealthy became even richer, larger amounts of their wealth would trickle down to the poor and so benefit everyone. As everyone was gaining it did not matter whether the gap between top and bottom was widening.

Subsequent work, however, cast doubt on this relationship. In particular, it was shown that with a larger number of countries the relationship was no longer present, as was also the case when income per individual rather than income per family (with no adjustment for family size) was used. A subsequent study by the same researchers (Ross and collaborators 2000), showed that the association they had reported for states in the USA was not seen among Canadian provinces.

Nonetheless, the belief that income inequality in a country is an important determinant of overall health has persisted. One reason is that the mechanisms proposed are intuitively attractive. In particular, the strong association between homicide and income inequality in the US seems easily explicable. However the major mechanisms proposed is that knowledge of one's relative position in society leads to psychosocial stress, and subsequently to illness.

The following extract from a paper by Lynch and colleagues (2001) addresses this relationship. You will see that the authors refer to the Gini coefficient.

The Gini coefficient is a measure of income inequality. Consider a society in which income was distributed perfectly equally. If you plotted a graph of the cumulative percentage of individuals (or households, depending on what you were interested in) against the cumulative percentage of income, you would get a straight line (AB in Figure 4.3). But in practice, this never happens. Typically the poorest receive quite a bit less than 10 per cent of the overall income (illustrated by the dots – representing deciles – and the curved line). The Gini coefficient is simply a mathematical representation of this situation, calculated as the area ABC (shaded) divided by the area ABD. The smaller it is, the more equal is the distribution of income.

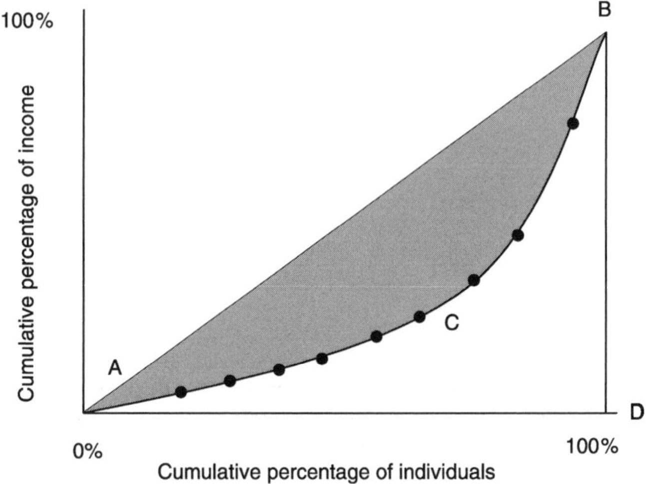

Figure 4.3 The Gini coefficient

Activity 4.3

As you read the extract, consider the following questions:

1 What are the main challenges faced in describing patterns of income inequality in a country?

2 What do the authors mean by the term 'social capital'?
3 The authors found a strong correlation between the Gini coefficient and life expectancy when they compared all 22 countries. Why was this?
4 What explained the association between income inequality and child mortality?
5 The authors describe the USA as the exception, not the rule. Why?
6 What does this paper add to the debate on the relationship between income inequality and health?

Income inequality, the psychosocial environment and health: comparisons of wealthy nations

Important questions remain about the underlying empirical evidence to support claims that countries with more income inequality and poorer psychosocial environment have worse population health. Previous research has been based on small numbers of countries and limited health indicators, such as life expectancy – a synthetic, overall measure of population health which can mask differences in the age and cause of death structure between countries. Across Europe, between country differences in the cause of death structure have been shown to be important in interpreting differences in the extent of within country health inequalities.

We aimed to assess associations between income inequality and low birthweight, life expectancy, self-rated health, and age-specific and cause-specific mortality among countries providing data in wave III of the Luxembourg Income Study (LIS). The LIS is widely regarded as the premier study of income distribution in the world. We have also examined how aspects of the psychosocial environment were associated with between-country variations in health.

Methods

Country selection

Wave III (1989–92) of the LIS provides the most recent, complete income inequality data available and includes 23 countries – Taiwan, Czech republic, Hungary, Israel, Poland, Russia, Slovak republic, Australia, Belgium, Canada, Denmark, Finland, France, Germany, Italy, Luxembourg, Netherlands, Norway, Spain, Sweden, Switzerland, UK, and USA. Taiwan was excluded because health data were not available. We first examined income inequality and life expectancy among the remaining 22 countries. However, all subsequent analyses were limited to 16 countries after excluding Russia, Poland, Hungary, Slovak and Czech republics, and Israel. We limited the sample because the period under study witnessed the break-up of the Soviet Union, collapse of other eastern bloc governments, and the continuing struggles in Israel. Such social instability may directly affect both income inequality and measures of the psychosocial environment thus making comparisons with countries having more stable political, economic, and social institutions difficult to interpret.

Assessment of income inequality

We used the Gini coefficient, based on equivalised household disposable income, as our measure of income inequality. This is a standard measure providing an overall estimate of inequality that ranges from 0 to 1 – higher values mean greater inequality.

Assessment of the psychosocial environment

We used data from the 1990–91 wave of the World Values Survey (WVS) to generate measures of the quality of the psychosocial environment. The WVS was conducted through face-to-face interviews of nationally representative samples in 43 countries and collected data on political, cultural, economic, and civic beliefs, and other aspects of life. All measures were weighted to generate valid national estimates. 'Distrust' was measured by the question 'generally speaking, would you say that most people can be trusted or that you can't be too careful in dealing with people.' 'Belonging to organisations' and 'volunteering' was the mean number of organisations to which respondents reported belonging and doing unpaid work. Both these questions were asked in regard to a variety of organisations – social welfare, religious, education/cultural, political, local community, third world development/human rights, conservation/environment, professional, youth, recreation, women's groups, peace, animal rights, health-related, or other groups. Mean perceptions of 'control' were assessed from a question on how much 'freedom of choice and control you feel you have over the way your life turns out'. 'Belonging to a trade union' was the per cent of respondents reporting trade union membership. We had a priori distinguished 'belonging to trade unions' from belonging to other types of organisations because of the specific role trade unions play in affecting socioeconomic policies and in mediating social class relations. We also included an additional social indicator from the UN Human Development Report – 'females in government' – which represents the per cent of elected seats in national government held by women.

Assessment of health outcome

Life expectancy at birth (1991–93) was taken from the WHO's statistical information system. Mortality rates were calculated from age-specific and sex-specific numbers of deaths and population counts from the WHO mortality database. All-cause death rates were standardised in 5-year age groups using the new European Standard populations for men and women. We calculated rates for all ages combined and age groups <1, 1–14, 15–44, 45–64, and 65 years plus. Standardised mortality rates were also computed for the following causes of death: coronary heart disease, stroke, lung cancer, breast cancer, prostate cancer, diabetes, infectious, chronic obstructive pulmonary disease, cirrhosis, unintended injury, and homicide. We compared mortality rates for 1989–92 for all countries except Germany, where only 1990–92 data were available. Rates of low birthweight (<2500 g) were obtained from WHO's statistical information system and were available for 1991–93 for all study countries except Canada and the USA (for which 1989–90 rates were used). Low birthweight data were not available for the Netherlands. Self-rated poor health was taken from the WVS, and represents the per cent of the population reporting their health to be 'fair, poor, or very poor'. All outcomes were calculated from pooled rates for the years described above except for self-rated health which was based on point prevalence for the 1990–91 group of the WVS survey.

Statistical analyses

We calculated Pearson correlation coefficients for associations between income inequality, measures of social capital, and health outcomes. All analyses were weighted by population size and adjusted for gross domestic product, using the Penn World Tables purchasing power parity.

Results

We first examined data on income inequality and life expectancy for 22 countries in the wave III LIS database, in figure 4.4, which shows that income inequality was strongly and negatively associated with life expectancy (p=0·0001). However, this association was largely induced by the data point for Russia, where the level of income inequality vastly exceeded all other countries. For the reasons explained above all subsequent analysis excluded Russia, Poland, Hungary, Czech and Slovak republics, and Israel.

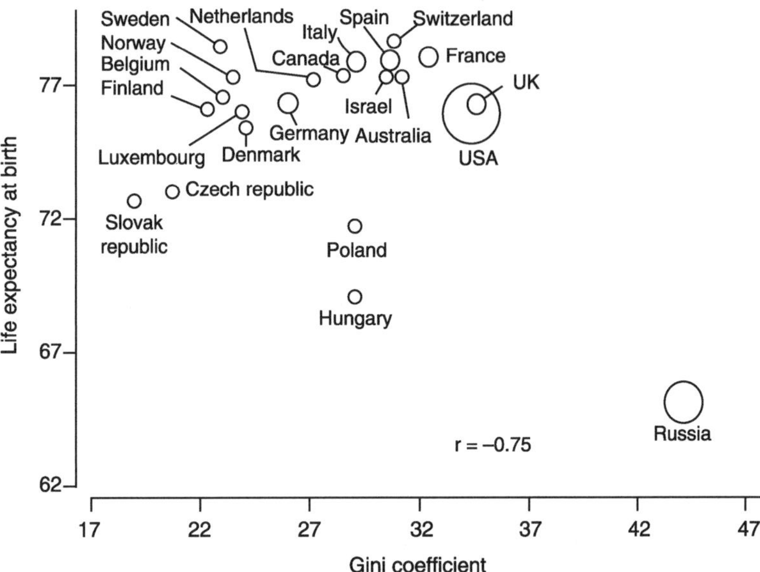

Figure 4.4 Income inequality (gini coefficient) and life expectancy for all 22 countries reporting to the Luxembourg Income Study, for the period 1989–91

Source: Lynch and collaborators (2001)

Table 4.1 shows sex-specific associations of income inequality with mortality by age and cause, and with life expectancy, for 16 countries. Higher income inequality was strongly associated with greater mortality among infants, and more moderately associated with mortality among those aged 1–14 years in both sexes. Associations between income inequality and mortality declined with age at death, and then reversed, so that among those aged 65 years or older, higher income inequality was moderately, but not conventionally significantly, associated with lower all-cause mortality. Income inequality was not related to life expectancy differences. In analyses not shown, exclusion of the USA substantially diminished the associations between income inequality and child mortality (eg, female infant mortality from *r*=0·69 to *r*=0·26).

Income inequality was inconsistently associated with specific causes of death. Among women, higher inequality was at least moderately associated with higher rates of homicide, lung cancer, chronic pulmonary obstructive disease, infectious disease, and unintentional deaths under age 1 year. However, it was also moderately associated with lower stroke and suicide rates among women. For men, higher inequality was associated with high rates of homicide, infectious disease, and unintentional death from ages 0–14 years, but it was also associated with lower stroke mortality. Income inequality was not associated with CHD, breast or prostate cancer, cirrhosis or diabetes. Exclusion of the USA removed associations between income inequality and deaths from unintentional injury, infectious disease, and homicide (data not shown).

Table 4.1 Correlation weighted by population size between income inequality (gini coefficient) with mortality and life expectancy OECD among 16 countries (1989–92), adjusted for gross domestic product per capita

	Women	*p value*	*Men*	*p value*
Mortality by age				
<1 year	0·69	0·004	0·74	0·002
1–14 years	0·53	0·04	0·60	0·02
15–44 years	0·46	0·09	0·45	0·09
45–64 years	0·35	0·20	0·09	0·75
>65 years	–0·41	0·12	–0·47	0·08
All ages	–0·28	0·32	–0·26	0·34
Mortality by cause				
Coronary heart disease	0·03	0·93	–0·04	0·88
Stroke	–0·46	0·09	–0·56	0·03
Lung cancer	0·65	0·01	0·21	0·44
Breast cancer	0·04	0·89	..	..
Prostate cancer	..	..	–0·16	0·57
Diabetes	–0·21	0·45	–0·05	0·85
Infectious	0·50	0·06	0·47	0·08
Chronic obstructive pulmonary disease	0·63	0·01	0·12	0·68
Cirrhosis	–0·31	0·26	–0·32	0·25
Unintentional				
<1 years	0·48	0·07	0·46	0·08
1–14 years	0·35	0·20	0·49	0·06
15–44 years	0·44	0·10	0·34	0·22
45–64 years	0·23	0·41	0·07	0·79
>65 years	–0·35	0·20	–0·20	0·47
Suicide	–0·49	0·07	–0·28	0·31
Homicide	0·66	0·01	0·65	0·01
Life expectancy	0·04	0·89	–0·11	0·70

Source: Lynch and collaborators (2001)

Low birthweight and poor self-rated health were available only for both sexes combined. Higher income inequality was strongly associated with a greater proportion of low birthweight infants (r=0·79, p=0·001). This association was reduced with exclusion of the USA. Income inequality was only moderately associated with poorer self-rated health (r=0·46, p=0·12).

Table 4.2 shows that belonging to organisations, distrust, and control were unrelated to mortality at any age. However, countries that had greater trade union membership and political representation by women had better child mortality profiles. For instance, lower male infant mortality was associated with greater trade union membership and female political representation. Similar but weaker patterns emerged for mortality between ages 1–14 years. No social indicators were strongly related to mortality at higher ages, except volunteering, which was related to lower mortality among elderly people.

Measures of the quality of the psychosocial environment showed generally weak and somewhat inconsistent associations with cause-specific mortality. Greater distrust was associated with lower CHD mortality among both women and men. Since distrust and control were strongly negatively correlated, higher levels of perceived control were also significantly correlated with higher CHD mortality in both men and women. Distrust was also moderately associated with greater cirrhosis and unintentional injury deaths under 1 and above 65 years of age. Belonging to organizations was associated with lower cirrhosis among men and women. The amount of volunteering was negatively associated with stroke and cirrhosis mortality. Associations with measures of social capital were unchanged by excluding the USA. Greater trade union membership and having more women in government were both moderately associated with lower unintentional injury death, especially among the young. None of the psychosocial indicators were associated with female or male life expectancy. Only trade union membership and per cent women in government were associated with reduced rates of low birthweight. Poor self-rated health was only associated with volunteering.

Discussion

Our findings seem consistent with a previous study that compared the USA and Canada. Although the extent of inequality was strongly related to health differences between US metropolitan areas, there was no association between income inequality and mortality across such areas in Canada. Evidence comparing states and cities within the USA has been used extensively to support the income inequality psychosocial environment theory of population health. It seems likely that the USA is the exception, not the rule, and it is possible that evidence drawn from studies within the USA has less direct applicability to other wealthy nations. Higher income inequality within the USA is overwhelmingly associated with more unequal distribution of many powerful determinants of health. This may not be the case in other wealthy countries where there has been more widespread and more evenly distributed social investments in public health relevant goods and services. As we have argued elsewhere, there is no necessary association between income inequality and population health – it may depend on the distribution of other health-relevant resources and exposures that exist within a country. For example, low CHD in southern Europe may be related to high prevalence and low social inequality in healthy diets, while the relatively low life expectancy of Danish women is likely related to the historical patterns of relatively high prevalence and low social inequality in smoking. Understanding how different countries generate particular patterns and trends in population health is likely to be historically and culturally contextualized. It may not be income inequality or the quality of the psychosocial environment that drives population health in these stable healthy nations. Rather, what may be most important are the current and historical links between income inequality and the distribution of health relevant resources and exposures, and how these links have played out over the life course of different birth cohorts. Levels of health within a country are the product of complex interactions of history, culture, politics, economics, and the status of women and ethnic minorities. These complex interactions might not be adequately described by current levels of income inequality or aggregate indicators of the psychosocial environment.

Table 4.2 Correlations between mortality, life expectancy, low birthweight, self-rated health, and distrust, organisation membership, volunteering, control, trade union membership, and the % of women elected to national government among OECD countries (1989–92), adjusted for gross domestic product per capita and weighted by population size

Women	*Distrust (n=14)*	*p value*	*Belonging to organisations (n=13)*	*p value*	*Volunteering (n=12)*	*p value*	*Control (n=14)*	*p value*	*Belonging to trade union (n=14)*	*p value*	*% women in government (n=16)*	*p value*
Mortality by age												
<1 years	0·07	0·82	–0·21	0·51	0·25	0·47	0·14	0·64	–0·56	0·04	–0·63	0·01
1–14 years	0·12	0·70	0·13	0·70	0·23	0·49	0·32	0·29	–0·52	0·07	–0·41	0·13
15–44 years	0·36	0·22	–0·10	0·76	0·05	0·89	0·10	0·75	–0·38	0·20	–0·37	0·18
45–64 years	–0·33	0·28	0·24	0·45	–0·31	0·36	0·40	0·18	0·15	0·62	–0·19	0·50
>65 years	–0·33	0·28	0·19	0·56	–0·59	0·06	0·28	0·35	0·40	0·17	0·43	0·11
All ages	–0·33	0·27	0·20	0·53	–0·59	0·06	0·33	0·27	0·36	0·23	0·33	0·24
Mortality by cause												
CHD	–0·61	0·03	0·30	0·35	–0·14	0·67	0·63	0·02	0·46	0·11	0·16	0·56
Stroke	–0·29	0·33	0·02	0·95	–0·55	0·08	0·23	0·45	0·31	0·29	0·44	0·10
Lung cancer	–0·44	0·13	0·17	0·59	0·53	0·10	0·54	0·06	–0·06	0·84	–0·46	0·08
Breast cancer	–0·21	0·49	0·37	0·23	–0·22	0·51	–0·10	0·75	0·20	0·50	–0·12	0·68
Diabetes	–0·08	0·78	–0·04	0·91	–0·13	0·69	–0·02	0·95	–0·26	0·39	0·19	0·51
Infectious	0·26	0·39	0·01	0·96	0·33	0·32	0·11	0·71	–0·39	0·19	–0·38	0·16
Chronic obstructive pulmonary disease	–0·32	0·29	0·18	0·57	0·13	0·70	0·42	0·15	–0·16	0·61	–0·51	0·05
Cirrhosis	0·50	0·08	–0·58	0·05	–0·66	0·03	–0·37	0·22	–0·28	0·35	0·16	0·57
Unintentional												
<1 years	0·63	0·02	–0·33	0·29	0·10	0·76	–0·15	0·64	–0·59	0·03	–0·46	0·08
1–14 years	0·21	0·49	0·02	0·94	0·30	0·38	0·23	0·44	–0·40	0·18	–0·30	0·27
15–44 years	0·34	0·25	–0·28	0·37	0·37	0·27	0·18	0·55	–0·54	0·06	–0·42	0·12
45–64 years	0·42	0·16	–0·31	0·34	0·42	0·20	–0·09	0·77	–0·28	0·35	–0·24	0·38
>65 years	0·53	0·06	–0·33	0·29	–0·25	0·46	–0·78	0·002	0·07	0·82	0·18	0·52
Suicide	0·34	0·26	–0·04	0·89	–0·38	0·25	–0·45	0·12	0·45	0·13	0·39	0·15
Homicide	–0·03	0·93	–0·01	0·98	0·40	0·22	0·37	0·22	–0·42	0·16	–0·45	0·09
Life expectancy	0·45	0·12	–0·33	0·29	0·41	0·20	–0·44	0·13	–0·31	0·30	–0·14	0·62
Low birthweight (both sexes combined)	0·07	0·84	0·13	0·70	0·22	0·55	0·22	0·49	–0·57	0·05	–0·71	0·005
Self-rated poor health (both sexes combined)	0·47	0·11	–0·36	0·25	–0·80	0·003	–0·29	0·33	–0·17	0·58	0·29	0·34

Men												
Mortality by age												
<1 years	0·20	0·51	–0·23	0·47	0·19	0·58	–0·02	0·95	–0·58	0·04	–0·73	0·002
1–14 years	0·13	0·67	0·01	0·98	0·23	0·50	0·32	0·28	–0·57	0·04	–0·48	0·07
15–44 years	0·39	0·18	–0·31	0·33	0·23	0·50	0·13	0·67	–0·52	0·07	–0·34	0·21
45–64 years	0·41	0·16	–0·21	0·51	0·39	0·24	–0·04	0·88	–0·15	0·63	–0·05	0·87
>65 years	–0·32	0·28	0·34	0·29	–0·51	0·11	0·11	0·73	0·48	0·10	0·43	0·11
All ages	–0·06	0·84	0·17	0·59	–0·53	0·09	0·13	0·67	0·25	0·42	0·27	0·33
Mortality by cause												
CHD	–0·63	0·02	0·36	0·25	–0·11	0·74	0·55	0·05	0·53	0·06	0·23	0·41
Stroke	–0·15	0·62	–0·08	0·81	–0·60	0·05	0·04	0·90	0·31	0·30	0·50	0·06
Lung cancer	–0·07	0·83	0·33	0·30	0·27	0·43	–0·19	0·52	–0·34	0·26	–0·39	0·15
Prostate cancer	–0·16	0·60	0·48	0·12	0·07	0·84	–0·003	0·99	0·52	0·07	0·22	0·43
Diabetes	–0·23	0·44	–0·01	0·97	–0·02	0·95	0·12	0·70	–0·25	0·41	0·09	0·74
Infectious	0·30	0·32	–0·06	0·85	0·24	0·48	0·13	0·68	–0·42	0·16	–0·33	0·12
Chronic obstructive pulmonary disease	–0·40	0·18	0·41	0·18	–0·11	0·74	0·34	0·25	–0·02	0·94	–0·16	0·58
Cirrhosis	0·56	0·05	–0·58	0·05	–0·71	0·01	–0·31	0·31	–0·30	0·31	0·19	0·49
Unintentional												
<1 years	0·67	0·01	–0·33	0·30	0·13	0·70	–0·22	0·48	–0·64	0·02	–0·47	0·08
1–14 years	0·12	0·71	–0·04	0·90	0·32	0·33	0·38	0·20	–0·52	0·07	–0·40	0·14
15–44 years	0·33	0·26	–0·36	0·26	0·33	0·31	0·21	0·49	–0·55	0·05	–0·30	0·27
45–64 years	0·28	0·35	–0·33	0·29	0·46	0·16	0·06	0·84	–0·22	0·47	–0·002	0·99
>65 years	0·47	0·10	–0·32	0·31	0·11	0·74	–0·60	0·03	–0·02	0·95	0·11	0·70
Suicide	0·35	0·25	–0·13	0·68	–0·08	0·81	–0·25	0·40	0·29	0·33	0·23	0·41
Homicide	–0·04	0·89	–0·07	0·84	0·40	0·23	0·28	0·36	–0·46	0·11	–0·45	0·09
Life expectancy	–0·14	0·65	–0·07	0·82	0·28	0·40	–0·21	0·49	0·13	0·68	0·06	0·82

All available data have been used but sample sizes differ because some questions in the WVS were not asked in some countries.

Source: Lynch and collaborators (2001)

Feedback

1 Current indicators of income inequalities may be of limited value. Some researchers have raised doubt about their accuracy for international comparison (for example, difficult to assess household income, income is a sensitive topic, different tools may have been used in different countries, difficulty with sampling, measurement bias, and so on). They may also be too simplistic, the authors suggesting that they do not take account of other important factors on health such as history, culture, politics, economics, women status and ethnic minorities.

2 Social capital is a multidimensional concept used to describe the total mix of relationships individuals have. It is a network of social relations characterized by norms of trust and reciprocity.

3 The association was largely due to the data from Russia as the level of income inequality largely exceeded that of the other countries. The number of data points being small, one such country can have an important effect on the correlation coefficient.

4 The association observed was mainly due to data from the USA as this country has a very high income inequality and poor child health.

5 Studies that compared states or cities in the USA have often shown strong relationships between inequality levels and health differences. However, this does not seem to be the case when we compare other wealthy countries where there have been more widespread and more evenly distributed social investments in public health relevant goods and services.

6 This study challenges the theory suggesting that differences in psychosocial environments are keys to explaining health differences among countries. It suggests that the understanding of differences in health patterns needs to be historically and culturally contextualized. The interactions between history, culture, politics, economics, women status and ethnic minorities need to be considered.

This chapter has concentrated on social inequalities in health, although there are many others, in particular in respect to access to services. For example, older people are often less intensely investigated and treated than younger people, even though they are equally able to benefit. Gender inequity also exists as exemplified in the South Asian context where gender discrimination at each stage of the female life cycle contributes to health disparity, sex selective abortions, neglect of girl children, reproductive mortality, and poor access to health care for girls and women (Fikree and Pasha 2004). Another factor is ethnicity. But all of these issues raise complex issues.

Activity 4.4

Read the following extract from a paper by Raj Bhopal (1997) on ethnicity and health, and answer the following questions:

1 Bhopal mentions the concept of 'black box epidemiology'. What do you understand by this concept?
2 What are the potential pitfalls of research on ethnicity and health, and how can they be avoided?

Is research into ethnicity and health racist, unsound, or important science? Research into ethnicity and health

Expectations of researchers

Scientists want to discover the causes and processes of disease, while health policy makers and planners want to meet the needs of ethnic minority groups. Historical analysis reveals motives such as a wish to reverse the health and social disadvantages of ethnic minority groups, curiosity about racial and ethnic variation, and an interest in ranking races and ethnic groups.

The message from most publications on ethnicity and health is that this opportunity must not be missed. Marmot and colleagues' report *Immigrant Mortality in England and Wales* opens with the statement: 'Studies of mortality of immigrants are useful for pointing to particular disease problems of immigrants, investigating aetiology and validating international differences in disease'.

Black box epidemiology

Does such research discover aetiology? Thousands of associations between racial and ethnic groups and disease have been published with the promise that they will help in elucidating aetiology. The data are usually published in the style of aetiological epidemiology to show relative frequency of disease by means of standardised mortality ratios or similar measures. Few variations have been explained in a way that gives new insight into aetiology.

Most ethnicity and health research is 'black box' epidemiology. Skrabanek argued that science must open and understand the black box. He cited a review of 35 case-control studies of coffee drinking and bladder cancer which failed to provide important information and likened such epidemiology to repeatedly punching a soft pillow.

We need to move from the repetitious demonstration of disease variations that have already been shown in research into ethnicity and health or in work on international variations or in social and sex variations and move to new territory. Studies of ethnicity and health should be able to provide models and contexts for advancing aetiological knowledge if questions for research are clearly articulated and pursued with sound methods.

Is such research unsound epidemiology?

Much research into ethnicity and health is unsound. The key variables of ethnicity and race are vaguely defined, and the underlying concepts are poorly understood and hard to measure. There is inconsistent use of terminology: for example, Asian, white, Caucasian, and Hispanic are common terms in research but have inconsistent and non-specific meanings. There are difficulties in collecting comparable data across cultural groups: for example, do questions on stress or alcohol consumption have equivalence across cultures? There are problems in recruiting representative and comparable population samples.

Data need to be adjusted for known confounding variables and interpreted with the recognition that adjustment is probably incomplete. Rigour is needed for sound epidemiology in ethnicity and health, but the literature is littered with elementary errors (see Table 4.3).

Table 4.3 Basic errors in epidemiological studies of ethnicity

- *Inventing ethnic groups* – A study labelled a group as Urdus on the basis of the language spoken, thus inventing an ethnic group
- *Not comparing like with like* – Inner city populations are different from whole population samples, but studies of ethnicity and health continue to focus on them for convenience
- *Lumping groups together* – A paper on smoking and drinking habits in British residents born in the Indian subcontinent did not describe sex and regional variations, creating the impression that smoking and drinking were unimportant in the 'Asian' population. As has been shown, smoking and drinking are important problems in some subgroups.
- *Not adjusting for confounding factors* – Inferences can change radically once interacting and confounding factors are accounted for

Harm from such research

Perceiving ethnic minorities as unhealthy – The perception that the health of ethnic minority groups is poor can augment the belief that immigrants and ethnic minorities are a burden.

The focus on a few 'ethnic' problems (such as high birth rates, 'Asian rickets,' the haemoglobinopathies, and congenital defects said to be linked to consanguinity) has been at the expense of major problems. Health education material for ethnic minority groups in the 1980s tackled birth control, lice, child care, and spitting, but there was nothing on heart disease and little on smoking and alcohol.

The comparative approach – Most research into ethnicity and health (including mine) is based on the comparative paradigm and presents data using the 'white' population as the standard. Inevitably, attention is focused on diseases that are commoner in ethnic minority groups than in the white population, thereby displacing problems like cancer and respiratory disease that are very common but less so than in the white population from their rightful place as high priorities for ethnic minority groups.

Ignoring quality of services – The misperception that the needs of ethnic minorities are so different from those of the majority that separate strategies are necessary (but which may not materialise) provides a rationale for national strategy to exclude consideration of ethnic minority groups. The promise of aetiological understanding has meant a focus on variation in diseases, as opposed to the quality of services. There is a huge gap in the research record on the quality of care received by ethnic minority groups.

Fuelling racial prejudice – Finally, racial prejudice is fuelled by research portraying ethnic minorities as inferior to the majority. Infectious diseases, population growth, and culture are common foci for publicity.

Conclusion

Knowledge of the interplay of cultural, genetic, and environmental factors is valuable, and research into race and ethnicity is one way to achieve it. Contemporary researchers also justify such research as necessary to help meet the needs of ethnic minority groups and point out that lack of data can hinder health policy. Inequalities in the health status of ethnic minority groups demand attention. For these reasons, scientists' interest in the relation between race, ethnicity, and health will increase.

Participation by ethnic minorities in research, policy making, and the development of services might be one safeguard against repeating the mistakes of the past.

Senior and I made nine recommendations to help make ethnicity a sound epidemiological variable (see Table 4.4). To these I would add (or re-emphasise) the following:

- Researchers, policy makers, and professionals in the subjects of race, ethnicity, and health should understand the ignoble history of race science and be aware of the perils of its return
- In the absence of consensus on the nature of ethnicity and race, researchers must state their understanding, describe the characteristics of both the study and comparison populations, and provide and justify the ethnic coding
- Editors must play a greater role in developing and implementing a policy on the conduct and reporting of research on race, ethnicity, and health
- There should be wide recognition that, like data on social class, information on race and ethnicity has a key role in raising awareness of inequalities and stimulating policy and action.

Table 4.4 Summary of recommendations to improve the value of ethnicity as an epidemiological variable (from Senior and Bhopal (1994))

- Ethnicity should be perceived as different from race and not as a synonym for it
- Ethnicity's complex and fluid nature should be appreciated
- The limitations of methods of classifying ethnic groups should be recognised, and reports should state explicitly how such classifications were made
- Investigators should recognise the potential influence of their personal values, including ethnocentricity
- Socioeconomic differences should be considered as an explanation of differences in health between ethnic groups
- Research on methods for ethnic classification should be given higher priority
- Ethnicity's fluid and dynamic nature means that results should not be generalised except with great caution
- Results should be applied to the planning of health services
- Observations of variations in disease should be followed by detailed examination of the relative importance of environmental, lifestyle, cultural, and genetic influences

Feedback

1 This means that, although we see an association between a given risk factor (here ethnicity) and an outcome, we cannot explain it, we do not understand the mechanism behind it. In the current example, we see health differences among ethnic groups but we do not know what factors might explain them.

2 The author describes various potential pitfalls:

- ethnicity is hard to define (for example, there are inconsistent and non-specific meanings used, ethnic groups invented, groups sometimes lumped together, and so on);
- its underlying concepts are poorly understood;
- it is hard to measure with accuracy or validity;
- there are inconsistent and non-specific meanings used;
- there are problems in recruiting representative and comparable population samples;
- adjustment for confounding factors and interactions is not always done;
- differences are rarely studied in details in an attempt to explain them (going beyond the 'black box');
- research on ethnicity and health can be 'harmful' (for example, if ethnic groups are

perceived as unhealthy, if the conclusions focus on a few 'ethnic' problems, if they minimize the importance of some problems, if the importance of the quality of care is forgotten, if it fuels racial prejudice).

Suggestions on how these can be avoided include:

- researchers should understand how research into race and health was misused in the past;
- ethnicity should be perceived as different from race and not as a synonym for it;
- the complex and fluid nature of ethnicity should be appreciated;
- the limitations of the methods of classifying ethnic groups should be recognised;
- researchers should provide a better description of the characteristics of their study and comparison populations and an explicit description of the ethnic coding used in their research;
- research on methods for ethnic classification should be given higher priority;
- researchers should recognise the potential influence of their personal values, including ethnocentricity;
- analyses should take account of potential confounders including socioeconomic status;
- results should not be generalised except with great caution;
- results should be applied to the planning of health services;
- ethnic minorities should be involved in research, policy making, and the development of services;
- a partnership between scientists from ethnic minority and ethnic majority groups should be developed;
- a wider and constructive debate on mounting criticisms should exist;
- the presentation and interpretation of research into ethnicity and health should change – from aetiological research to being a tool for assessing needs and inequality and for stimulating and guiding policy action (observations of variations in disease should be followed by detailed examination of the relative importance of environmental, lifestyle, cultural, and genetic influences);
- editors should have a greater role in developing and implementing a policy on the conduct and reporting of research on race, ethnicity and health.

Activity 4.5

Now think about your own country, or one in which you have worked, and identify any groups within the population of this country that are disadvantaged in relation to access to health care. Consider the reasons for this and the nature of any policy response. In particular, think of whether there is any direct or indirect discrimination (see list of key terms) that should be overcome. A potential source of help for this task is the website of the London Health Observatory – Ethnic minorities (http://www.lho.org.uk/HIL/Population_Groups/Ethnicminorities.htm (London Health Observatory 2005).

Feedback

The answer will obviously depend on the country you are considering. However you may wish to think of groups that are defined in terms of:

- Their social, demographic, or functional characteristics: elderly people, women, the poor, prisoners, disabled people, rural inhabitants, inner city inhabitants
- Minority populations: Australian aborigines, New Zealand Maoris, Native Americans, First Nation Canadians, African-Americans, Roma in central Europe
- New migrants: refugees and asylum seekers in industrialized countries

The reasons why discrimination exists are many and often reflect country-specific features. However you should consider concepts of citizenship (who is eligible), the size and political voice of the group concerned, attitudes to multi-culturalism, legal rights, etc.

Summary

In this chapter you were introduced to the concept of health inequalities, including the reasons behind them and the potential actions to tackle them. The chapter discussed the main developments in the debate about inequalities in health, and examined the evidence for and against the explanations proposed for the persistence of health inequalities in the UK in the 1970s. It also described how strengthening individuals and communities, improving access to services and encouraging macroeconomic and social changes could be used as actions for the development of a health strategy tackling health inequalities.

References

Bhopal R (1997) Is research into ethnicity and health racist, unsound, or important science? *Br Med J* **314**: 1751–6.

Fikree FF and Pasha O (2004) Role of gender in health disparities: the South Asian context. *Br Med J* **328**: 823–6.

Kaplan GA, Pamuk ER, Lunch JW, Cohen RD and Balfour JL (1996) Inequality in income and mortality in the United States: analysis of mortality and potential pathways. *Br Med J* **312**: 999–1003.

Kuh D and Ben-Shlomo Y (eds) (2004) *A life course approach to chronic disease epidemiology; tracing the origins of ill-health from early to adult life.* 2nd edn. Oxford: Oxford University Press.

Leon DA, Walt G and Gilson L (2001) International perspectives on health inequalities and policy. *Br Med J* **322**: 591–4.

Levine RS, Foster JE, Fullilove RE, Fullilove MT, Briggs NC, Hull PC, Husaini BA and Hennekens CH (2001) Black-white inequalities in mortality and life expectancy, 1933–1999: implications for healthy people 2010. *Public Health Rep* **116**: 474–83.

London Health Observatory (2005) *Health in London – Population groups – Ethnic minorities.* London, London Health Observatory (available at: http://www.lho.org.uk/HIL/Population_Groups/Ethnicminorities.htm, last visited 2 February 2005).

Lynch J, Smith GD, Hillemeier M, Shaw M, Raghunathan T and Kaplan G (2001) Income inequality, the psychosocial environment, and health: comparisons of wealthy nations. *The Lancet* **358**: 194–200.

Public Health Electronic Library (2005) *Glossary*. London: Health Development Agency and National Institute for Health and Clinical Excellence (available at: http://www.phel.gov.uk/glossary/glossary.asp, last visited 2 February 2005).

Robinson D and Pinch S (1987) A geographical analysis of the relationship between early childhood death and socio-economic environment in an English city. *Soc Sci Med* **25**: 9–18.

Ross NA, Wolfson MC, Dunn JR, Berthelot JM, Kaplan GA and Lynch JW (2000) Relation between income inequality and mortality in Canada and in the United States: cross sectional assessment using census data and vital statistics. *Br Med J* **320**: 898–902.

Senior P and Bhopal RS (1994) Ethnicity as a variable in epidemiological research. *BR Med J* **309**: 327–9.

Further reading

Bulletin of the World Health Organization (2000) Special issue on inequalities in health. *Bull World Health Org* **78**: 1–152. This series of papers explore inequalities in health with an international perspective.

Evans T, Whitehead M, Diderichsen F, Bhuiya A and Wirth M (eds) (2001) *Challenging Inequities in Health: From Ethics to Action*. Oxford: Oxford University Press. This is an excellent collection on health inequalities globally.

Healy J and McKee M (2004) *Accessing Health Care: Responding to Diversity*. Oxford: Oxford University Press. This book explores issues involved in providing health care to a wide range of diverse populations in many different countries.

Wilkinson R (1996) *Unhealthy Societies: The Afflictions of Inequality*. London: Routledge. This book develops the ideas of the author about the relationship between income inequality and health. While some of his conclusions are controversial, this book does provide a useful overview of the role of social cohesion in promoting health.

5 The impact of health care on population health

Overview

In the previous chapter you learned about the impact on the health of populations of activities and policies outside the health care sector. This chapter will now specifically discuss the role of the health care sector in promoting population health.

Learning objectives

By the end of this chapter you should be able to:

- **discuss the changing views on the contribution of health care to population health, citing examples from the main writers on this topic**
- **discuss ways of assessing the contribution of health care to health, including the concept of avoidable mortality and the use of specific indicators**
- **describe ways in which health services can be used to promote health more generally**

Key terms

Avoidable mortality Premature deaths that should not occur in the presence of timely and effective health care.

Health system A health system includes all the activities whose primary purpose is to promote, restore or maintain health (World Health Organization 2000).

Health system goals Improving the health of the population they serve, responding to people's expectations, providing financial protection against the cost of ill health (World Health Organization 2000).

Changing views on the role of health care

Prior to the twentieth century, it would have seemed ludicrous to most people that health services could contribute to better health at a population level. Whether one survived or died was seen largely as a matter of divine will. This began to change when, for example, Florence Nightingale (1820–1910) showed that it was possible to reduce substantially the mortality among soldiers injured in the Crimean War by applying strict sanitary routines in a hospital in Turkey. Ignaz Semmelweis (1818–1865) a Hungarian physician, also showed that something could be done when he instituted hand (and later equipment) washing with chlorinated water and reduced the death rate among mothers following childbirth.

Until then, with no anaesthesia, an inadequate understanding of infection, and only a very few pharmacologically active drugs, going in to hospital was, quite correctly, seen as a process that made death rather more likely. By the beginning of the twentieth century, however, things had changed. Anaesthesia was relatively safe, aseptic techniques were in use, as were new drugs such as sulphonamides.

Throughout the twentieth century, scientific knowledge, and with it advances in health care, steadily grew. The Second World War provided a major impetus for innovation in health care, as it did in areas such as aviation. It also led to a vast expansion in the number of people with surgical training, who subsequently pushed surgical techniques ever further. By the 1960s many commentators, viewing the shining new hospitals and health centres that were springing up in industrialized countries, were caught up in unprecedented optimism about what health care could achieve, predicting the end of, for example, infections and cancer.

In the mid-1960s, however, some contrary voices began to be heard. Thomas McKeown, Professor of Social Medicine in Birmingham, looked at the large decline in mortality that had occurred over the previous 100 years and argued that it had largely been due to broader social changes. For example, he showed that the largest declines in mortality had taken place before the introduction of effective treatments. One of his best-known examples is that of tuberculosis, where he could plot mortality against the introduction of specific interventions (Figure 5.1). He argued that the reduction in mortality was largely a function of improved nutrition during the nineteenth and early twentieth centuries.

Soon afterwards, another dissenting voice was heard. This was Ivan Illich, who in his book 'Medical Nemesis' argued that medicine was not only useless, but was actually harmful. He argued that patients suffered from side effects of drugs, hospital acquired infection, and the effects of poorly performed surgery. He saw the newly developed technology that allowed for a scatter gun approach to testing as leading to a situation in which apparent abnormalities (which may simply be the one in 20 tests that lie outside the 95 per cent confidence intervals conventionally used to signify the bounds of normality) lead to increasingly invasive investigations and treatment, each carrying an unnecessary risk. He describes the harm done to patients in this way as *clinical iatrogenesis* but also identifies what he sees as the dependency on medicine that is created, and the resulting diminution of autonomy for patients, as *social iatrogenesis*. Iatrogenesis is derived from the Greek, meaning physician (*iatros*) created (*genesis*). The concept of social iatrogenesis resonated

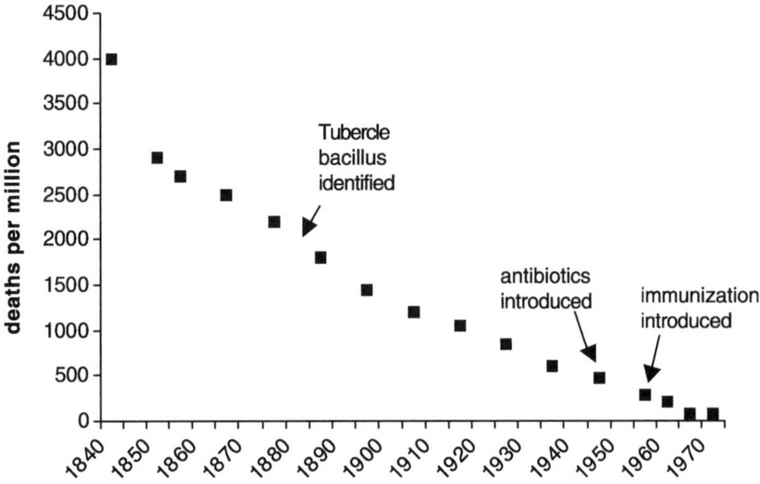

Figure 5.1 Decline in mortality from tuberculosis in England and Wales over time

Source: Derived from McKeown (1979)

with an emerging movement in mental health that challenged the widespread practice of institutionalizing people with psychiatric illness and the growing use of powerful drugs, which were seen by some as a means of social control of deviancy. Leading writers on this topic included the radical psychiatrist RD Laing and the libertarian commentator Thomas Szasz.

Inevitably, the views of McKeown and Illich have been highly controversial and several commentators have revisited McKeown's arguments. For example, Simon Sretzer argued that McKeown was wrong in some important aspects and, while individual health care may not have been very important during the period in question, public health interventions, such as improved housing to reduce overcrowding, clean water supplies, and implementation of regulations on quality of food played a much more important role than McKeown gave them credit for. Johan Mackenbach has examined changing mortality in the Netherlands between 1875–79 and 1970, and also came to a somewhat different conclusion. He agrees with McKeown that antibiotics were only introduced after mortality from infectious diseases had already fallen substantially. However he showed how their use was still associated with acceleration in the rate of decline. Thus, assuming a general introduction of antibiotics in the Netherlands around 1946, he estimated that between 1.6 and 4.8 per cent of the total decline in infectious disease mortality between 1875–79 and 1970 could be attributed to medical care. He also analysed the potential impact of improvements in surgery, anaesthesia and antenatal and perinatal care since around the 1930s. Taking account of all of these factors he estimated that between 5 and 18.5 per cent of the total decline in mortality between 1875–79 and 1970 in the Netherlands could be attributed to health care.

From a biomedical perspective, several physicians challenged Illich, conceding that in the past many treatments were useless or harmful (examples included the application of hot cups to the skin, the use of strong purgatives, and, an example quoted by Paul Beeson, rolling a cannonball on the abdomen). However, they argued that we had moved on from those times and that the treatments made available by the enormous growth in medical knowledge that had taken place in the 1960s and 1970s were much more likely to have been evaluated and found to be effective.

A rather less complacent view was taken by Archie Cochrane, who argued, in a landmark 1971 publication, 'Effectiveness and efficiency: random reflections on health services', that far too much contemporary health care remained unevaluated. He argued for much greater use of the randomized controlled trial, in which subjects are allocated, at random, to different treatments and the outcomes measured. In recognition of his pioneering work, the Cochrane Collaboration, an international collaboration dedicated to the systematic review of evidence of effectiveness in health care, was named after him.

Activity 5.1

Most of the commentators mentioned above were writing in the 1970s. Do you believe that their views still apply? Explain why.

Feedback

Clearly the world has moved on and many new treatments are available. For example, in the field of cancer there are many new chemotherapeutic agents, and some forms of cancer, such as childhood leukaemia and testicular cancer are effectively curable. The management of ischaemic heart disease has changed beyond recognition, with the introduction of thrombolysis, angioplasty, and effective methods of secondary prevention in those who have already suffered a heart attack. Similarly deaths from major trauma have declined, reflecting improved methods of resuscitation. Thus, Robert Beaglehole estimated that 42 per cent of the decline in deaths from cardiovascular disease in New Zealand between 1974 and 1981 could be attributed to advances in medical care and Luc Bonneaux and his colleagues showed that the long-term decline in mortality from coronary heart disease in the Netherlands between 1969 and 1993 accelerated significantly after 1987 coinciding with the wider availability of interventions such as coronary care units and thrombolysis.

However, arguably the greatest change has been that the criticisms voiced by Illich, Cochrane and others have been accepted (even if only reluctantly) and systems have been put in place in many countries to ensure that clinical iatrogenesis is reduced (such as surveillance of adverse effects of drugs and quality assurance programmes) and that interventions are based on evidence (for example, through technology assessment agencies).

Yet, we cannot assume that these changes have taken place everywhere. In many countries there are still health care workers who have been relatively untouched by the growth of evidence-based health care and whose practices are embedded in the past. There is a particular problem in some parts of the world, such as the countries of the former Soviet Union, where, primarily because of the long period of scientific isolation before 1990, many obsolete and ineffective interventions remain in common use.

But does it work in practice?

If we think that modern, evidence-based health care holds the potential to improve population health, can we assess whether it does. Although some organizations that should know better have attempted to judge the achievements of health care by looking at the overall levels of mortality, this is clearly oversimplistic. Clearly, a more sophisticated approach is needed.

Most work in this field builds on a study conducted by David Rutstein and colleagues, in which they proposed the concept of *unnecessary untimely deaths*. These were deaths from certain conditions that should be avoidable, on the basis of current medical knowledge, by timely intervention and that could therefore serve as an indicator for the quality of medical care. Medical care was defined in its broadest sense as prevention, cure and care, and including

> the application of all relevant medical knowledge [. . .], the services of all medical and allied health personnel, institutions and laboratories, the resources of governmental, voluntary, and social agencies, and the co-operative responsibility of the individual himself.
>
> Source: Rutstein and collaborators (1976)

Using this broad definition, they proposed a list covering over 90 conditions including childhood infections and diabetes. Rutstein and his team acknowledged that the chain of responsibility to prevent the occurrence of a case of death from any of the conditions they selected may be complex, and that the physician cannot be solely responsible for failures that result in a death. However, they argued that the physician nevertheless has a crucial role as being the 'one competent to provide the leadership and the professional guidance' to inform (community) action to prevent such events. Information on these events was therefore seen as providing an index of the quality of care delivered by health care providers, agencies and institutions or by health care sectors. Following this line of reasoning, their list includes not only conditions where the role of medical care appears to be obvious, as for example in the case of appendicitis, but also conditions where the contribution of medical care is usually believed to be small, such as lung cancer.

Charlton and colleagues subsequently adopted this approach and applied it at the community level. Accepting that we all must die some time (Benjamin Franklin famously said that 'only two things are certain, death and taxes') they imposed an upper age limit on 'avoidability' at age 65. They also reduced the rather comprehensive list created by Rutstein to 14 disease groups, chosen to reflect different aspects of health care including primary care, general practice referrals to hospitals and hospital care. Their work formed the basis for the European Community (EC) Concerted Action Project on Health Services and 'Avoidable Deaths' that resulted in the publication of the EC Atlas of 'Avoidable Death' in 1988. This document was later updated in 1993 and 1997. This work broadened the definition of health care to include collective health services such as screening and public health programmes, for example immunization. The conditions considered 'avoidable' were chosen on the basis of having 'identifiable effective interventions and health care providers'. Now named 'avoidable death indicators' these deaths were intended to 'provide warning signals of potential shortcomings in health care delivery'.

Since then the concept has been refined and extended, in particular by increasing the range of diseases included as new treatments become available and by increasing the upper age limit, as life expectancy increases generally.

There are now a large number of studies, from different countries. They show that, in almost all industrialized countries, deaths amenable to medical care have declined at a faster rate than those that are not so amenable. For example, Johan Mackenbach argues that, in the Netherlands between 1950 and 1984, improvements in deaths from amenable causes contributed almost three years to male life expectancy and almost 4 years to female life expectancy at birth.

The concept has also been used to compare countries, as in a study that found that about a quarter of the difference in mortality between east and west Europe in the 1980s could be accounted for by deaths from causes that were avoidable using existing forms of health care.

More recent work on avoidable mortality has increasingly focused on distinguishing more clearly between causes that are amenable to medical intervention, through secondary prevention and treatment ('treatable' conditions) and those amenable to interventions that are usually outside the direct control of the health services, through healthy public policies ('preventable' conditions). This approach was used in a study in Valencia in Spain. It showed how deaths from causes amenable to medical care fell between 1970 and 1990 but those amenable to national health policies (such as traffic injuries and lung cancer) rose.

Of course while the concept of avoidable mortality provides a broad picture of how things are changing, it says little about what might be causing any change. For this it is necessary to look in more detail at specific conditions. In general there are two types of indicator of health care performance. One involves looking at things that clearly should not happen. This might include the occurrence of cases of vaccine preventable disease, deaths after routine surgery, or deaths at young ages from conditions where death should not occur if care is adequate. The second group includes diseases for which both incidence and mortality can be measured. The best example is cancer registry data.

Imaginative use of these indicators makes it possible to look at different levels of the health care system (although always recognizing that health systems are complex, with each level continually interacting with others). For example, rates of measles infection (which should be prevented by immunization) indicate the quality of public health and primary care services. The existence, in some countries, of diabetic registers, makes it possible to compare survival, and to draw conclusions on the quality of primary (mainly) and secondary care and, specifically, the co-ordination between them (Figure 5.2).

The use of more specific indicators also makes it possible to identify when health systems are facing problems. For example, in the 1990s, deaths among young people with diabetes increased up to eight times in some countries of the former Soviet Union as supplies of insulin became erratic and existing health services faced growing financial pressures.

As this section has shown, there is now compelling evidence that health care can now play an important role in improving population health. To do so, however, it has to be related to the health needs of the population and to be based on evidence of effectiveness. The issues involved go beyond the scope of this book.

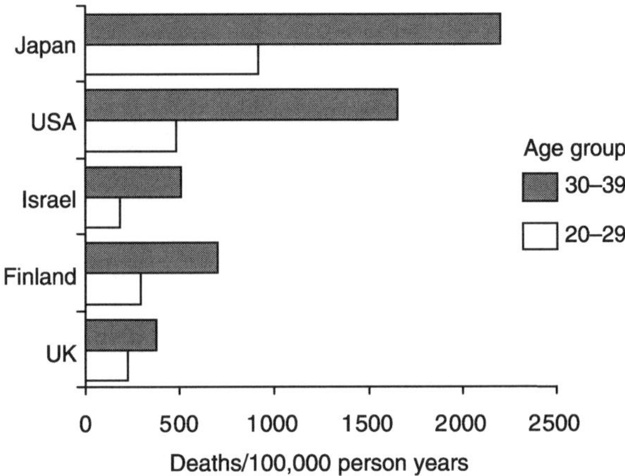

Figure 5.2 Age-specific all-cause death rates in cohorts of young people with diabetes
Source: derived from DERI (1995) and Laing and collaborators (1999)

How can health services be used to promote health?

The final section goes beyond the immediate consequences of diagnosis and treatment to ask whether health care facilities offer opportunities to promote health more generally.

One way to reach this objective is by designing facilities in ways that promote health, both physical and mental. In a classic study of patients undergoing cholecystectomy in a Pennsylvania hospital, those given rooms with windows looking out on trees and lawns had shorter postoperative hospital stays and required less pain relief than matched controls in similar rooms with windows facing a brick building wall (Ulrich 1984). It is easy to forget that patients do care about their surroundings. Results of focus groups indicate concerns about the view from beds, especially among bedridden patients, the quality of washing facilities, privacy, and the ability to control noise levels. Other aspects of the environment are also important, with a German study identifying colour preferences for rooms, furnishings and bed linen, in that case beige, white, green and pink (of course, given the importance of cultural norms, we cannot assume that the same colours would be selected elsewhere – what colours do you think would be preferred in your country?). One manifestation of the benefits of a therapeutic design is the international movement entitled the Planetree model.

It is also important that health services meet the needs of those who cannot make their voices heard, the people who are often invisible to policy makers, such as the homeless, illegal migrants and people with disabilities, or those with invisible diseases, in particular mental health problems but also many chronic diseases. For example, in a British study, most hospital lifts were inaccessible to those with limited mobility or with visual or hearing impairments. Surprisingly, health care facilities are often inaccessible to people in wheelchairs.

Another way for health services to promote health is to send consistent messages. For example, if we accept that the decline in deaths from heart disease reflects improvements in clinical care, and also in people's diet, then it seems strange that we spent vast amounts to unblock someone's coronary arteries using angioplasty but then let people block them up again with fried food and a lack of fresh fruit and vegetables. Similarly, given that tobacco consumption is among the leading causes of premature death in industrialized countries, and harms not only those who are smoking but also those around them, it seems strange that we still permit smoking in many health care facilities. Many hospitals have successfully banned smoking on their premises; their experiences demonstrate that it just requires commitment by managers and health professionals to do so (McKee and colleagues 2003).

Yet health care professionals are especially well placed to bring about change. They are still (for the most part) respected sources of advice. A systematic review of smoking cessation strategies found that one in 35 smokers given brief advice to give up by a physician will do so, and if nicotine replacement therapy is added, this increases to one in 17. Similarly, brief interventions by physicians are effective in reducing consumption by problem drinkers.

It is also important to recall the saying often attributed to Hippocrates 'Primum non nocere' – or 'first do no harm'. The struggle against infection has always been finely balanced, with humans remaining only slightly ahead over the past century as micro-organisms mutate in response to our actions. Antibiotic resistant infection is a growing problem in industrialized countries but rates vary enormously, in general, within Europe. Indeed, rates are low in Scandinavia and high in Southern Europe. Antibiotic resistant infection is clearly linked to prescribing policies and poses a major threat to the way we provide health care in the future. Yet many hospitals still have inadequate or inaccessible hand-washing facilities and physicians often fail to wash their hands between patients even where there is a clear risk of cross-infection.

Finally, it is important to remember that patients are not the only people who use health care facilities. Public health professionals should also be concerned about the health needs of staff.

For example, it is estimated that, within the European Union (EU) work-related injuries in the health care sector are 34 per cent higher than the average across all sectors. Increased flexibility of work and insecurity of employment in the health sector have been associated with excessive fatigue, high rates of burnout, reduced employee morale, absenteeism and high turnover. Beyond the immediate impact on individuals working in health care this may also have implications for the quality of care they deliver.

Read the following extract by Yusuf (2002) in which he discusses ways of reducing the burden of cardiovascular diseases.

Two decades of progress in preventing vascular disease

In the mid-1950s, myocardial infarction and strokes were not considered to be preventable. This view persisted until the early 1980s. Over the past two decades, reliable data have emerged indicating that smoking cessation, β-blockers, antiplatelet agents, inhibitors of angiotensin-converting enzyme (ACE), and lipid-lowering agents (today's HPS results), each reduce the risk of vascular events to a moderate but important degree. Today's issue of *The Lancet* has two reports from the MRC/BHF Heart Protection Study (HPS), a large and well-designed 2×2 factorial randomised trial that reliably evaluates the effects of cholesterol-lowering with simvastatin and a cocktail of antioxidant vitamins in preventing vascular events.

The results of cholesterol-lowering with simvastatin are a culmination of experimental and epidemiological studies as well as randomised trials over the past 30–40 years. Early trials of cholesterol-lowering were not convincing because the available interventions (drugs or diet) lowered cholesterol to only a modest degree, the interventions were not well-tolerated, or the studies lacked adequate statistical power. With the discovery of statins, large reductions in cholesterol concentrations were easily and safely achievable, and this finding led to a series of trials that demonstrated benefits in selected populations. The MRC/BHF-HPS extends the knowledge to much broader populations. A 1 mmol difference in LDL led to a 25 per cent reduction in relative risk of vascular events (coronary heart disease and strokes) overall. This reduction is probably an underestimate of the true benefits that 40 mg simvastatin would confer, because a substantial proportion of patients in the placebo group also received a statin as the results of other trials became available during the HPS. Therefore, the real benefits are likely to be somewhat larger, perhaps around a one-third reduction in relative risk.

Clear benefits were also seen in several subgroups of patients who were poorly represented in previous trials. These subgroups include those over 75 years of age, women, those with concentrations of LDL below 2·5 mmol/L, individuals with diabetes and no vascular events, and those with known cerebrovascular or peripheral arterial disease. The reduction in ischaemic stroke, without an excess of haemorrhagic stroke is noteworthy, and confirms the findings from previous trials. The reductions in vascular events were observed in addition to other effective therapies, such as aspirin, β-blockers, and ACE inhibitors.

The implications of these findings are profound. Cholesterol-lowering with a statin is of value in much broader populations than currently recognised, including those with 'low' and 'normal' lipid values. Thus, practically all patients with vascular disease today in western countries will benefit from statins. Perhaps clinicians will choose to initiate and continue treatment with statins in high-risk individuals without routine lipid measurements. The extremely low rates of myopathy and increases in liver enzymes confirm the safety of simvastatin used at 40 mg a day. The lack of liver toxicity suggests that in most patients, muscle or liver enzymes need not be measured routinely. Minimising measurements of lipids and muscle or liver enzymes will simplify the clinical use of statins, and reduce the costs associated with their use. The current results from the HPS study on efficacy and safety were obtained with simvastatin at 40 mg a day. Higher doses of simvastatin may not be as safe, and the recent withdrawal of cerivastatin on safety grounds emphasises the importance of using specific drugs at doses proven to be both effective and safe.

The HPS trial, with three other major trials, also shows the lack of efficacy of antioxidant vitamins in preventing vascular complications. Indeed the small increases in LDL and triglycerides with vitamins in HPS call for caution, as it could well be that prolonged use of these antioxidant vitamins (at least in western populations without nutritional deficiencies) is not only ineffective but may also potentially lead to some increase in vascular disease. Therefore the routine use of such vitamins in large doses should be discouraged.

The lack of benefit of antioxidant vitamins in several large randomised trials contradicts the claims from observational studies that suggested protection against cardiovascular disease and cancers. Several other contradictions between the randomised trial results and the observational data are highlighted by the HPS results. For example, observational studies have described no consistent relation between lipid concentrations and ischaemic strokes, and some have even suggested an increase in haemorrhagic strokes at low concentrations of lipid. Yet an important reduction in ischaemic strokes, with no excess in haemorrhagic strokes, is seen with lipid-lowering in the HPS trial. Furthermore, observational studies have suggested lower rates of fractures with statins and vitamins, higher rates of obstructive airways disease at low cholesterol concentrations, lower rates of cataracts, and lower rates of dementia with both interventions – yet none of these observations have been confirmed by randomised trials, including HPS. These apparent contradictions are likely due to confounding from other factors that may be associated with use of vitamins or statins, which cannot be adequately adjusted for in observational studies. These findings emphasise the need to generally view claims of treatment benefit from observational studies with considerable scepticism, unless confirmed by large well-designed randomised trials.

The past 25 years have seen the establishment of aspirin, β-blockers, ACE-inhibitors, and lipid-lowering therapies to lower the risk of future vascular events, by about a quarter each, in high-risk patients. The benefits of each intervention appear to be largely independent, so that when used together in appropriate patients it is reasonable to expect that about two-thirds to three-quarters of future vascular events could be prevented. Add to this the potential benefits of quitting in smokers (which lowers the risk of myocardial infarction by a half), and blood-pressure lowering (a 10 mm Hg reduction in systolic blood pressure could reduce the risk of vascular events by a quarter) in hypertensive patients, and it may be possible to lower the risk of future events by more than four-fifths in high-risk individuals. Therefore, the potential gains from the combination of currently known preventive strategies are large. Given that over 80 per cent of cardiovascular disease occurs in developing countries, a priority is to make these interventions affordable, accessible, and convenient (perhaps even a combination pill). Ensuring that patients worldwide receive these treatments will lead to substantial clinical and public health benefits.

The next extract by Robert Beaglehole (2001) also discusses ways of reducing the burden of cardiovascular diseases but from a different approach.

Activity 5.2

As you read the extract below by Robert Beaglehole (2001) make notes comparing and contrasting his policy implications with those of Yusuf (in the extract above).

Global cardiovascular disease prevention: time to get serious

This year there will be an estimated 56 million deaths globally. The two leading causes, coronary heart disease and stroke, will be responsible for 7·0 million and 5·5 million deaths, respectively. For demographic reasons, most of these deaths occur in the poorer regions of the world. The pattern will probably be unchanged in 2020.

Causes of cardiovascular disease

The proximal causes of the cardiovascular disease epidemics are well known. The major risk factors – inappropriate diet and physical inactivity (as expressed through unfavourable lipid concentrations, high body mass index, and raised blood pressure), together with tobacco use – explain at least 75 per cent of new cases of cardiovascular disease. In the absence of these risk factors, cardiovascular disease is a rare cause of death. The optimum levels of cardiovascular disease risk factors are known; unfortunately, only about 5 per cent of the adult population of developed countries are at low risk with optimum risk factor levels.

There is now a strong case for diverting scientists, the bodies that fund them, and the journals that publish their work, away from aetiological research and towards the more challenging task of identifying the best ways of enabling people and populations to lower their risk of cardiovascular disease.

Prevention priorities

The important policy question now, especially for less-developed countries, is the appropriate balance between primary and secondary prevention and between the population and high-risk approach to primary prevention. The only strategy with the potential to greatly increase the proportion of the population at low-risk status is the population-wide approach to primary prevention. All other strategies will, at best, only restrain the epidemics; they will not prevent them. The challenge is to implement the population approach to primary prevention, that is, to shift the population risk factor distributions to the left. Since the aim should be reduction of population risk, and since 95 per cent of the population is not at the optimum risk level, most resources should be directed towards this aim. This challenge will require strong government leadership including fiscal, taxation, and other cross-sectoral policies appropriate for less-developed countries. The real challenge is to redirect resources to population-wide measures, away from strategies directed towards individuals.

Evidence is available in support of the policies needed for the task of shifting risk factor distributions. Data from the Asia Pacific Cohort Studies Collaboration, for example, indicate that a 2 per cent reduction of mean blood pressure (about 3 mm Hg in blood diastolic pressure), achieved by a shift of the blood pressure distribution to the left, has the potential to prevent 1·2 million deaths from stroke (about 15 per cent of all deaths from stroke) and 0·6 million from coronary heart disease (6 per cent of all deaths from coronary heart disease) every year by 2020 in the Asia Pacific region alone. Reductions in mean population blood-pressure values of this magnitude have been achieved in the USA, and could readily be achieved in many populations by reducing the salt content of manufactured food. Favourable shifts in the population distributions of abnormal blood lipid concentrations could be achieved by the maintenance of healthy diets in the face of urbanisation, and the promotion of the traditional Mediterranean diet. The promotion of physical activity is a public health priority, especially in the context of nutritional abundance, and to counter the pandemic of obesity; serious attention should be given to the environmental determinants of obesity and physical inactivity.

Control of the tobacco industry remains an absolute health priority for all countries. The two main aims in tobacco control are to support the expressed desire of most adult smokers in many countries to give up smoking, and to reduce the uptake of smoking by young people. Achievement of the adult cessation goal will have a major positive effect on the burden of the tobacco pandemics in a relatively short time; strong government action –

ie, the provision of subsidised cessation therapies – is needed. Smoking cessation by health workers and in patients with clinical cardiovascular disease are two obvious immediate priorities. The long-term aim is for smoke-free societies; the health effect of successful population-based youth programmes will not, however, be evident for decades. The relations between risk factors and disease events are continuous, and most events occur in people in the middle range of the risk factor distribution who are not normally judged high risk. The effort expended on measuring risk factors in individuals is, therefore, questionable. Since most of the population is at risk in developed countries, and because this strategy is particularly inappropriate for less-developed countries, promotion of the measurement of risk factors, such as blood pressure and cholesterol concentrations, should be stopped, except for surveillance purposes. Perhaps high-risk status can be assessed simply with information on age, family history, past history of disease, and smoking status. On the basis of these questions, health professionals might be able to identify people who would warrant tobacco cessation help and cheap blood pressure and cholesterol lowering medication, even in the absence of knowledge of their biomedical risk factor levels. There is, after all, increasing evidence of benefits at all levels of risk factors in high risk individuals. These issues are of special relevance to less-developed countries, where resources used for individual risk assessment could be used for the primary aim of reducing population risk or for treatment. In these countries, only cheap and effective secondary preventive interventions should be used – that is, aspirin after myocardial infarction.

Advancement of global cardiovascular disease prevention needs strong international leadership and a willingness to work with communicable disease control initiatives in rebuilding public health infrastructures. WHO is again assuming this role, but support is also needed from non-governmental organisations.

Feedback

Beaglehole argues that the major and well known risk factors for cardiovascular disease (inappropriate diet, physical inactivity and smoking) explain up to 75 per cent of new cases of cardiovascular disease. For this reason research should divert its efforts away from aetiological studies into new risk factors towards identifying ways that are suitable to reduce levels of risk factors in populations (that is, the public health approach). In view of the high burden of cardiovascular disease worldwide and the knowledge about factors causing this burden already accumulated he strongly argues that available resources and policy strategies should be directed towards the population approach to primary prevention ('Measures seeking to prevent the initial occurrence of a disease by personal and communal efforts'), that is, increasing the proportion of the population at low risk, rather than promoting further the individualistic approach, that is, identifying and treating individuals at high risk.

Yusuf reviews the progress that has been made in preventing (cardio)vascular disease over the last 20 years, focusing on the benefits gained from treating high-risk individuals through secondary prevention efforts ('Measures seeking to arrest or retard disease through early detection and appropriate treatment or to reduce the occurrence of and the establishment of chronicity'). Recognizing that about 80 per cent of the global burden of cardiovascular disease occurs in developing countries he argues that the priority should be to make secondary prevention interventions affordable, accessible and convenient to ensure that patients worldwide will benefit from treatment.

The arguments given by Beaglehole and Yusuf emphasize different approaches that are ultimately aimed at reducing the global burden of cardiovascular disease. There is no right or wrong answer; both approaches are valid, moreover, they complement each other in achieving this aim. The perspective adopted by either writer very much reflects the work they are involved in as will the perspective you may have adopted in reading the two papers. Again, both visions have advantages and disadvantages; a comprehensive and effective strategy to combat the global burden of cardiovascular disease will adopt an approach balancing both views.

Activity 5.3

Infant mortality has traditionally been used as a key measure of population health in international comparisons. It is commonly regarded as a sensitive indicator of living conditions and of the coverage and quality of health care in a given country. In England, for example, infant mortality was chosen as one key indicator within the National Health Services (NHS) Performance Framework that is also viewed as supporting the UK's national health inequalities target to narrow the gap in infant mortality rates between children of fathers in manual social groups and the population as a whole. However, aggregate measures such as infant mortality provide only limited information about the determinants of health in early life. They may conceal different trends in neonatal and postneonatal mortality as postneonatal mortality is strongly related to socioeconomic factors while neonatal mortality may more closely reflect the quality of medical care.

Read the following extract from a paper by Koupilová and collaborators (1998) to get acquainted with the association of socioeconomic factors with infant mortality.

Neonatal mortality in the Czech Republic during the transition

Introduction

Since the mid 1960s, the health of the people of central and eastern Europe has lagged behind that of those living in the west. The reasons for this gap are complex and there is still considerable debate about their relative importance, in particular the contributions of socio-economic circumstances and health care.

So far, most research has concentrated on the health of adults. There has been less research on the effects of the transition on children. One reason for this is that easily available aggregate figures, such as infant mortality, have shown relatively little change during this period. Furthermore, in the absence of more detailed information on who is dying, it is difficult to interpret any changes that did occur.

There is, however, a powerful argument for examining in detail changes in mortality in early life. In the continuing debate about the relative-importance of socio-economic factors and quality of health care as explanations for the east-west gap in mortality, patterns of neonatal mortality offer an opportunity to begin to disentangle this issue. Any change in neonatal mortality may be due to a difference in the distribution of birth weights, which will largely reflect changes in socio-economic factors, and survival at a particular birth weight, which is much more closely related to the quality of medical care.

This paper examines how neonatal mortality has changed in the Czech Republic during the transition. It compares them with corresponding values from Sweden, a country with one of the lowest neonatal mortality rates in Europe.

Material and methods

Czech Republic

The material consists of information on all singleton live born infants reported to the Czech Statistical Office in 1989–1991 and in 1994–1995. Data for 1992–1993 were not available. The Czech Republic uses the WHO definition of live birth. One hundred per cent of births are attended by health personnel, and virtually all births occur in hospitals. All live born infants with birth weight of 500 + g were included in the register up to 1994; live born infants of birth weight less than 500 g are included from 1995 ($n = 6$ in 1995). To make the data sets comparable, we only analyse births of 500 g and over. Information on single or multiple birth, birth weight, and mother's place of residence is also available from the register. Birth weight is rounded to the nearest 10 g.

There were 380633 singleton live births reported to the Czech Federal Statistical Office in 1989–1991. In 1994–1995, the number of singleton live births reported to the Czech Statistical Office was only 198592, reflecting a substantial decline in fertility rates compared to the earlier period.

In order to study neonatal and postneonatal mortality, data from the birth registry were linked to the death register, using the unique personal numbers. The linkage was successful for nearly 90 per cent of infant deaths.

Although no formal evaluation of the quality of data from the Czech birth registry has been available, the register is virtually complete and it is generally believed that the quality of the information is good. There was no indication that the quality of data in the register changed significantly over the study period.

Sweden

The Swedish Medical Birth Registry of the National Board of Health and Welfare provides medical information, based on hospital records, on more than 99 per cent of all infants born in Sweden since 1973. This register collects data on year of birth, child's sex, single and multiple birth, weight at birth, and other characteristics. As in the CR, the WHO definition of live birth is used in Sweden. Data on infant deaths are also available from the Birth Registry database.

The quality of data from the Swedish Medical Birth Registry has been judged to be of good quality. The birth weight measurements are rounded to the nearest 10 g. Data on birth weight was available for 99.9 per cent of singleton live births.

Over the period 1989–1991, 351796 singleton live births were reported to the Swedish birth register. In order to make the Swedish and Czech data sets fully comparable, 21 live births weighing less than 500 g were excluded.

Statistical methods

The standard definition of neonatal deaths (deaths from 0–27 days) was used. Birth weights were aggregated into 250 g bands. In comparisons, the indirect method of standardisation was used to adjust for differences in birth weight distribution.

Results

Changes in neonatal mortality

Between the two periods, the neonatal mortality rate fell from 5.6 to 3.8 per thousand live births (Table 5.1). As in other countries in the region, there was a dramatic fall in births, from 128008 in 1990 to 94034 in 1995.

Table 5.1 Live births and deaths in neonatal period by birth weight

Birth weight (g)	*Live births (No (%))*	*Neonatal deaths (No (%))*
Sweden 1989–1991		
<1500	1 956 (0.6)	398 (36.1)
1500–2499	10 379 (3.0)	229 (20.8)
2500+	338 934 (96.3)	411 (37.2)
Not known	506 (0.1)	65 (5.9)
Total	351 775 (100.0)	1 103 (100.0)
Czech Republic 1989–1991		
<1500	2 339 (0.6)	937 (43.9)
1500–2499	15 729 (4.1)	552 (25.8)
2500+	362 565 (95.3)	648 (30.3)
Total	380 633 (100.0)	2 137 (100.0)
Czech Republic 1994–1995		
<1500	1 324 (0.7)	355 (47.3)
1500–2499	7 788 (3.9)	150 (20.0)
2500+	189 474 (95.4)	245 (32.7)
Total	198 586 (100.0)	750 (100.0)

Restricted to singleton live births. Sweden 1989–1991, and Czech Republic 1989–1991 and 1994–1995.

Source: Koupilová *et al.* (1998)

There was only a slight, and somewhat contradictory, change in the distribution of birth weights during this time. Mean birth weight increased by 23 g, but there was also a slight increase in the proportion of total births that were under 1500 g. Applying the birth-weight specific mortality rates seen in 1989–1991 to the number of births in each birth weight category in 1994–1995 indicates the neonatal mortality rate that would have occurred if the distribution of birth weight had not changed. This gives a figure of 1180 deaths, compared with the 750 that did occur, and equates to a neonatal mortality rate of 5.9 per thousand. This indicates that the effect of changing birth weight alone would have been to cause a deterioration in the neonatal mortality rate, rather than the improvement that was observed.

Further examination indicates that the observed improvement is actually due to improved rates of survival at all birth weights, although the percentage reduction is greatest in those under 2500 g (Table 5.2).

The figures can be rearranged to show how much of the fall in the neonatal mortality rate, from the predicted 5.9 (on the basis of the new birth weight distribution) to the observed 3.8 per thousand is due to changes in survival in each birth weight category. This shows that 80 per cent of the overall reduction is due to improvements in survival of those born at under 2500 g.

As noted above, even after these improvements, neonatal mortality in the Czech Republic

Table 5.2 Birth weight and neonatal mortality, Czech Republic 1989–1991 and 1994–1995

	Period	*Birth weight*		
		< 1500 g	*1500–2499 g*	*> 2500 g*
Neonatal mortality rate/1000	1989–1991	400.6	35.1	1.8
	1994–1995	268.1	19.3	1.3
% Reduction		33	45	27
Actual deaths in 1994–1995		355	150	245
Predicted deaths using 1989–1991 rates		577	271	332
Difference between actual and predicted		222	121	87
% Contribution to total decline in neonatal mortality		52	28	20

Source: Koupilová *et al.* (1998)

remains higher than that in other parts of Europe, with the rate in Sweden one of the lowest in Europe (Table 5.3). If the birth weight specific mortality rates from Sweden in 1989–1991 are applied to births in the Czech Republic in 1994–1995, the predicted number of deaths would have been 711, compared with the 750 observed. The Czech neonatal mortality rate would then be 3.6 per thousand, which is still somewhat higher than the Swedish figure of 3.0.

Table 5.3 Birth weight and neonatal mortality, Czech Republic and Sweden

	Country/period	*Birth weight*		
		< 1500 g	*1500–2499 g*	*> 2500 g*
Neonatal mortality rate/1000	Cz 1994–1995	268.1	19.3	1.3
	Sw 1989–1991	203.5	22.1	1.2
Sweden as % of Czech		75.9	114.6	93.8
Actual deaths in 1994–1995		355	150	245
Predicted deaths using Swedish rates		285	166	260
Difference between actual and predicted		70	–16	–15

Source: Koupilová *et al.* (1998)

Analysis by region shows that the relative positions of Prague and the rest of the Czech Republic have reversed. In 1989–1991, the neonatal mortality rate in Prague was 5.71 compared with 5.60 in the rest of the country. By 1994–1995 the rate in Prague had fallen to 3.21 but that in the rest of the country had only fallen to 3.84. If, however, during the later period, the birth weight specific survival rates seen in the rest of the country had pertained in Prague, its neonatal mortality rate would only have fallen to 4.2.

In the first period, neonatal mortality among babies under 1500 g was only slightly lower in Prague than in the rest of the country and, for babies born between 1500 and 2499 g it was actually higher. By the second period, Prague was considerably outperforming the rest of the country in both birth weight categories. This was because the relative reduction in deaths at low birth weights was much greater in Prague than in the rest of the country (Table 5.4). The reasons for the greater percentage reduction in deaths at heavier birth weights outside Prague are unclear.

Table 5.4 Birth weight and neonatal mortality, Prague and the rest of the Czech Republic

Region/period	*Birth weight*		
	< 1500 g	*1500–2499 g*	*> 2500 g*
Neonatal mortality rate/1000			
Prague 1989–1991	376.8	37.4	1.7
Other 1989–1991	403.8	34.9	1.8
Prague 1994–1995	179.7	15.6	1.5
Other 1994–1995	277.6	19.6	1.3
Number of deaths saved in 1994–1995 compared with predicted using 1989–1991 rates (% reduction)			
Prague	34 (60)	16 (59)	2 (5)
Other	188 (36)	105 (43)	84 (28)

Source: Koupilová *et al.* (1998)

By 1994–1995, the neonatal mortality among low birth weight babies in Prague had fallen to well below that in Sweden in 1989–1991 but it remained much higher in other parts of the country.

Discussion

This study provides important new insights to the east west gap in mortality in Europe and the effects of transition. It confirms the scale of the reduction in birth rate but also shows that there has been a slight change in the distribution of birth weight, with a net effect that would, in the absence of other factors, have led to an increase in neonatal mortality. This did not happen and, indeed, neonatal mortality fell markedly. This was due to an improvement in survival at all birth weights but especially among those born at under 2500 g. This is the group whose survival is most amenable to health care interventions.

The improvement was not, however, uniform throughout the country and was much greater in Prague, which, like any capital, has the greatest access to neonatal intensive care facilities.

Two possibilities arise. The first is that the fall in birth rate has allowed a higher proportion of infants to obtain access to scarce intensive care facilities than would previously have been possible. A second is that the opening of borders and the reform of the system of financing health care has increased availability of modem equipment and drugs. On the basis of the information available it is not possible to disentangle these two factors although it is likely that they have both played a part.

The comparison with Sweden offers an indication of the scope for further improvements. This suggests that achievable survival rates at each level of birth weight could only be expected to have a very small effect on overall neonatal mortality in the Czech Republic and any improvement is likely to be seen outside Prague.

These findings have important implications for policy. Neonatal mortality in the Czech Republic remains higher than in many countries of western Europe but, if it is to improve further, it will require a combination of policies. One set should address the determinants of low birth weight, such as maternal nutrition and smoking, although it should be recognised that beneficial effects may take more than one generation to be fully manifest. The second set should seek ways of reducing regional inequalities in the quality of care for low birth weight babies.

Finally, aggregate data such as these can only indicate the existence of a problem and suggest possible avenues for further exploration. What is now required is a system to identify specific amenable factors, such as the confidential inquiries into neonatal deaths that have been established elsewhere.

Causality

The question of whether one thing causes another is at the heart of epidemiology. In an ideal world, we would take a group of people, divide them into two groups at random, so that each group was identical, in every way, to the other, and expose one to the factor in question while keeping the other group unexposed. This is essentially what we do when we test the effectiveness of drugs (the randomized (because which individual receives the intervention is decided randomly) controlled (because there is a control group to compare with) trial). In risk factor epidemiology this is not so easy. Think about the practicalities and ethical issues involved in, say, looking for the effects of smoking or diet. As a consequence, we often have to look for associations between potential risk factors and diseases, for example, the observation in the 1950s that people who smoke seemed to be especially likely to get lung cancer. However, just because two things are associated, it does not mean that they are related causally, in other words, that one causes the other. They may simply occur in the same people – lots of risk factors cluster (thing about the things people who live in deprived areas are exposed to).

Epidemiologists have, inevitably, given this issue some thought. In 1965 Sir Austin Bradford Hill developed a series of nine criteria of causality. When applying them it is still necessary to use judgement: not all might apply in a given set of circumstances and as Bradford Hill said, these are not hard and fast rules. However, if only a few, or none do, you should think carefully about whether a causal relationship really exists.

The criteria are:

Strength of association: A strong association is more likely to be causal (although a weak association can be too)
Consistency: Where an association is seen consistently in different circumstances it is more likely to be causal. Again, inconsistency does not exclude causality as something may be causal only in certain circumstances, such as people with particular genetic make-up.
Specificity: The cause should lead to a single, rather than multiple outcomes. This criterion has since been criticized and is generally seen as not very helpful as it is clear that some factors, such as tobacco, cause many diseases.
Temporality: Exposure to the cause should occur before the outcome.
Biological gradient: There should be a dose-response curve – the greater the exposure, the greater the risk of disease. There are, of course, exceptions.
Biological plausibility: It should make sense in the light of what is known about biological mechanisms. Of course, epidemiological research may stimulate research in basic science that may revise what is known about biological mechanisms.
Coherence: It should be consistent with common sense. Given that tobacco is inhaled and not painted on the skin or eaten, it makes sense that it causes lung cancer and not skin or colon cancer.

Experimental evidence: This is rarely available for humans but animal studies may help.
Analogy: For example, if one drug can cause birth defects then it is plausible that another one might.

Clearly these criteria are not perfect, and they have been criticized by some. For example, Ken Rothman favours the view that scientists should simply report the evidence and leave it to others to make judgements suggesting that scepticism is preferable in science. However, for those who feel that we have an obligation to make a judgement, these criteria may help.

Activity 5.4

Now look at Figure 5.3 which shows trends in infant, neonatal, and postneonatal mortality in east and west Germany between 1972 and 1997. Analyse these trends and prepare a briefing note (of no more than 800 words) for the German health minister that answers the following questions:

1 What do the figures tell us about health care in east and west Germany?
2 What do they tell us about other factors that may have influenced trends?
3 Make a recommendation on whether infant mortality is an appropriate indicator for quality of health care, justifying your point of view.

Feedback

1 Both parts of Germany experienced considerable declines in the infant mortality rate (IMR) between 1972 and 1997. Until 1980, infant mortality was higher in west Germany than in east Germany; since then, IMR was very similar in both parts.

The decline in infant mortality was due to a decline in both neonatal and postneonatal mortality in both parts of Germany although the pattern differed between the two countries. Thus, neonatal mortality (NMR), although initially (until 1978) higher fell much more steeply in the west, resulting in higher NMR in the east from 1978 onwards until 1995, when rates became similar to those in the west. Until 1990, postneonatal mortality (PNMR) was consistently higher in west Germany than in the east, where rates had fallen steeply already in the early 1970s. In 1990, east Germany experienced a small increase in PNMR, which soon fell again to become similar to PNMR in the west by 1997.

2 Based on the observed declining trends in infant mortality one may conclude that both countries experienced improvements in living standards and health care, both impacting on infant health. However, since NMR was lower in the west throughout the 1980s one may speculate that access to and/or quality of peri/neonatal care may have been better in west Germany in the 1980s than in the east since NMR is usually more closely related to health care. To support this statement one would need to look at additional data, for example birthweight-specific neonatal mortality. In contrast, looking at PNMR one may conclude that access to and/or quality of postnatal care may

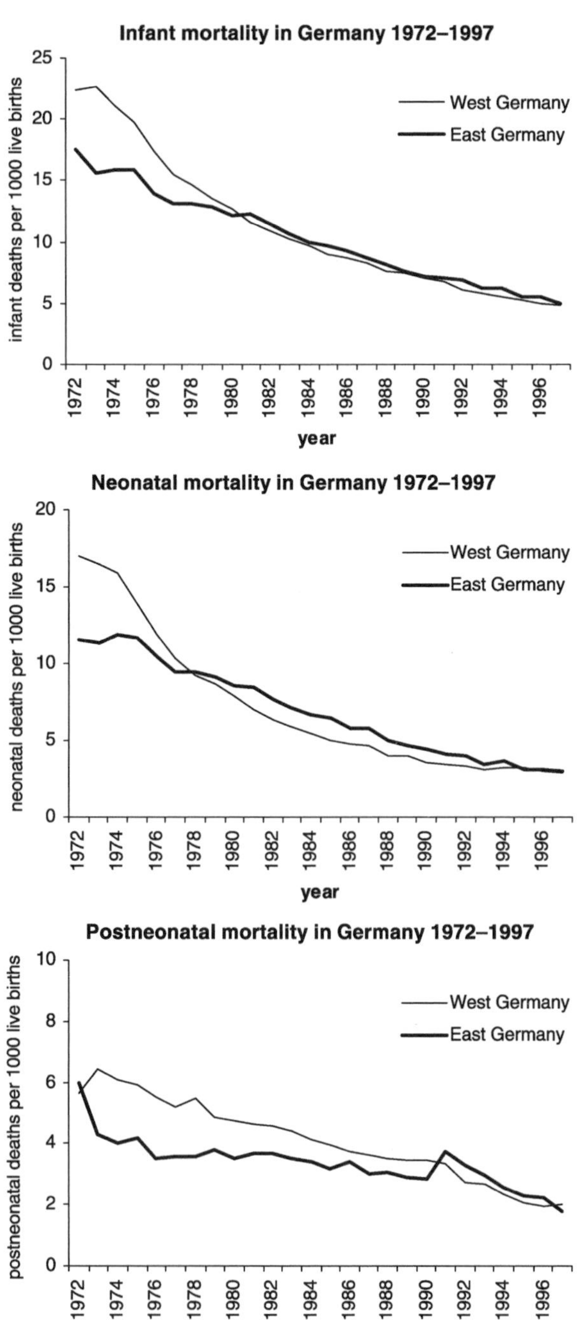

Figure 5.3 Trends in infant, neonatal and postneonatal mortality in East and West Germany between 1972 and 1997.

Source: Nolte (2000)

have been superior in the east throughout much of the 1970s and 1980s. One may wish to look at the causes of death to explore this assertion further, for example, looking at the frequency of sudden infant death (SID) or data on utilization of postnatal care.

Finally, in looking at IMR across different countries one needs to be aware of possible limitations of data comparability regarding completeness of registration of live births and deaths. For example, until 1990 east Germany used a definition of a live birth which was more restrictive (the definition requires the presence of a heart beat *and* breathing) than that used in the west (the definition requires the presence of a heart beat *or* breathing *or* pulsating umbilical cord). As a consequence, infant mortality in east Germany was slightly underestimated.

3 Following from the above: Infant mortality can be a good indicator of the quality of medical care but:

- it should be looked at in association with other measures, such as avoidable mortality.
- you should ideally take account of differences in underlying factors that increase the risk of a death in infancy. This, as several groups noted, can most easily be done by adjusting for differences in birth weight. Low birth weight is associated with adverse socioeconomic factors.

Source of data on health care systems in Europe

The Health Systems in Transition Profiles (HiTs) provide comparative and analytical views into health care systems in Europe. These reports are produced by the European Observatory on Health Systems and Policies, in which LSHTM is a partner, along with the London School of Economics, the governments of Finland, Greece, Norway, Spain and Sweden, the European Investment Bank, the Open Society Institute, and the World Bank. In addition to the HiTs, the Observatory produces overviews of issues relating to health systems (such as health care funding), the role of hospitals, and regional overviews (such as one on health and health care in central Asia).

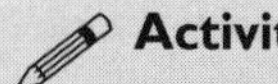

Activity 5.5

The HiTs can be obtained freely from the Observatory web site. They are about 80 to 120 pages long so you will probably want to read them online rather than printing them out.

Go to the Observatory web site (http://www.euro.who.int/observatory, European Observatory on Health Systems and Policies 2005). Select 'HiT country profiles'.

Select the HiT for Albania. Browse through the document and find the following information (take advantage of this exercise to see the type of information provided in the HiTs – they all use the same format):

1 Percentage of the state budget allocated to the Ministry of Health
2 Number of hospital beds per 1000 population in 2000 in Albania and Germany

Feedback

1 47.5 per cent of the state budget of Albania is allocated to the Ministry of Health

2 3.2 for Albania and 6.4 for Germany

Summary

You should now be familiar with the main views and issues related to the role of health care in promoting and ensuring the health of a population. The chapter examined the changing views on the contribution of health care to population health. It discussed different approaches used to assess the contribution of health care to health, and described how health services can be used to promote health.

References

Beaglehole R (2001) Global cardiovascular disease prevention: time to get serious. *The Lancet* **358**, 661–3.

Diabetes Epidemiology Research International (DERI) Study (1995) International analysis of insulin-dependent diabetes mellitus mortality: a preventable mortality perspective. *Am J Epidemiol* **142**, 612–18.

European Observatory on Health Systems and Policies (2005) *Home page*. Brussels, European Observatory on Health Systems and Policies (available on http://www.euro.who.int/observatory, last visited 2 February 2005).

Koupilová I, McKee M, Holčík J (1998) Neonatal mortality in the Czech Republic during the transition. *Health Policy* **46**, 43–52.

Laing SP, Swerdlow AJ, Slater SD, Botha JL, Burden AC, Waugh NR, Smith AW, Hill RD, Bingley PJ, Patterson CC, Qiao Z, Keen H (1999) The British Diabetic Association Cohort Study, I: all-cause mortality in patients with insulin-treated diabetes mellitus. *Diabet Med* **16**, 459–65.

McKee M, Gilmore A, Novotny T (2003) Smoke-free hospitals. *Br Med J* **326**, 941–2.

McKeown T (1979) *The role of medicine: dream, mirage or nemesis?* Oxford: Blackwell.

Nolte E, Brand A, Koupilová I, McKee M (2000) Neonatal and postneonatal mortality in Germany since unification. *J Epidemiol Community Health* **54**, 84–90.

Rutstein DD, Berenberg W, Chalmers TC, Child CG, Fishman AP, Perrin EB (1976) Measuring the quality of medical care. *N Engl J Med* **294**, 582–8.

Ulrich RS (1984) View through a window may influence recovery from surgery. *Science* **224**, 420–1.

World Health Organization (2000) *The World Health Report 2000. Health system improving performance*. Geneva: World Health Organization.

Yusuf S (2002) Two decades of progress in preventing vascular disease. *The Lancet* **360**, 2–3.

Further reading

Frampton SB, Gilpin L, Charmel PA (eds) (2003) *Putting patients first: Designing and practicing patient-centered care*. San Francisco: Jossey-Bass. For those who would like to read about the international movement entitled the Planetree model.

Mackenbach JP (1996) The contribution of medical care to mortality decline: McKeown revisited. *J Clin Epidemiol* **49**, 1207–13.

6 Assessing the impact on population health of policies in other sectors

Overview

In Chapter 5 you learned about how health care can contribute to making a population healthier. In this chapter, you will now examine how to determine the effects on the health of the public of activities and policies in non-health sectors, such as transport, agriculture or the environment. This chapter will introduce health impact assessment (HIA), its principles, uses, advantages, limitations, and how it is performed.

Learning objectives

By the end of this chapter you should be able to:

- **describe the broad determinants of health and recognize the range of policy sectors that influence population health**
- **explain how public health can have a role in addressing these wider determinants of health in policy making**
- **describe the key elements of a HIA process**
- **outline the application of HIA to policies from the non-health sector, illustrated by examples of HIA worldwide**
- **comment on the strengths and limitations of current HIA methods in helping policymakers decide on priorities and activities**
- **have a basic understanding of how HIA can be applied in a real policy making situation**

Key terms

Health inequalities Differences in health experience and health status between countries, regions and socioeconomic groups.

What is health impact assessment?

The most quoted definition of health impact assessment (HIA) was developed at a consensus conference of the World Health Organization (WHO):

> HIA is a combination of procedures, methods, and tools by which a policy, programme, or project may be judged as to its potential effects on the health of population and the distribution of those effects within the population.
>
> Source: World Health Organization European Centre for Health Policy and World Health Organization Regional Office for Europe (1999)

All definitions highlight that HIA is concerned with the health of populations and attempts to predict the future consequences of health decisions that have not yet been implemented.

The purpose of HIA

HIA is a flexible and adaptable approach helping those developing and delivering policies. It is intended to influence decision-makers so that policies, projects and programmes in all areas lead to improved public health, or do no harm to population health (Lock 2000).

HIA can influence decisions in four ways:

1. By raising awareness among decision-makers of the relationship between health and other factors such as the physical, social and economic environment, so that they consider health effects in their planning;
2. By helping decision-makers identify and assess the potential impact of a specific proposal on population health and well-being, and on the distribution of those effects within the population (that is, issues of equity by considering health inequalities or the impact on specific vulnerable groups);
3. HIA can also identify practical ways to improve and optimize the outcome of proposals, by producing a set of evidence-based recommendations which feed into the decision-making process;
4. By helping stakeholders affected by policies to participate and contribute to decision-making.

Whatever approaches or methods are used, it is important to maintain a clear focus on the ultimate purpose of HIA. This is to inform and influence subsequent decision-making. HIA is not merely a research tool, it is a political tool to aid decision-making.

HIA within the context of a broad health model

The HIA approach is grounded in the broad determinants of human health. These include personal, social, cultural, economic, environmental and other factors that influence the health status of individuals and populations. You will have covered some of these earlier in the book, for example in Chapters 3 and 4.

Activity 6.1

Think about the determinants of human health. Then, list some examples of determinants for each of the following categories:

- Pre-conceptual/in utero:__________
- Behavioural/lifestyle:__________
- Psycho-social environment:__________
- Physical environment:__________
- Socioeconomic status:__________
- Provision of and access to public services:__________
- Public policy:__________
- Global policy issues:__________

Feedback

You will find below a few examples of health determinants. The list is of course not exhaustive (it could almost be endless) and you may have provided other good examples. This exercise simply reminds us that health is determined by a complex combination of factors affecting all aspects of our lives, many of which will interact. This is important to consider in many aspects of public health practice and especially in HIA, where we would inadequately be able to look at the health effects of wider policy if we limited our analysis to impacts on death and incidence of medically defined disease.

- Pre-conceptual/in utero: maternal health, health of foetus during pregnancy
- Behavioural/lifestyle: diet, smoking, physical activity, risk taking behaviour (for example, unsafe sex, illicit drugs)
- Psycho-social environment: community networks, culture, religion, social inclusion
- Physical environment: air, water, housing, noise, waste
- Socioeconomic status: employment, education, training, household income
- Provision of and access to public services: transport, shops, leisure, health and social services
- Public policy: economic, welfare, crime, agriculture, health policies
- Global policy issues: international trade, European Union policy, multi-national industries (for example for tobacco, food, oil)

This broad model of health helps realize that virtually every area of human activity influences health, and therefore that most public or political decisions have the potential to impact on health both positively and negatively. This obviously means that the greatest scope for improving the public's health often lies outside the control of the health services, through interventions in economic, housing, agriculture, transport, education and other 'non-health' areas.

In most countries the interface between the health and non-health sectors is still fairly limited, for example, to links between health care and social care, and public health and environmental health. Health is not routinely on the agenda of other ministries or agencies. However, the financial burden of negative health impacts of their policies usually falls on the health sector.

Policies and programmes, and the way they are implemented, represent important influences on people's health and well-being. HIA is one concept that has emerged to identify those activities and policies likely to have major impacts on the health of a population. It is increasingly proposed as a way of bringing together stakeholders from diverse backgrounds (including those from the public, private and voluntary sectors as well as the community) to identify and address how the development and implementation of a policy or programme will affect the wider determinants of health.

Many health determinants are interrelated and there are several cross cutting issues that affect health (for example poverty). The systematic nature of HIA recommends that health impacts are considered by way of a number of categories. The categories cover a series of intermediate factors that are determinants of health, through which changes due to a policy or project can impact on people's health. The precise categories used and their component parts may vary according to the nature of the proposed policy, programme or other development thus providing sufficient flexibility in the application of the health impact assessment concept in different circumstances. The categories of health determinants used in Activity 6.1 illustrate one example of such a classification.

Activity 6.2

Explain, using an example of your choice, how certain policies unrelated to health can have a negative impact on the health sector.

Feedback

Numerous policies set by ministries other than health ministries can have indirect negative effects on the health of populations.

For example, the British and US Ministries of Trade promote Tobacco Multi-national companies overseas. Yet, it is Ministries of Health that have to treat people with smoking-related disease (approximately 20 per cent of the burden of disease in the USA).

Another example is the European Union Common Agricultural Policy (CAP) which determines which crops are grown, and the prices they are sold at in the 25 countries of the European Union (EU). Certain CAP regimes maintain the livelihoods of farmers by subsidizing production of 'unhealthy crops' such as tobacco and high fat dairy products. Often this production is extra to that which is consumed by people in Europe creating surpluses, for example of butter fat which is sold cheaply to food companies to produce high-fat processed food. The CAP also determines the prices of crops imported from other (usually developing) nations, thus affecting livelihoods and thus socioeconomic status of people worldwide.

Historical background of HIA

The basic concepts of HIA are not new and they will be familiar to those working in public health. HIA builds on and brings together many existing methods and disciplines including policy appraisal, risk assessment, stakeholder analysis, evidence-based health care, and environmental impact assessment.

HIA has its roots in two main developments:

1 The promotion of healthy public policy; and
2 Environmental impact assessment.

Healthy public policy was a key component of the Ottawa charter for health promotion. The concept included policies designed specifically to promote health (for example, banning cigarette advertising) and policies not dealing directly with health but acknowledged to have a health impact (for example, transport, education, economics).

The WHO Health for All programme (adopted in 1977 and launched at the Alma Ata Conference in 1978) and the WHO's healthy cities programme (launched in 1988) stimulated interest in the important part local authorities and communities can play in improving health, including urban regeneration strategies. More recently this has been updated as the WHO global health policy 'Health for All for the 21st Century' which includes a recommendation to undertake HIA.

Sustainable development plans by national and local authorities have further added to wider policy initiatives, which have implications for improving population health. These initiatives have been strengthened by increased public awareness of social and environmental effects on health. The open debate of these issues at international, national, and local levels has dramatically increased between the mainly environmental focus of the UN Earth summit in Rio de Janeiro (in 1992), and the recent World Summit on Sustainable Development in Johannesburg (in 2002) whose agenda had a much greater focus on poverty and human health issues (United Nations 2003).

The principles of HIA are similar to social impact assessment and environmental impact assessment (EIA). Initially it developed as a natural extension of these methods. Many countries, including the countries of the EU and the USA have a legal requirement to carry out EIA. There is currently no statutory duty in law in any European country to undertake HIA. However, article 129 of the Maastricht treaty (signed in 1992) and article 152 of the Amsterdam treaty (signed in 1997) require the EU to check that policy proposals do not have an adverse impact on health or create conditions that undermine health promotion. The European Commission is developing HIA as part of its public health work, but it is unlikely to be mandatory.

It has been argued that procedures for HIA could be most easily introduced with the inclusion of health in existing processes for EIA. While health effects are currently supposed to be dealt with within the EIA legislation, they are actually poorly assessed or not at all. There are some initiatives that are attempting to strengthen the health consideration in other impact assessments. One approach is so-called 'integrated impact assessment tools'. For example, some governments and the EU are in the process of developing such an integrated approach for screening new proposals. Another approach is to strengthen the health component of Environmental Assessment. For example, in a new European legal protocol on Strategic Environmental Assessment (World Health Organization Regional Office for Europe 2001). Mostly HIA has developed as an independent tool for promoting public health in policies, and programmes.

What has HIA been used for?

HIA has been used in many countries in the world and for various types of policies and programmes in a wide range of policy sectors. We will examine this in Activity 6.3.

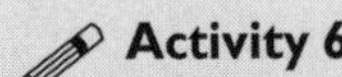

Activity 6.3

What are the main policy sectors or projects that HIA has been applied to? To explore this you are invited to search for and read examples of completed HIAs of programmes, projects or policies at both local and national levels. You can select examples by searching the following websites for subjects or countries that interest you. It may be best to start with the HIA gateway website or WHO website (see those listed below). While exploring these websites, you will see that HIA can be used for different purposes. Prepare a list of the main applications of HIA.

1. Health Development Agency: http://www.hiagateway.org.uk (Health Development Agency 2005). This site is the easiest place to start. It was launched in December 2000, revised in September 2002, and is rapidly evolving. It has numerous links and HIA resources, including an introductory guide, many examples of HIA toolkits and case studies, as well as links to reviews of evidence. It focuses mainly on the UK but has links to HIA worldwide.
2. World Health Organization HIA website: http://www.who.int/hia/en/ (World Health Organization 2005). This is a new website set up in 2003 and has increasing worldwide examples and links.
3. Liverpool University. International Impact Assessment consortium: http://www.ihia.org.uk/ (Liverpool University 2005).
4. National Institute for Public Health and the Environment. Health Impact Assessment Database: http://www.hiadatabase.net/ (National Institute for Public Health and the Environment 2005).

Feedback

Your summary of the main applications of HIA may include:

1 *Urban and transport planning*: Urban regeneration schemes and policies: for example in London and Wales. Transport strategies: for example in Scotland, Merseyside, London.

2 *Political lobbying*: There was for example the input of a rapid HIA to the Public Inquiry into the Manchester Airport Second Runway expansion.

3 *National Policy Appraisal*: Examples can be found in The Netherlands, Canada and Thailand.

4 *Environmental HIA (often called EHIA)*: Examples can be found in New Zealand, Australia, Central and Eastern Europe (through National Environmental Health Action Plans). This usually covers issues such as waste disposal, air quality and transport, water pollution.

5 *Developing country polices and programmes*: This has mainly been used to appraise donor aid projects (for example, World Bank, Asian Development Bank, UN Food and Agriculture Organisation). Examples include agricultural and water policies and the World Commission on Dams. The method was based on a more medical model of health, considering health impacts in five main disease categories: communicable disease, non-communicable disease, nutrition, injury, and mental disorder. The likelihood of specific health risks related to the project was considered and risk reduction strategies proposed. More recently the approach taken in developing countries has adopted a broader view of the determinants of health.

This list and the one you prepared confirm that HIA covers a wide range of policy sectors.

Methods of HIA

It should be clear that HIA is a multidisciplinary, intersectoral process within which a range of evidence about the health effects of a proposal is considered in a structured framework. It takes into account the opinions and expectations of those who may be affected by a proposed policy. Evidence for the potential health impacts of a proposal are analysed and recommendations for improving health are fed into the decision-making process.

HIA has been undertaken in a range of different ways. The choice of the approach depends on the timeframe and resources available. There are many different toolkits and methods proposed (many of which can be accessed via the weblinks given above). This can appear confusing for a newcomer. However, in many ways this is not as important as it seems, as all methods have similarities. It also serves to highlight the inherent flexibility of HIA, and the ability to adapt the process to the requirements of the particular circumstances.

Core stages of the HIA process

There is a general consensus about the core stages of HIA which are summarized in Figure 6.1. These stages are briefly described below. Further details can be found in various methodological guides available (see the list of optional readings and additional resources given at the end of the session). It should be noted that not every HIA necessarily has to follow this framework rigidly. HIA is a flexible approach which can be adapted to the specific circumstances.

Screening: Systematic screening of policies and programme proposals provides a quick preliminary assessment of the relevance to health of the proposals. It is an

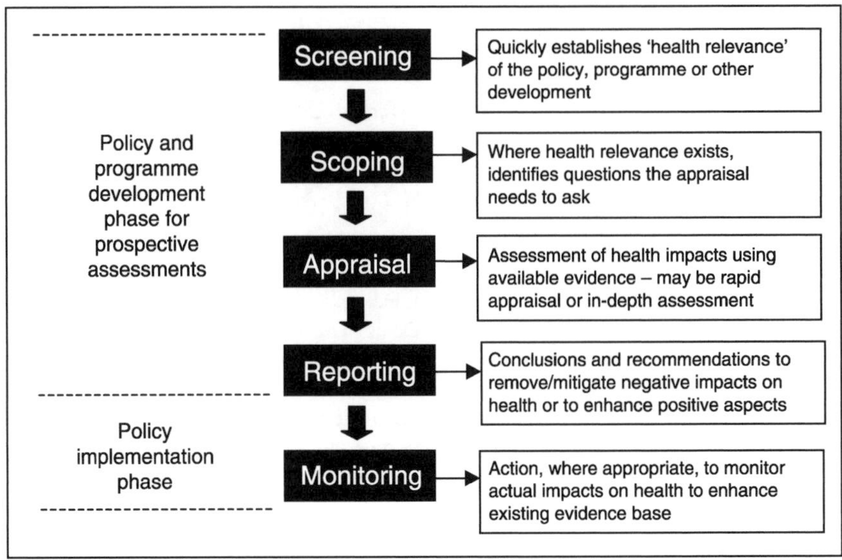

Figure 6.1 A schematic representation of an HIA process

important first stage of the health impact assessment and can be done with or without the assistance of screening tools and checklists. It enables any significant issues relating to health to be identified and a decision to be made on whether or not there is a need for more detailed assessment to take place.

Scoping: If there is felt to be a need for further consideration of the health impacts or potential impacts, the scoping stage identifies the questions that need to be addressed in the assessment process, and the scope of the HIA for example, the geographical area, the population and the timescales to be covered.

Appraisal: The appraisal stage itself also has in-built flexibility. It can take the form of a rapid appraisal, which might be done over the course of a few days, or an in-depth appraisal, which may require a period of weeks or several months. The appraisal may include quantitative and/or qualitative assessments that cover both risks and hazards to health, and opportunities to help people to improve their health by adjusting elements of the proposals or by integrating new elements within it.

Reporting recommendations to decision-makers: The conclusions of the appraisal and assessment are reported to those responsible for the decision-making and should meet political timeframes. The report should make any recommendations necessary to remove or to mitigate any negative impacts on the health of a population or on specific groups within a population. Similarly, the report should identify ways on which the proposal could be enhanced in order to positively encourage and support people to improve their health and well-being.

Using evidence to make recommendations

A key consideration in HIA is identifying and assessing potential evidence. Evidence for actual or potential impacts can come from many sources including epidemiological evidence, local routine data sources from health and other sectors, and qualitative sources of data collection (some of which may be gathered specifically for the HIA). Due to the nature of the broad determinants of health, the evidence base available to support the HIA process may be of poor quality, detailed but still inconclusive, incomplete or difficult to locate. Unfortunately epidemiology and related health sciences, which could contribute to HIA, are currently limited in their ability to explore outcomes other than death or disease incidence, and are unable to quantify causal pathways and the multiple interactions between risk factors. This emphasis on health determinants means that HIAs will confront considerable uncertainty in making definitive conclusions about potential health impacts. For many policies, especially those implemented at a national level where even the immediate effects are often unclear, the causal pathways are very complex, with the current evidence base patchy and often irrelevant to concrete policy options. For this reason, HIA practitioners have to acknowledge the constraints of only being able to make recommendations based on the 'best available' evidence given the time and other resource limitations.

There is much debate about what is the 'best available' evidence. Many scientists argue that quantified estimates are more influential but it should be remembered that not everything that can be quantified is important, that things should not be quantified if not done robustly, and that not everything that is important can be quantified. So in HIA it is accepted that evidence from a variety of sources is necessary.

However, this creates its own problems. Prioritizing and making recommendations using evidence from different sources and methodologies is fraught with difficulty. HIA also has to be aware that the evidence can be mixed, contradictory or limited, and so an important part of the process is involving key stakeholders to ensure that any recommendations are based on a clear understanding of their different perspectives, and are reached by consensus.

Other methodological difficulties

Several issues are unresolved in the methodology of HIA. Although there is increasing agreement about the wide variety of factors that influence health, the comparative importance of these varies across professional and public views. In order for HIA to be a valid tool, a shared definition of health is needed. This affects the ability to measure health impacts in various settings. At present, different models measure health impacts in different ways. Most use some checklist procedure, which uses the perceived determinants of health as markers for changes in health risks for example, using employment levels as a marker for the status of community health. The difficulty with this is that causal pathways are so complex that it is not often possible to say if an outcome will definitely be good or bad for the health of a population. Will a development such as replacing a derelict industrial site with new offices increase local employment? And if it does will this improve health? Such health indicators can potentially measure progress towards possible health improvement but this is not necessarily equivalent to a measure of health impact.

One of the major criticisms of HIA is that the methods of collecting and analysing evidence are not sufficiently rigorous to withstand scrutiny and challenge. The current evidence base for many health determinants is inadequate for accurately informing a process of assessment. In completed studies the principal sources of evidence have come from literature reviews and qualitative methods. A range of data sources including economic, epidemiological, quantitative, and qualitative information should be routinely taken into account. However, often the most useful information is not being routinely collected. Seldom is there going to be the time or money available for collection of primary data. Although it may be preferable for decision-makers to have a quantitative measure of health impact, the limitations of qualitative estimates may have to be accepted as the best evidence available. This may limit the strength of the recommendations an assessment can make both in terms of the certainty and size of an impact.

HIA aims to influence the decision-making process in an open, structured way. To do this it has to acknowledge that assessing and ranking evidence is not a wholly objective process and involves a series of value judgments. There are no evaluated methods for prioritizing evidence from different sources, and political imperatives are likely to affect the outcome. The balance between objective evidence and subjective opinion should be explicitly recognized in reports of assessments. In evidence-based medicine there is a weighted hierarchy of epidemiological evidence, with randomized controlled trials at the top. Obviously this is not useful in assessments where evidence comes from a range of quantitative and qualitative sources. There is a need for developing a new framework for gathering, interpreting, and prioritizing evidence from different origins for evidence-based policy making.

The findings of a HIA are often limited by financial and time costs. There is a need for a balance between rigorous methods that require specialist skills and high levels of resources and those that can be used more easily and cheaply. The two approaches are not mutually exclusive and can be combined in a continuum of options for assessment, which includes preliminary project screening, rapid appraisal, and in-depth assessment. The decision of which method to use may relate to whatever will have most weight in influencing the decision-making process in a timely way. Ultimately there will have to be a trade-off between costs and quality to make the impact assessment a realizable goal.

Benefits of using HIA

Activity 6.4

Despite the current limitations of the methods, process evaluation has shown that HIA leads to many benefits for 'healthy decision making'. Suggest what these benefits might be.

Feedback

The benefits of the HIA include:

- Providing a mechanism for health to inform decision-making
- Improving intersectoral working
- Creating a structured approach for demonstrating the broad health agenda to other agencies/ policy sectors
- Raising community awareness of health
- Encouraging and enabling public participation in decision-making
- Increasing the transparency of some aspects of decision-making

The way forward

HIA is a developing process worldwide, at local, regional and national levels. It can be usefully used by public health departments, policymakers, community groups, non-governmental organizations and individuals working in a range of settings to push public health issues up the political agenda. Its flexibility often means that it can be easy to integrate into existing processes. However, it is important to plan before introducing it. Important things to consider include:

1 Identifying and using existing public health expertise and resources
2 Raising awareness about HIA, and the broad determinants of health across health and non-health sectors
3 Looking for opportunities to use HIA to promote intersectoral approaches to health improvement, for example public or political concern
4 Deciding on your approach: rapid or in-depth, projects or policies
5 Managing the expectations of the HIA process and its outcomes: remember there is no single, perfect method; HIA is not a decision-making tool, it helps inform decision-making; there are insufficient resources to do an in-depth HIA of every project/ policy.

Activity 6.5

Designing and conducting a HIA of a new agricultural policy

In this activity you will design a rapid HIA of a new agricultural policy. This exercise is deliberately not set in any specific country in order to allow you to think about the issues in the place where you live. These types of policies have been introduced in both Europe and developing countries. Although some issues will vary depending on the context (that is, the level of economic development, geography and climate) there are also core issues that will be the same (such as access to food, employment, environmental factors).

By working through the three questions described below you will outline the key public health issues that the HIA needs to cover, the main people that it should involve and the types of information that should ideally be collected to present a report and recommendations on the health issues to the Ministry of Agriculture (see scenario below).

You will be able to do this using your own knowledge and experience as well as the materials provided. You are not expected to use any other resources.

Practical points to consider before you start

Experience of previous HIAs has shown the value of rapid appraisal sessions. Evaluation of these activities has also identified some potential problems or barriers that it is important to dispel before you start:

- You may feel that you need to become an expert in the process of HIA or agriculture, and that you lack the experience or knowledge necessary. **THIS IS NOT TRUE!** Like any piece of work the focus remains on answering the task you are set, and you should concentrate on the practical things that you are being asked to do. An HIA will appraise policies not just on the basis of the evidence, but also in the light of your views and your knowledge gained through a variety of experience and information. However, if you want to see at another example of a HIA looking at agriculture and food, you can check the papers from Gabrijelcic and collaborators (2004) and Lock and collaborators (2003) (both available on the net). You can read them before or after the activity as they are not required to do it.
- Some of you may feel that you need more information about specific aspects of the Policy before you can reach a view. If you are not careful, this may result in getting stuck on one point of detail. Try to avoid this. If you feel you are unable to decide on one aspect then note this down, and move forward to the next issue.
- You only need to use the materials provided to you, and it is not expected that you read any more references.

You should set aside approximately one and a half hours to do this activity.

Think broadly about the effects of agriculture, and have fun!

Organization of the work

The exercise includes 3 components:

1 Policy appraisal: apply a 'determinants of health' framework to the policy proposals, to identify the range of public health issues the HIA should consider and which ones you believe may potentially have positive and negative effects on population health.
2 Conduct a stakeholder analysis to identify the key people affected by the policy who should be involved in the HIA.
3 Outline a rapid appraisal of the policy and decide what information you would want to collect to make an analysis of the likely health impacts. You will use this information to propose three recommendations to promote public health.

Scenario

You work in the Public Health Department of the Ministry of Health. You have been asked to conduct a rapid HIA of the possible health effects of a new national policy proposed by the Ministry of Agriculture. This policy aims to increase agricultural productivity and farmers' income. Its objectives are as follows:

1 to increase growth of cash crops for sale or export: including fruits and vegetables, tobacco and non-food crops.
2 to increase productivity through two mechanisms: a) intensification of land use by enforced purchase and amalgamation of the current pattern of small holdings and

family farms, and b) technical education and support to increase the use of improved technology (including fertilizers, pesticides, mechanization and irrigation techniques).

Questions to answer

1 What health determinants should be considered when planning a HIA of this policy? Consider the policy proposal and identify what health determinants may be affected. You should remember that health impacts can be both positive and negative, so you need to include both 'risks to health' and issues positively affecting well-being. You can develop a table such as Table 6.1. Some examples are given in it to help you start, but these are not exhaustive.

Table 6.1 Health determinants to consider for the new agricultural policy

Category of health determinants	*Area of health impact*	*Type of impact (indicate whether positive or negative)*
Pre-conceptual/ in utero	Maternal nutrition	
Behavioural/ lifestyle	Diet	
Psycho-social environment	Cultural impact	
Physical environment	Land use Water	
Socioeconomic status	Employment	For example, merging of small family farms may remove the source of nutrition from subsistence farmers and families (negative) Commercial farms may become source of employment and income (positive)
Provision of and access to public services		
Public policy		
Global policy issues	Global trade agreements, e.g. Common Agricultural Policy	

2 Who are the stakeholders that the HIA should involve? Most HIAs aim to involve stakeholders that may be affected by or that can influence the policy or project, to allow their opinions to input into decisions. Stakeholder analysis can be used to ensure that stakeholders who normally have low impact or influence 'can be heard' as part of the decision-making process (assuming that the HIA and community involvement are conducted well, which is another problem!). A stakeholder analysis is one technique you can use to identify and assess the importance of key people, groups of people, or institutions that may influence the success of your activity or project. It should be used early in the HIA or other types of project planning. Stakeholder analysis can also be used to develop the most effective support possible for any project and reduce any obstacles to successful implementation.

To conduct a stakeholder analysis you can follow the following steps:

- Develop a **Stakeholder Analysis Table** such as Table 6.2
- Identify all the people, groups, and institutions that will affect or be affected by the policy and list them in the column under 'Stakeholder' (column 1).

Table 6.2 Stakeholder analysis for the new agricultural policy

Stakeholder	*Interest(s) in the project*	*Assessment of Influence*
Ministry of Agriculture	Policy proponent, increased production, increased revenue, improved agricultural practices	A

- Once you have a list of all potential stakeholders, review the list and identify the specific interests these stakeholders have in the policy. Consider issues like: the policies benefit(s) to the stakeholder; the changes that the policy might require the stakeholder to make; and the policy activities that might cause difficulty or conflict for the stakeholder. Record these under the column 'Stakeholder Interest(s) in the Project' (column 2).
- Now review each stakeholder listed in column one. Ask the question: how important are the stakeholder's interests to the success of the proposed policy? Consider:
  a) The role the key stakeholder must play for the project to be successful, and the likelihood that the stakeholder will play this role
  b) The likelihood and impact of a stakeholder's negative response to health implications

  Assign 'A' for extremely important, 'B' for fairly important, and 'C' for not very important. Record these letters in the column entitled 'Assessment of Influence' (column 3).

3 Conduct a rapid HIA of the proposed policy. This requires you to look in more detail at some aspects of the proposed policy. Choose three issues that you identified in Table 6.1. You also need to outline what information and evidence you would want to collect to make an analysis of the likely health impacts. Use a table such as Table 6.3 to assist you.

Table 6.3 Information and evidence to be collected for the HIA

Policy-related issue	*Potential effects of policy*	*Health determinants which may be affected*	*Evidence required and sources of information to assess potential health impacts*	*Relevant stakeholders*

Then outline three clear recommendations that result from this rapid appraisal. You need to identify ways in which the proposed policies could potentially be strengthened to support and promote public health. You should consider ways to both maximize potential positive impacts on health, and to minimize potential negative impacts on health. This should also consider the relevant stakeholders.

Feedback

There is no 'correct' response to this type of rapid HIA exercise. HIA aims to include stakeholder opinion as one part of the information which directs the appraisal of evidence, hence there could be a number of different answers depending on the people involved and their perspective.

You should propose the evidence required to support your statements. Obviously what you will be able to do will be limited by the time and evidence available. It is difficult to replicate these issues in a paper based exercise. However, it is crucial not to be speculative (that is, prioritize the issues you want if the evidence does not justify it), nor just repeat political rhetoric.

In an HIA you must interpret the policy or project details to identify issues which have potential or known health effects. You then need to back up this 'hypothesis' of a health impact by citing evidence to support your conclusions.

You will increasingly learn that policymakers often say they make 'evidence-based policy' although they use evidence very selectively. In contrast, anyone challenging policy or plans (such as in an HIA) needs to cite as much detailed evidence as possible to ensure their conclusions are robust. The responses to the questions you had to answer are meant as a guide, you may have come up with others.

1 What health determinants should be considered when planning a HIA of this policy?

When considering the proposed policy you need to understand how agricultural can affect the health of different people in different ways. It is important to think broadly about the range of issues, not just nutrition. These include:

a) Access to and availability of food:
  - food production – change in types of food produced
  - food marketing and distribution, changes in patterns of marketing and distribution (that is, from local to regional, national or international)
  - access to different foods by specific population groups, on the basis of their age, socioeconomic status, living in urban/rural areas

b) Methods of agricultural production including:
  - use of pesticides and agrochemicals
  - intensive agriculture techniques and intensive land use for limited types of crops.

c) Working and living conditions of those involved in the food chain and their families including:
  - owners of small farms, family gardens or subsistence farmers
  - agricultural workers in large farms
  - food processing workers
  - distributors and retailers – owners and workers running market stalls, small shops and large outlets, such as supermarkets

d) Socioeconomic factors and employment:
- rural poverty – including subsistence farmers or small family farmers who supplement their income in other ways
- high rates of unemployment and low rates of pay in agricultural communities
- the effect of the supermarket retail sector on what the producer is paid for products
- the effect of global trade policies on the price of agricultural products on world markets

e) Travelling patterns and need for travel by different means/modes of transport
- increasing transport of food stuffs long distances to 'market'

f) Tourism and niche markets including:
- agri-tourism
- production of local products 'on farm' for specialized markets (for example, expensive handmade cheese)

You might have come up with a table similar to Table 6.4.

Table 6.4 Health determinants to consider for the new agricultural policy

Category of health determinants	*Area of health impact*	*Type of impact (indicate whether positive or negative)*
Pre-conceptual/ in utero	Maternal nutrition	Could be positive or negative health impact. If the policy focuses on cash crops, could reduce availability of subsistence food locally, however if small farmers benefited from increased productivity and income this may offset the reduction in home food production
Behavioural/lifestyle	Diet	The most direct effect between agriculture and health is nutrition. If the fruits and vegetable are available locally could improve diet and health (positive). However, this could also reduce local availability of food (negative, see below).
	Accidents and injury	Increased mechanization or use of pesticides without adequate training (negative impact on rates accidents and poisonings)
Psycho-social environment	Cultural impact	This will depend on whether the crops grown are part of the normal local diet. Often farming of cash crops for export causes change in food grown from local fruits and vegetables to those required by the market (that is, negative impact on food availability)
Physical environment	Water	1. Increased use of pesticides may cause pollution of water supplies (negative). If severe this may cause issues such as: 2. Food safety: Need to ensure what crops are grown with what water, for example, potential microbial contamination of salads if the water used for irrigation is untreated wastewater (negative). Also heavy metal accumulation in soil or plant uptake (negative). 3. Irrigation may increase production (positive) but only if this does not deplete home water sources (negative).

	Land use	Will the policy force farmers to sell or merge small farms into large intensively farmed units (for example as the Common Agricultural Policy (CAP) favours). Intensification can lead to increased soil pollution if use of agrochemicals is poorly managed (negative). But intensification can increase production (which could increase food supply, positive).
	Transport pollution	Increasing exports will involve increased transport of foods long distances. There may be some local increases in air pollution around processing and warehouse sites (negative).
Socioeconomic status	Employment	For example: Merging of small family farms may remove source of nutrition from subsistence farmers and families and increase unemployment (negative). Commercial farms may become a source of employment and income (positive). Agricultural processing industries may have positive effects (employment) but also potential negative effects if poor occupational health (dust induced lung diseases etc).
Provision of and access to public services	Occupational and primary care health services, agricultural education services	Occupational health services and agricultural technical education services (positive impact by reduction of accidental injuries and poisonings from new technology and agrochemical use).
Global policy issues	Global trade agreements for example Common Agricultural Policy (CAP)	The CAP effects the price that products can be imported into the European Union, often causing developing countries to accept lower prices for their products. So commercial production may not benefit local farmers (negative).

2 Who are the stakeholders that the HIA should involve?

Table 6.5 provides you with an example of a stakeholder analysis for the new agricultural policy.

3 Conduct a rapid HIA of the proposed policy.

Table 6.6 provides you with some examples of HIA for the proposed policy.

For more information, you may be interested to read the paper from Lock and collaborators (2003).

Examples of recommendations that could have resulted from the above policy issues include:

a) Agrochemical use on farms must be accompanied by official training in safe handling, and occupational health inspections to ensure the correct safety equipment is worn, and that agrochemicals are stored safely (that is, correctly labelled).

Table 6.5 Stakeholder analysis for the new agricultural policy

Stakeholder	*Interest(s) in the project*	*Assessment of influence*
Ministry of agriculture	Increased production, intensification of farming	A
Farmers (commercial)	Increased production, increased profits	A
Farmers (family or subsistence)	Increased income or fulfilling family nutritional needs	B
Retailers – local markets	Will it affect local food supply?	B
Food processors	Increased opportunities for processing products for export or sale, increased profits	A
Retailers – supermarkets	Increased dependable supply of fruits and vegetables for their national or global market	A
Consumers	Will it affect the type and quantity or produce available for local consumers?	C
Rural population	Will it increase or decrease unemployment?	C
Ministry of Health	Probably have little interest except food safety issues	C
Rural primary care	Will there be greater risks to the population, will this result in more demand for local health services?	C
Rural education and training services	Is there resources for holding adequate education for those remaining in the more technical agricultural production?	C
Regional development agencies	How will this feed into regional development plans?	B

b) Any compulsory merging of small farm units should not totally remove the ability of a rural family to continue home-growing of food. Subsistence farmers should be assisted in finding other sources of employment or income by rural education and extension schemes.

c) The effects on the local rural populations of increased traffic to transport the produce to market should be minimized. This should aim to reduce road traffic accidents and air pollution.

Table 6.6 Information and evidence to be collected for the HIA

Policy-related issue	*Potential effects of policy*	*Health determinants which may be affected*	*Evidence required and sources of information to assess potential health impacts*	*Relevant stakeholders*
Increased use of pesticides and agrochemicals.	1. Increased productivity could be positive (increased income, increased food grown) but it depends on who will benefit. 2. Negative health impacts resulting from accidental poisoning, or environmental contamination due to overuse of agrochemicals, for example, water quality.	Behavioural/ lifestyle – food consumption, accidents and injury. Physical environment – water quality.	1. Amount of crops grown before and after similar schemes elsewhere. Long term sustainability of increased production, for example, from literature reviews. 2. Surveillance data for current rates of accidental poisonings amongst farm workers. Literature review of the rates of accidental injury with increasing pesticide use, and ways of minimizing hazards.	1. Commercial farmers, farm workers, Ministry of agriculture. 2. Farm workers, agricultural technical education workers, occupational health.
Change in land use could cause loss of small family farms.	May reduce access to essential food source or income for many families.	Cultural, socio-economic.	Survey of how much food eaten is home grown. Also household budget surveys of how much a low income family spends on food, and where the food supply comes from.	Farm workers and their families, consumers.
Intensification of agricultural production.	A source of local employment (although due to efficiency of intensive methods likely to be less farm workers than current land use). Increased mechanization and transport of products – could increase accidents and pollution.	Socioeconomic, physical environment – transport related.	Current rates of road traffic accidents.	Commercial farmers, family farmers, retailers, Ministry of agriculture.

Summary

This chapter introduced you to HIA. It first described the range of policy sectors that influence the main determinants of health, and how public health can have a role in addressing these wider determinants of health in policy making. It then examined the key elements of a HIA process and described different applications of HIA to policies from the non-health sector. The strengths and limitations of the current HIA methods in helping policymakers decide on priorities and activities were then described. Finally, the last activity provided you with a practical example of how HIA can be applied in a real policy making situation.

References

Gabrijelcic M, Zakotnik J and Lock K (2004) Health impact assessment: implementing the CAP in Slovenia after Accession. *Eurohealth* **10**, 17–21 (available at: http://www.euro.who.int/Document/Obs/Eurohealth10_1.pdf, 2 February 2005).

Health Development Agency (2005) *Health impact assessment gateway*. London: Health Development Agency (available at http://www.hiagateway.org.uk, last visited 2 February 2005).

Liverpool University (2005) *IMPACT – International health impact assessment consortium*. Liverpool, Liverpool University (available on http://www.ihia.org.uk/, last visited 2 February 2005).

Lock KJ (2000) Health Impact Assessment. *Br Med J* **320**, 1395–98.

Lock K, Gabrijelcic-Blenkus M, Martuzzi M, Otorepec P, Wallace P, Dora C, Robertson A and Zakotnic JM (2003) Health impact assessment of agriculture and food policies: lessons learnt from the Republic of Slovenia. *Bull WHO* **81**, 391–8 (available at: http://www.scielosp.org/pdf/bwho/v81n6/v81n6a05.pdf, last visited 6 January 2005).

National Institute for Public Health and the Environment (2005) Health impact assessment database. Bilthoven: *National Institute for Public Health and the Environment* (available on http://www.hiadatabase.net/, last visited 2 February 2005).

United Nations (2003) *Johannesburg Summit 2002. World Summit on Sustainable Development in Johannesburg*. New York: United Nations.

World Health Organization Regional Office for Europe (2001) *Health impact assessment as part of strategic environmental assessment*. Copenhagen, World Health Organization Regional Office for Europe.

World Health Organization (2005) *Health impact assessment (website)*. Geneva: World Health Organization (available on http://www.who.int/hia/en/ last visited 2 February 2005).

World Health Organization European Centre for Health Policy and World Health Organization Regional Office for Europe (1999) *Gothenburg consensus paper. Health impact assessment. Main concepts and suggested approach*. Brussels: European Centre for Health Policy.

Further reading

Birley MH (1995) *The health impact assessment of development projects*. London: HMSO. Although slightly dated, this book is the original approach developed for developing countries. It contains useful examples.

Bulletin of the World Health Organization (2003) Volume 81, Number 6, 387–472. This is a special edition of the journal devoted to articles about HIA from around the world.

Kemm J, Parry J and Palmer S (2004) *Health impact assessment*. Oxford: Oxford University Press. [This is the most up to date and definitive book on HIA, giving an in-depth perspective on HIA theory, techniques and applications. It has multiple examples from all around the world.]

Phoolcharoen W, Sukkumnoed D and Kessomboon P (2003) Development of health impact assessment in Thailand: recent experiences and challenges. *Bull WHO* **81**, 465–7.

SECTION 2

Major determinants of health

7 The changing nature of infectious disease

Overview

At the beginning of the twenty-first century, infectious diseases remain a major global public health problem. Public health measures that can both detect and respond to known and unknown risks, linked to the development and monitoring of prevention and control programmes, are crucial to better health worldwide. In this chapter you will learn about how measures to reduce infectious diseases have changed over time. You will also be introduced to the changing patterns of infectious diseases and to the factors underlying these changes, and how these in turn have influenced the way we have tried to contain infectious diseases.

Learning objectives

After completing this chapter you will be able to:

- **describe some of the measures used to contain infectious diseases historically**
- **describe the nature of how infectious diseases are changing**
- **describe factors behind the changing profile of infectious diseases**
- **comment on the shifting relationship between the state and individuals in controlling infectious diseases**

Key terms

Germ theory The theory that all contagious diseases are caused by micro-organisms.

The evolution of human disease and our understanding of it

Infectious diseases have afflicted mankind since the dawn of civilization. Understanding the history of the interrelationship between the agents responsible and their host provides insights into current trends in infectious diseases, some understanding of how environmental and social changes impact upon disease, and how responses to public health threats are frequently mirrored in the past.

The human race originated in the tropical climate of Africa and was affected by the same parasites as other primates in these areas. As these early hunters migrated into more temperate zones, then the infectious agents they were exposed to changed. During this period humans might have been relatively free of infectious diseases.

Thereafter, as hunting gave way to agriculture, populations grew and stabilized. The development of agriculture, and with it a situation in which domestic animals lived in close proximity to humans, created the opportunity for many zoonotic infections (such as measles, which may have arisen from distemper in dogs or rindepest in cows) to spread to humans. The increase in population size and density provided the ideal conditions for further person-to-person spread of infectious micro-organisms. Humans, food, and water became established reservoirs for many infectious agents.

As civilizations developed further and trade routes became established the movements of people and goods carried new pathogens to susceptible populations. Explorers and armies performed similar functions. Epidemics of infectious diseases such as plague, smallpox, and typhus devastated communities, reduced armies to waste, and generated fear and foreboding.

Of course, a good understanding of disease and its causes is necessary to develop appropriate responses. But before the role of micro-organisms in the causation of disease was understood, responses to epidemics of disease often focused on individuals or groups of individuals perceived as the originators of disease. History is replete with examples of people being subjected to severe measures to protect the wider population. The Jewish population in Europe was especially vulnerable as their observance of strict laws on food preparation often spared them infections that affected the remainder of the population. In response to the threat of plague, for example, 900 Jews were burned alive at Strasbourg in 1349, even before the plague arrived. The perceived association of minority populations and disease, in a climate of irrational fear, has been a common feature of responses to infectious diseases for many centuries.

Control of infectious diseases became possible through the work of Robert Koch and Louis Pasteur and the isolation and identification of etiologic agents. The epidemiology and clinical picture of infectious diseases could then be described, measures to support control introduced, and the impact of these measures determined. The understanding of the 'germ theory', first plausibly articulated in the 1870s, improved. As a result, the focus of measures to contain disease became narrower. This focus sometimes highlighted the inherent tension between the individual and public health, as noted in Chapter 1. Examples include the following:

- In England the Contagious Diseases Acts of the 1860s were aimed at countering sexually transmitted infections in the armed forces through the compulsory medical inspection of 'streetwalkers' in garrison towns and ports;
- The forcible removal of children with suspected polio to specially outfitted pavilions in New York in 1916;
- The detention for life of Mary Mallon ('Typhoid Mary') on North Brother Island (in the East River in New York City) in 1915 (she died in 1938);
- The incarceration of 30,000 prostitutes during World War I in the United States.

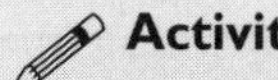

Activity 7.1

Think about other legal measures that might be used to control infectious diseases. List some examples.

Feedback

There are numerous other legal measures that have been used or that are currently being used to control infectious diseases. These include for example:

- The power to tax and spend (for example spending on treatment of the human immunodeficiency virus (HIV))
- The power to alter how information is received (through health promotion activities – an example might be restrictions on the use of explicit language in campaigns to control sexually transmitted diseases)
- Direct regulation of individuals (removal of freedom to decline treatment for tuberculosis, for example)
- Indirect regulation through litigation (or tort) (for example, promoting improved infection control to reduce wound infection rates from methicillin-resistant *Staphylococcus Aureus* (MRSA))
- Deregulation (for example, removal of legal obstacles for brothels)

For other examples, see also Gostin (2001).

Activity 7.2

The advent of effective anti-microbial agents along with the establishment of the principles and practice of immunization hailed a new era. In 1948, George Marshall, then US Secretary of State, proclaimed that the conquest of all infectious diseases was imminent. This optimism persisted for several decades. It later appeared that this optimism was not so much wrong, or even premature, as misconceived. Explain why this might be the case. Illustrate your explanation with a few examples.

Feedback

This misconception was related to a simpler view of the relationship between infectious agents and human beings than we hold today. Relationships between humans and the microbial world are hugely complex and dynamic. The milieus in which parasites and host operate are informed by political, cultural, institutional and environmental forces.

Examples that illustrate this misconception include diseases such as the acquired immune deficiency syndrome (AIDS) and severe acute respiratory syndrome (SARS), the re-emergence of ancient diseases such as tuberculosis or diphtheria, the recognition that infectious agents might play a role in the genesis of many diseases previously not considered infectious, and the increasing anxiety that biological weapons may pose a substantial threat to public health.

The global burden of infectious disease

Infectious diseases are a major cause of ill health and death, affecting particularly children. In 2002 they caused 14.9 million deaths, accounting for 26 per cent of total global mortality. They also accounted in 2002 for almost 30 per cent of the total disability adjusted life years (DALY) lost worldwide.

Activity 7.3

In this activity you will take a closer look at mortality and at the burden of disease due to communicable diseases.

Tables 7.1 and 7.2 give information on the main causes of death and disease burden by WHO region. Using data from these tables, answer the following questions.

1 Identify in which regions deaths from infectious diseases are highest. Take into account the total number of deaths from infectious diseases, mortality rates (go back to chapter 3 if you don't remember how to calculate mortality rates), and the proportion of deaths due to infectious diseases.

2 Identify in which regions the burden of disease due to infectious diseases is highest (consider the total number of DALYs and the proportion of DALYs due to infectious diseases).

Feedback

1 Mortality from infectious diseases is clearly highest in Africa where we see the highest number of deaths in absolute terms and the highest mortality rate for infectious and parasitic diseases (837 deaths per 100,000 population). Mortality from infectious/parasitic diseases or respiratory infections affects one in a hundred persons in Africa (1003 deaths per 100,000 population). Deaths from infectious diseases are also relatively high in South-East Asia (mortality rates: 184 per 100,000 for infectious/parasitic diseases and 276 per 100,000 for infectious/parasitic diseases and pulmonary infections taken jointly) and the Eastern Mediterranean region (190 per 100,000 for infectious/parasitic diseases and 260 per 100,000 for infectious/parasitic diseases and pulmonary infections taken jointly). In comparison, the death rate from infectious/parasitic diseases is only 22 per 100,000 population in Europe (although this hides regional differences within Europe that are not shown in Table 7.1).

The proportion of all deaths due to infectious diseases is also highest in Africa where more than half of all deaths are due to infectious or parasitic diseases (52.7 per cent) and 63 per cent to infectious/parasitic diseases or pulmonary infections. This compares with only 2 per cent and 5.1 per cent respectively in Europe. A relatively high proportion of deaths from infectious/parasitic diseases is also found in South-East Asia (19.9 per cent) and the Eastern Mediterranean region (23.0 per cent).

2 A pattern similar to that described above is found when we look at the burden of disease due to infectious diseases. Over 187 millions DALYs are lost yearly in Africa due to infectious or parasitic diseases and 35.6 millions lost due to respiratory infections.

Table 7.1 Deaths by cause in WHO regions, estimates for 2002

	Total		*Africa*	*The Americas*	*South-East Asia*	*Europe*	*Eastern Medit.*	*Western Pacific*
Population (000)	*6 224 985*		*672 238*	*852 551*	*1 590 832*	*877 886*	*502 824*	*1 717 536*
	(000)	*% total*	*(000)*	*(000)*	*(000)*	*(000)*	*(000)*	*(000)*
Total number of deaths	57 029	100	10 664	5 962	14 657	9 564	4 152	11 940
Infectious and parasitic diseases	10 904	19.1	5 625	397	2 922	195	953	804
Respiratory infections	3 963	6.9	1 118	226	1 474	288	354	498
Maternal and perinatal conditions	2 972	5.2	785	191	1 184	68	370	370
Nutritional deficiencies	485	0.9	143	61	189	12	53	27
Neoplasms	7 270	12.7	419	1 145	1 178	1 871	296	2 347
Diabetes mellitus, nutritional/endocrine disorders	1 354	2.4	116	303	306	290	118	219
Neuropsychiatric disorders	1 112	1.9	90	240	267	256	89	167
Cardiovascular diseases	16 733	29.3	1 036	1 928	3 911	4 927	1 079	3 825
Respiratory diseases	3 702	6.5	257	398	874	404	155	1 609
Digestive diseases	1 968	3.5	157	284	502	389	152	480
Other non communicable conditions	1 521	2.7	187	237	389	188	175	342
Injuries	5 168	9.1	741	540	1 467	792	392	1 229

Source: Adapted from World Health Organization (2004)

Table 7.2 Burden of disease in disability-adjusted life years (DALYs) by cause in WHO Regions, estimates for 2002[1]

	Total		*Africa*	*The Americas*	*South-East Asia*	*Europe*	*Eastearn Medit.*	*Western Pacific*
Population (000)	*6 224 985*		*672 238*	*852 551*	*1 590 832*	*877 886*	*502 824*	*1 717 536*
	(000)	*% total*	*(000)*	*(000)*	*(000)*	*(000)*	*(000)*	*(000)*
Total number of DALYs	1 490 125 643	100	361 376 478	145 586 527	426 572 902	150 321 605	139 079 337	264 879 260
Infectious and parasitic diseases	350 332 571	23.5	187 448 845	11 890 388	88 952 900	5 665 026	32 410 088	23 671 157
Respiratory infections	94 603 349	6.3	35 595 347	3 315 928	33 026 019	3 115 191	10 818 791	8 653 688
Maternal and perinatal conditions	130 966 679	8.8	33 104 006	9 319 806	50 542 629	3 554 015	16 654 594	17 602 104
Nutritional deficiencies	34 416 632	2.3	9 573 867	2 124 420	12 127 757	1 703 909	4 490 404	4 360 317
Neoplasms	77 293 663	5.2	4 914 205	11 405 860	14 070 924	17 445 197	4 183 809	25 151 663
Diabetes mellitus & nutritional/ endocrine disorders	24 155 400	1.6	2 404 904	5 753 643	5 893 601	3 169 056	2 095 680	4 751 614
Neuropsychiatric disorders	193 278 495	13.0	17 897 036	35 787 391	48 313 777	29 348 996	15 019 744	46 533 897
Cardiovascular diseases	148 190 083	9.9	10 910 418	15 173 288	42 987 030	34 417 792	12 059 668	32 413 230
Respiratory diseases	55 153 199	3.7	5 482 583	7 968 078	15 630 419	6 735 413	3 719 707	15 535 384
Digestive diseases	46 475 768	3.1	5 103 566	5 543 889	14 205 642	7 396 276	4 031 778	10 111 155
Other non communicable conditions	153 268 686	0	18 138 712	17 440 027	45 275 063	16 825 972	16 113 431	39 121 304
Injuries	181 991 119	12.2	30 802 990	19 863 809	55 547 140	20 944 762	17 481 643	36 973 747

[1] Figures computed by WHO to assure comparibility, they are not necessarily the official statistics of WHO Member States, which may use alternative rigorous methods.

Source: Adapted from World Health Organization (2004)

This compares with only 5.7 millions and 3.1 millions respectively in Europe. The burden of disease due to infectious diseases is also relatively high in South-East Asia. In this region, almost 90 millions DALYs are lost due to infectious or parasitic diseases and 33 millions due to respiratory infections. The third region with the highest disease burden due to infectious diseases is, as expected, the Eastern Mediterranean region (32.4 millions and 10.8 millions DALYs lost respectively to infectious/parasitic diseases and respiratory infections).

Results for the proportion of total DALYs lost due to infectious diseases are similar with the highest values observed in Africa (51.9 per cent for infectious/parasitic diseases and 9.8 per cent for respiratory infections), followed by South-East Asia (20.9 per cent and 7.7 per cent) and the Eastern Mediterranean region (23.3 per cent and 7.8 per cent). The lowest proportions are found in Europe where 3.8 per cent of total DALYs are accounted for by infectious/parasitic diseases and 2.1 per cent by respiratory infections.

Emergent and re-emergent infectious diseases

The nature of infectious diseases is changing not only in terms of magnitude and the inability of science to provide all the answers but also for the following three reasons. First, 'new' diseases, most notably HIV/AIDS and SARS, resulting from apparently new organisms are occurring. Second, 'ancient' diseases such as tuberculosis and diphtheria are re-emerging as serious threats to public health (often having 'disappeared' only in affluent western societies). Third, novel agents are being implicated in the causation of a number of clinical syndromes (for example parvovirus, human T-cell lymphotropic viruses I and II, and a number of human herpes viruses).

In a similar vein, the causative agent has been better defined, such as Legionnaires' disease and Lyme disease. Progress in the identification of micro-organisms through advances in molecular biology and epidemiology have led to the discovery that infectious agents may be responsible for diseases previously considered non-transmissible, such as a number of cancers, peptic ulcer disease, reactive arthritis and atherosclerosis. Examples of pathogenic microbes and the diseases they cause are given in Tables 7.3 and 7.4.

The spectre of drug resistant organisms, unresponsive to anti-microbial agents, has emerged over the past 60 years. Multi-drug resistance of infectious micro-organisms is a major global health problem. Strains of resistant *Mycobacterium tuberculosis* have been reported from all countries in the world. Outbreaks of resistant *Staphylococcus aureus*, including methicillin resistant *Staphylococcus aureus* (MRSA), threaten health care provision with potentially huge economic costs. Resistant *Salmonella* species have arisen from excessive use of antibiotics in the food industry with serious consequences for human health. Other examples of drug resistant infectious agents are provided in Table 7.5.

The costs of outbreaks of infectious diseases have been high (Table 7.6). The epidemic of bovine spongiform encephalitis is estimated to have cost approaching

Table 7.3 Examples of pathogenic microbes and the diseases they cause since 1973

Year	*Microbe*	*Type*	*Disease*
1973	Rotavirus	Virus	Infantile diarrhea
1977	Ebola virus	Virus	Acute hemorrhagic fever
1977	Legionella pneumophila	Bacterium	Legionnaires' disease
1980	Human T-lymphotrophic virus (HTLV1)	Virus	T-cell lymphoma/leukemia
1981	Toxin-producing Staphylococcus aureus	Bacterium	Toxic shock syndrome
1982	Escherichia coli O157:H7	Bacterium	Hemorrhagic colitis; hemolytic uremic syndrome
1982	Borrelia burgdorferi	Bacterium	Lyme disease
1983	Human Immunodeficiency virus (HIV)	Virus	Acquired Immuno-Deficiency Syndrome (AIDS)
1983	Helicobacter pylori	Bacterium	Peptic ulcer disease
1989	Hepatitis C	Virus	Parentally transmitted non-A, non-B liver infection
1992	Vibrio cholerae O139	Bacterium	New strain associated with epidemic cholera
1993	Hantavirus	Virus	Adult respiratory distress syndrome
1994	Cryptosporidium	Protozoa	Enteric disease
1995	Ehrlichiosis	Bacterium	Severe arthritis?
1996	nvCJD	Prion	New variant Creutzfeldt-Jakob disease
1997	HVN1	Virus	Influenza
1999	Nipah	Virus	Severe encephalitis
2003	Coronavirus	Virus	SARS

Source: Adapted mostly from Department of Health (2002)

Table 7.4 Diseases associated with infectious agents

Disease/syndrome/disorder	*Agent*
Chronic gastritis	H pylori
Peptic ulcer	H pylori
Guillain-Barre syndrome	Campylobacter jejuni
Bell's palsy	Borrelia burgdorferi, Herpes simplex virus
Tropical spastic paraparesis	HTLV-1
Haemolytic uraemic syndrome	E coli 0157
Throbotic thrombocytopenic purpura	E coli 0157
Polyarteritis nodosa	Hepatitis B virus
Insulin dependent diabetes	Enterovirus
Atherosclerosis	Chlamydia pneumoniae, cytomegolovirus
Reactive arthritis	Salmonella spp., Yersinia spp., Chlamydia trachomatis
Human T-cell leukaemia	HTLV-1
Hairy cell leukaemia	HTLV-2
Hepatocellular cancer	Hepatitis B and C
Cervical cancer	HPV
Burkitt's lymphoma	EBV
AIDS-related CNS lymphoma	EBV
Kaposi's sarcoma	HHV8
AIDS-related body cavity lymphoma	HHV8
Castleman's disease	HHV8

$40 billion, decimating the British beef industry. The financial cost of the epidemic of HIV is beyond comprehension.

The picture of infectious disease changes as effective therapeutic measures are developed and become adopted in practice. For example, the clinical picture of HIV has changed dramatically for those able to access HAART (Highly Active Anti-Retroviral Therapy) in ways analogous to the improvement in prognosis for diabetics with the introduction of insulin.

Table 7.5 Examples of drug-resistant infectious agents and percentage of infections that are drug resistant, by country or region

Pathogen	*Drug*	*Country/Area*	*Percentage of drug-resistant infections*
Streptococcus pneumoniae	Penicillin	United States	10–35
		Asia, Chile, Spain	20
		Hungary	58
Staphylococcus aureus	Methicillin	United States	32
	Vancomycin	United States	0
Mycobacterium tuberculosis	Any drug	United States	13
		New York City	16
	INH + RIF*	United States	2
		New York City	5
Plasmodium falciparum malaria	Chloroquine	Kenya	65
		Ghana	45
		Zimbabwe	59
		Burkina Faso	17
	Mephloquine	Thailand	40
Shigella dysenteriae	Multidrug	Burundi, Rwanda	100

* Resistance to isoniazid (INH), rifampicin (RIF), and/or other drugs.

Source: Institute of Medicine (1997)

Table 7.6 Examples of economic impact of major infectious disease outbreaks

Year	*Country*	*Disease*	*Cost (US$)*
1979–94	New York City	Tuberculosis	Over 1 billion
1990–8	Malaysia	Nipah virus	540 million
1991	United Kingdom	Bovine Spongiform Encephalopathy (BSE)	38 billion
1994	India	Plague	2 billion
1997	Hong Kong	'Bird flu'	22 million
1998	Tanzania	Cholera	770 million
1999	New York	West Nile Fever	Almost 100 million
1999	Russian Federation	Tuberculosis	Over 4 billion
2003	China, Hong Kong, Canada	Severe Acute Respiratory Syndrome (SARS)	15 billion

Source: Adapted from selected WHO reports

Factors affecting the growth and spread of infectious diseases

As noted above, factors beyond the immediate relationship of microbe and pathogenic host defences influence the growth and spread of infectious diseases. For example international travel and commerce is known to be associated with the spread of malaria, cholera, and pneumococcal pneumonia.

Activity 7.4

Take a moment to think about other potential factors contributing to the growth and spread of infectious diseases worldwide. Prepare a list of these factors. If possible, give examples of infectious diseases they have been associated with.

Feedback

There are numerous factors that you could have listed. These can be classified into seven main groups:

1 Demographic changes and human behaviours

Population growth: Despite falling birth rates in some developed countries and the dramatic impact on survival of the HIV/AIDS epidemic in others, the world population is growing at a rate of approximately 1.5 per cent per annum. It is likely that by 2030 the world population will be 8 billion. Overcrowding will increase and this will promote the spread of infectious diseases, including dengue/dengue hemorrhagic fever and giardiasis.

Poverty: Approximately one quarter of the world's population live in extreme poverty, surviving on less than $1 per day and most of these people live in Asia and sub-Saharan Africa. The share and number of people living on less than $2 per day – a more relevant threshold for middle-income economies such as those of East Asia and Latin America – is roughly similar. These figures translate into the stark fact that some 2 billion persons suffer from under-nutrition or malnutrition, lack access to basic health care, and access to safe water. The links between poverty, malnutrition, and infectious diseases are clear.

Population movements: People who flee their home countries out of a fear of persecution join a larger stream of migrants who leave in search of opportunities for work, education, reunification with family members, or for other reasons. It has been estimated that at the end of the twentieth century some 150 million people were living outside the country of their birth, amounting to about 2.5 per cent of the world's population, or one out of every 40 people. Two million people cross international borders every single day, about a tenth of humanity each year. And of these, more than a million travel from developing to industrialized countries each week. Many of these migrants live in overcrowded conditions and, as in centuries before, epidemics result from transmission through rapid person-to-person spread amongst susceptible populations or through the carriage of vectors.

Human behaviours: Changes in behaviour, including sexual behaviour and injecting drug use, are associated with changes in the incidence of several infectious diseases. Increases in sexually transmissible infections in eastern Europe has followed marked socio-economic and behavioural changes. Most notably, the past two decades has seen

HIV spread across the world. Sexual, vertical, and parenteral transmission is devastating communities. Hepatitis B is similarly transmitted. 'Non-compliance' by health care workers, patients, drug producers, and health care systems is resulting in drug resistant organisms. For example, outbreaks of multi-drug resistant tuberculosis that emerged often resulted in non-compliance of one or more of the actors/institutions.

2 Technological development

The epidemic of BSE, which by 2001 had afflicted over 179,000 cows in Great Britain, has been ascribed to technological changes in the animal and human food chain which dated from the 1980s. By October, 2001, 101 people had become sick and died from variant Creutzfeldt-Jacob disease (vCJD). Both vCJD and BSE are transmissible spongiform encephalopathies and it is likely that they are linked.

The development and application of new technologies may have deleterious effects. Another example is the link between air conditioning systems and legionella outbreaks. Other infections that have been associated with technological development include toxic shock syndrome, nosocomial (hospital-acquired) infections, and hemorrhagic colitis/haemolytic uremic syndrome.

3 Economic development and land use: associated with Lyme disease, malaria, plague, rabies, yellow fever, Rift Valley fever, schistosomiasis

Development projects such as the building of dams, irrigation schemes, hydroelectric power plants, and roads, which are intended to improve social well-being, may have negative effects that include the displacement of people, chronic food deficiency, and the development of new and more pernicious forms of poverty. The Nam Pong dam in Thailand resulted in substantial increases in local rates of liver fluke and hookworm morbidity – the result of poor waste disposal and poor living conditions of resettled people.

4 Microbial adaptation and change

Immunological responses of hosts may vary in response to changes in micro-organisms. An example is antigenic *drift* resulting from spontaneous mutations that result in minor changes in the amino acid sequence of proteins. The changes result in mutant strains of the virus then becoming selected in the population by their ability to infect partially immune hosts. By contrast antigenic *shift*, which occurs much less frequently, involves replacement of the main neutralizing antigen by a different protein acquired as a result of genetic change when some of the genetic coding of the micro-organism is exchanged for a code from another agent (for example, by transfer of plasmids, which are small fragments of DNA). Major epidemics often result from antigenic drift because the host has little immune protection, such as the 1918 influenza pandemic. (The SARS epidemic illustrated the frailty of global public health systems to meet the challenge of an emergent pathogen that readily crosses international borders – SARS is considerably less transmissible than influenza.)

5 Breakdown of health infrastructure or public health policy

In the 1990s a massive epidemic of diphtheria occurred throughout the countries of the former Soviet Union. Diphtheria had been well controlled in the Soviet Union for more than 2 decades after universal childhood immunization was initiated in the late 1950s. However from the mid 1980s changes in the immunization schedule to incorporate fewer doses of lower antigenic content, an increasing number of contraindications to vaccination and decreased public confidence in the vaccination programmes led to levels of vaccination coverage below 70 per cent in most areas. In 1990 epidemic diphtheria re-emerged in the Soviet Union with the highest incidence rates in adolescents and adults aged 40–49 years reaching a peak in 1994–95. Other infectious diseases associated with the breakdown of public health include rabies, tuberculosis, trench fever, whooping cough (pertussis), and cholera.

6 Climate changes

Global warming over the next century will result in increases in food productivity in some areas and falls in others. Some low-lying areas will suffer flooding and loss of agricultural land and contamination of fresh water supplies. Migration of large populations is likely to result. Five hundred million people currently live at or near sea level. Changes in temperature will result in different distributions of vectors. Mosquitoes will survive in previously mosquito-free regions introducing diseases such as malaria and dengue, cholera and yellow fever.

7 Warfare/terrorism/conflict

Wars and conflicts create environments that micro-organisms exploit. The movements of large numbers of people, unhygienic living conditions, malnutrition, and the destruction of public infrastructures encourage diseases and their spread.

The pollution of water supplies and catapulting of diseased human corpses into besieged cities are early examples of biological warfare. The British, in the eighteenth century, distributed smallpox-infected blankets to North American Indians. But it was not until the twentieth century that research and development of biological warfare activities increased. By the 1940s a joint programme between the United States, United Kingdom and Canada sought to produce an anthrax bomb. Through the cold war the Soviet Union maintained programmes to develop biological weapons, sometimes leading to accidental releases that caused many fatalities; by the 1980s advances in genetic engineering were being harnessed to produce, for example, strains of plague resistant to antibiotics.

Since the first Gulf War in 1991 there has been increasing concern about biological weapons. This has resulted in considerable investment in detection, identification, and protection measures. The events of September 11th 2001 in the USA and the subsequent distribution of anthrax through the US postal service has raised anxiety further. This is reflected in plans to immunize 500,000 key personnel in the USA against smallpox.

Control of infectious diseases – the state and individual responsibilities

As can be inferred from the sections above, the variables that influence the relationship between man and infectious agents are interrelated. What remains largely unclear, however, is what should be the appropriate responses to the changing nature of infectious diseases. The core principles of infectious diseases control and the resources available may be inadequate to assert 'control' even if that were theoretically possible. The complexity of the interrelationships between variables demands responses that go beyond those that focus on the hosts and organism but encompass socio-economic, cultural, and political imperatives.

Indeed, notions of globalization challenge infectious diseases in ways that are becoming starker. The roles and responsibilities of states and their often limited ability to control infectious diseases that have the potential to cross borders and threaten populations resident in other states is a potential source of tension. This was brought home during the SARS epidemic and has influenced the development of the international health regulations (international laws that aim to control transnational spread of disease). The role of the WHO is also being redefined by these tensions and challenges.

The tension between the individual and society plays out in several arenas when we contemplate responses to infectious diseases. For example, the free movements of peoples across borders may be inhibited, the quarantine of migrants potentially carrying infectious micro-organisms (for example returning soldiers, economic migrants, refugees from epidemics) – powers to quarantine cities in the United States has been suggested in the event of biological threat. Compulsory immunization may be deemed an appropriate measure in countries where it is not already in place.

Likewise, compulsory treatment or isolation of those who pose a threat might be considered where individuals either decline treatment or are untreatable respectively.

The following activity will help you to think about this perennial tension and contemplate the responsibilities of the state to provide for the well-being of individuals and of individuals to comply with measures to reduce the threat they might pose in the context of re-emergent tuberculosis.

Activity 7.5

Paul Farmer has been at the forefront of the campaign to see the emergence of infectious disease as a response to social inequity. Now read the following extract from one of his papers (Farmer 1996) and answer the following questions:

1 What, in Farmer's view, explains the relative lack of visibility of many infectious diseases?

2 Take one of the examples quoted by Farmer (Argentinian and Bolivian haemorrhagic fever) and sketch a chain of events that has led to its emergence as a problem.

3 Farmer quotes Anthony McMichael as saying 'Modern epidemiology is oriented to explaining and quantifying the bobbing of corks on the surface waters, while largely disregarding the stronger undercurrents that determine where, on average, the cluster of corks ends up along the shoreline of risk'. What do you understand by this statement? Do you agree with it?

4 Can you think of examples other than those mentioned by Farmer of global or regional policies that have had consequences for the pattern of infectious diseases?

Infections and Inequalities: The Modern Plagues

The past decade has been one of the most eventful in the long history of infectious diseases. The sheer number of relevant publications indicates explosive growth; moreover, new means of monitoring antimicrobial resistance patterns are being used along with the rapid sharing of information (as well as speculation and misinformation) through means that did not exist even 10 years ago. Then there are the microbes themselves. One of the explosions in question – perhaps the most remarked upon – is that of 'emerging infectious diseases'. Among the diseases considered 'emerging', some are regarded as genuinely new; AIDS and Brazilian purpuric fever are examples. Others have newly identified etiologic agents or have again burst dramatically onto the scene. For example, the syndromes caused by Hantaan virus have been known in Asia for centuries but now seem to be spreading beyond Asia because of ecologic and economic transformations that increase contact between humans and rodents. Still other diseases grouped under the 'emerging' rubric are ancient and well-known foes that have somehow changed, in pathogenicity or distribution. Multidrug-resistant tuberculosis (TB) and invasive or necrotizing Group A streptococcal infection are cases in point.

In studying emerging infectious diseases, many make a distinction between a host of phenomena directly related to human actions – from improved laboratory techniques and scientific discovery to economic 'development', global warming, and failures of public health – and another set of phenomena, much less common and related to changes in the microbes themselves. Close examination of microbial mutations often shows that, again, human actions have played a large role in enhancing pathogenicity or increasing resistance to antimicrobial agents.

The study of anything said to be emerging tends to be dynamic. But the very notion of emergence in heterogeneous populations poses questions of analysis that are rarely tackled, even in modern epidemiology, which 'assigns a primary importance to studying interindividual variations in risk. By concentrating on these specific and presumed free-range individual behaviors, we thereby pay less attention to the underlying social-historical influences on behavioral choices, patterns, and population health' (McMichael 1995). A critical (and self-critical) approach would ask how existing frameworks might limit our ability to discern trends that can be linked to the emergence of diseases.

A critical approach pushes the limits of existing academic politesse to ask harder and rarely raised questions: What are the mechanisms by which changes in agriculture have led to outbreaks of Argentine and Bolivian hemorrhagic fever, and how might these mechanisms be related to international trade agreements, such as the General Agreement on Tariffs and Trade and the North American Free Trade Agreement? How might institutional racism be related to urban crime and the outbreaks of multidrug-resistant TB in New York prisons? Similar questions may be productively posed in regard to many diseases now held to be emerging.

Questions for a critical epistemology of emerging infectious diseases

Ebola, TB, and HIV infection are in no way unique in demanding contextualization through social science approaches. These approaches include the grounding of case histories and local epidemics in the larger biosocial systems in which they take shape and demand exploration of social inequalities. Why, for example, were there 10,000 cases of diphtheria in Russia from 1990 to 1993? It is easy enough to argue that the excess cases were due to a failure to vaccinate. But only in linking this distal (and, in sum, technical) cause to the much more complex socioeconomic transformations altering the region's illness and death patterns will compelling explanations emerge.

Standard epidemiology, narrowly focused on individual risk and short on critical theory, will not reveal these deep socioeconomic transformations, nor will it connect them to disease emergence. 'Modern epidemiology' observes one of its leading contributors, is 'oriented to explaining and quantifying the bobbing of corks on the surface waters, while largely disregarding the stronger undercurrents that determine where, on average, the cluster of corks ends up along the shoreline of risk' (McMichael 1995).

Research questions identified by various blue-ribbon panels are important for the understanding and eventual control of emerging infectious diseases. Yet both the diseases and popular and scientific commentary on them pose a series of corollary questions, which, in turn, demand research that is the exclusive province of neither social scientists nor bench scientists, clinicians, or epidemiologists. Indeed, genuinely transdisciplinary collaboration will be necessary to tackle the problems posed by emerging infectious diseases. As prolegomena, four areas of corollary research are easily identified. In each is heard the recurrent leitmotiv of inequality:

Social inequalities

Study of the reticulated links between social inequalities and emerging disease would not construe the poor simply as 'sentinel chickens', but instead would ask, What are the precise mechanisms by which these diseases come to have their effects in some bodies but not in others? What propagative effects might social inequalities per se contribute?

Social inequalities have sculpted not only the distribution of emerging diseases, but also the course of disease in those affected by them, a fact that is often downplayed.

Transnational forces

Travel is a potent force in disease emergence and spread, and the current volume, speed, and reach of travel are unprecedented. The study of borders qua borders means, increasingly, the study of social inequalities. Many political borders serve as semipermeable membranes, often quite open to diseases and yet closed to the free movement of cures.

Research questions might include, for example, What effects might the interface between two very different types of health care systems have on the rate of advance of an emerging disease? What turbulence is introduced when the border in question is between a rich and a poor nation?

The dynamics of change

Can we elaborate lists of the differentially weighted factors that promote or retard the emergence or re-emergence of infectious diseases? It has been argued that such analyses will perforce be historically deep and geographically broad, and they will at the same time be processual, incorporating concepts of change. Above all, they will seek to incorporate complexity rather than to merely dissect it.

Critical epistemology

Many have already asked, What qualifies as an emerging infectious disease? More critical questions might include, Why do some persons constitute 'risk groups,' while others are 'individuals at risk'? These are not merely nosologic questions; they are canonical ones.

Finally, why are some epidemics visible to those who fund research and services, while others are invisible? In its recent statements on TB and emerging infections, for example, the World Health Organization uses the threat of contagion to motivate wealthy nations to invest in disease surveillance and control out of self-interest – an age-old public health approach acknowledged in the Institute of Medicine's report on emerging infections: 'Diseases that appear not to threaten the United States directly rarely elicit the political support necessary to maintain control efforts'. If related to a study under consideration, questions of power and control over funds, must be discussed. That they are not is more a marker of analytic failures than of editorial standards.

Reference

McMichael A (1995) The health of persons, populations, and planets: epidemiology comes full circle. *Epidemiology* **6**: 633–6.

Feedback

1 Farmer suggests that infectious diseases that attract more attention are those that represent a threat for wealthier nations (for example the United States), thus stimulating investment in disease surveillance and control. Diseases that do not seem to represent such a threat – although they might be very important in other countries – do not lead to the same support and thus to a lack of visibility.

2

→ Increased national prosperity
  → Ecological changes and degradation of land and water resources
  → Increased transport and consumption of energy
→ Increased movement from rural to urban areas with resulting uncontrolled urban growth
→ Increased illegal housing and slums
→ Poor/unsanitary living conditions
→ Reduced access to health care
  → Increased vulnerability to diseases
→ Increased possibility of mosquito breeding in stored water and non-biodegradable trash
  → Increased risk of infection
→ Constant movement within the country/region helps spread the disease
→ Lack of resources for epidemiological and vector control programmes and for treatment

3 Epidemiology usually examines the more direct causes of diseases (as in Farmer's example: the fact that a lack of vaccination was explaining an excess in the number of cases of diphtheria in Russia from 1990 to 1993), disregarding the more distal complex causes of diseases (in the above example the complex socioeconomic transformations altering the region's illness and death patterns).

4 The European Common Agricultural policy provides agricultural subsidies to EU countries. Markets for some developing nation products are thus restricted which leads to poverty, inequalities in health and accompanying infectious diseases.

Economic policies advocated by the international community to create market economy in Russia lead to great inequalities, economic hardship for many, high unemployment amongst the young, drug use, alcoholism, crime, high incarceration rates, and a rise in infectious diseases rates such as tuberculosis and HIV.

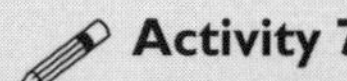

Activity 7.6

This activity now considers infectious diseases within the context of human rights.

A member of the European Parliament is concerned about the increase in tuberculosis in Eastern Europe, Asia and Africa, and interested in controlling tuberculosis within the European Union (EU) borders. He has heard that non-adherence to treatment is a cause of drug resistant tuberculosis. He is thus advocating that all individuals with tuberculosis who will not or cannot comply with treatment be isolated until non-infectious and received mandatory treatment until cured. Now read the following extracts of papers from Sepkowitz (1996) ('How contagious is tuberculosis?'), Gasner and collaborators (1999) ('The use of legal action in New York City to ensure treatment of tuberculosis'), and Hurtig and collaborators (1999) ('To what extent does the proposed policy or programme represent "good public health"?') and answer the questions that follow.

How contagious is tuberculosis?

One of the many lessons learned in the course of the now-passing resurgence of tuberculosis in the United States is how little about *Mycobacterium tuberculosis* we really understand. In the 1970s, with tuberculosis apparently poised on the brink of eradication, basic investigation – ranging from drug development to inquiry into pathogenesis and immunologic response – more or less ceased. After all, reliable 6-month treatment courses for cure had been established, and case numbers were dropping.

The scientific community therefore was caught flat-footed as tuberculosis reemerged in the 1980s and affected a new population – those with HIV infection – with startlingly high rates of disease and death. Researchers realized it was time to go back to the drawing board but found there was relatively little on the drawing board to explain the current events.

Much of our current understanding of the transmissibility of tuberculosis derives from inference and accident rather than from intentional scientific study. Published reports on various community outbreaks of tuberculosis have been particularly helpful in understanding the transmissibility of tuberculosis; in these reports, investigation of a cluster of cases has elucidated an important principle of disease transmission. In addition, numerous meticulous community-bases studies have demonstrated repeatedly that a single variable – the AFB (acid-fast bacilli) smear status of the source case – strongly predicts which patients are the most contagious. Beyond these observations, however, much has been left to speculation.

The group headed by Riley also noted that transmission was decreased when the mouth was covered while coughing. This simple intervention is often overlooked as attention is focused on the current elaborate strategies for decreasing transmission, such as sophisticated filters on masks, ultraviolet light sterilization of air, and negative pressure ventilation in rooms.

Our understanding of the transmission of tuberculosis is further hampered by our reliance on the tuberculin skin test to identify latently infected and newly infected individuals. Numerous investigations of outbreaks have been complicated by the relatively poor sensitivity and specificity of this old test. Improved understanding of the transmission of tuberculosis may await the development of a more reliable test for diagnosing individuals who are infected with *M. tuberculosis*.

Use of RFLP (restriction fragment-length polymorphism analysis) and other molecular techniques may provide the additional technologic advantage needed to better comprehend the principles of transmission. On the other hand, it may be that one more modern technique will fall short of completely unlocking the mysteries of tubercle bacillus.

The use of legal action in New York City to ensure treatment of tuberculosis

In 1992, New York City reported 3811 cases of tuberculosis, nearly three times the number of cases reported 15 years before. As part of a comprehensive response, the New York City Department of Health expanded services for patients with tuberculosis and in 1993 updated the Health Code to permit compulsory actions to protect the public health. The commissioner of health could issue orders compelling a person to be examined for suspected tuberculosis, to complete treatment, to receive treatment under direct observation, or to be detained for treatment.

Although there was widespread support for these changes, there was concern that the department would use its new powers as a means of social control, and some believed it was unfair to detain patients when their ability to comply voluntarily with treatment was affected by lack of adequate housing, primary health care, and services for substance abusers. The fear was that patients with a history of drug or alcohol abuse or homelessness would be singled out for legal action. In fact, some groups, including civil liberties organizations and organizations advocating for patients with the acquired immunodeficiency syndrome (AIDS), unsuccessfully supported a challenge to the regulations in court, seeking to require the department to exhaust every less restrictive option before ordering detention, rather than allowing it the discretion to skip steps.

New York City's tuberculosis-control program has been highly successful; new cases decreased by 54.6 per cent and cases of multidrug-resistant disease by 87.3 per cent between 1992 and 1997.

In the first two years of the program, less than 2 per cent of all patients with tuberculosis in New York City, and a minority of patients with substance abuse, homelessness, or a history of incarceration, required confinement for the completion of treatment. For 75 per cent of patients ordered to receive directly observed therapy and 76 per cent of patients who did not comply with such mandatory treatment who received a warning letter, detention was not necessary. The success of these interventions indicates that if detention is undertaken too quickly, patients' liberty may be limited unnecessarily. Although the power of the Department of Health to omit steps that are less restrictive than detention to ensure treatment was upheld by the courts and was important for patients who might otherwise have eluded outreach efforts and continued to spread tuberculosis, this power was used sparingly. The success of mandatory directly observed therapy is based on the credible threat of detention; noncompliant patients are warned that failure to adhere to the treatment regimen could result in detention. New York City is fortunate to have two hospitals with secure wards in which to detain patients, thus avoiding the serious ethical problems raised by the prospect of having to jail patients with tuberculosis.

Even though many patients had a history of noncompliance, advanced tuberculosis disease, and multidrug resistance, the use of orders for mandatory directly observed therapy or detention resulted in a completion rate of 96 per cent. The concern that the power to detain patients would result in the discriminatory detention of patients who were homeless or who were substance abusers was not realized. Although the proportion of patients who had a history of incarceration, substance abuse, or homelessness was high, the great majority of patients with both tuberculosis and social problems did not require any form of regulatory action. Since data collection was more complete for patients covered by regulatory orders than for other patients, the actual proportions of nondetained patients who had these characteristics may have been higher than indicated by the available data.

Detention was used only when it was judged necessary to protect the public health. Patients who were detained posed a serious risk to the public health. As compared with outpatients receiving mandatory observation of treatment, they were infectious for a longer period, left hospitals against medical advice more often, and were more likely to have cavitary disease. These were the patients the law was intended to reach – those with a history of repeated hospitalizations who did not accept directly observed therapy voluntarily, were not able to complete treatment without detention, and were likely to spread disease. Because information on adherence for the entire group of patients with tuberculosis was not available, we cannot prove that every patient who was repeatedly noncompliant with therapy was subject to regulatory action and that there was no bias in issuing orders. However, careful monitoring of all patients, including those treated by private physicians, resulted in rates of completion of therapy among patients without multidrug-resistant tuberculosis of 89 per cent in 1993 and 94 per cent in 1994. Among the patients who received any regulatory order, the data indicate that there was no racial or social bias with regard to detention. We are confident that there was no serious bias and that virtually all patients who did not comply with treatment and who could be located were issued regulatory orders.

The costs of the detention program were substantial, but they were considerably below the expenses that were averted. The costs of hospitalization during detention for patients described in this study totaled nearly $3 million (New York City Department of Health: unpublished data). In addition, the costs of staff to run the detention program included salaries for a program coordinator, a physician to review records and appear in court, and nine outreach workers to collect and review medical records of patients referred for regulatory action, prepare orders, monitor patients for whom orders had been issued, and respond to telephone inquiries. During this period, one Health Department lawyer reviewed all orders from a legal perspective, and additional legal staff represented New York City in the hearings for individual patients. Thus, at its height, the regulatory program probably cost nearly $2 million per year, including the costs of hospital care.

Although the costs of the program were high, the economic benefits appear to have been higher. Before the advent of regulatory intervention, ineffective and repeated hospitalization for the 304 patients ultimately ordered to receive treatment cost a total of more than $25 million (New York City Department of Health: unpublished data). By curtailing such costs, as well as preventing the spread of tuberculosis, the regulatory interventions saved substantial direct costs.

Comparison with other programs is difficult because of the different criteria for detention, the different definitions of psychosocial variables, and the dissimilar detention facilities. Nevertheless, since New York City has more than twice as many cases of tuberculosis and many times as many cases of multidrug-resistant disease as any other city in the United States, its detention program has been the most active, detaining almost as many patients in two years as Massachusetts did in five years. However, the percentage of patients detained was lower in New York than in other jurisdictions.

As New York City's total number of cases of tuberculosis has declined, so has the number of patients detained. Only 44 patients were detained in 1997, once again representing approximately 2 per cent of the total (New York City Department of Health: unpublished data). This decrease probably reflects both the program's success in identifying and completing the treatment of nearly all patients with existing disease and the decreased incidence of tuberculosis. In its implementation of the law, the Department of Health gave patients numerous less restrictive alternatives, reserving detention for the small number of patients who were truly unwilling or unable to adhere to treatment. Patients were evaluated on the basis of their histories with respect to tuberculosis, not on the basis of their social characteristics. Detention remained a last resort to cure patients, but, when applied, it was highly successful in ensuring complete treatment.

Extract from Hurtig and collaborators (1999)

To what extent does the proposed policy or programme represent 'good public health'?

Public health strategies for the control of infections concentrate on disease rather than 'well-being'. From a biomedical perspective, TB control strategies are 'rational' approaches developed from good science. As only people with sputum-positive pulmonary tuberculosis are regarded as being infectious to others, and because control needs to prevent transmission to the wider public, public health interventions are targeted at cases of *infectious* TB only. Forms of TB that are considered non-infectious, such as extra-pulmonary TB or TB in children, are not, therefore, seen to be public health issues. While 'rational' from a positivist, biomedical point of view, the human rights approach would question this perspective. What message does this give to the parents of children with tuberculosis? What message does it give to people with extra-pulmonary disease?

There is an inherent contradiction in the public health approach to the control of infectious diseases like tuberculosis. While the interest of a programme is ultimately the good of the population, the strategy focuses on the individual patient, who is treated without reference to the social conditions that frame his or her life. Take, for example, a TB programme that simply focuses on the act of directly observing patients take their medication, without taking into account the economic and social factors that are associated with the disease. A patient in this situation may be forced to discontinue treatment because a) she cannot travel to the clinic every other day for DOT (directly observed therapy short course), either because she lacks resources herself or because her household has refused to support her; b) she may not be able to tell her family that she has TB because a TB diagnosis may precipitate divorce or obviate her marriage chances; c) she is feeling too unwell to travel the sometimes long distances over difficult roads; and/or d) she simply cannot afford to take the time out of daily life. Such a programme is unlikely to achieve the hoped for results. Before the obstacles to a particular treatment regimen can be cleared away, patients have to understand the system, and the system must be consistent with the underlying health beliefs and social norms of the community. The programme will also need to take account of the practical realities of everyday life which play a role in the ability of people to adhere to any treatment regimen.

Is the proposal policy or programme respectful and protective of human rights?

In reviewing the human rights articles from the perspective of current TB control activities, several broad concepts need to be considered: stigma, treatment, adherence to medication, limitations of freedom, education and living conditions. Seeing TB control from a different perspective and addressing these issues with greater sensitivity will lead to better care of TB patients.

Discussion

The human rights/public health framework encourages a different perspective on the standard biomedical approach to disease control in order to develop improved ways of dealing with diseases like tuberculosis. A concentration on the individual, without an understanding of the wider socio-economic and cultural issues that frame their lives, is likely to create ineffective interventions-interventions which fail to 'provide the conditions in which people can be healthy'. TB patients can only be expected to comply with treatment if they are able to do so. Therefore, in any given setting, the key dimensions of social, economic and physical access to TB services need to be assessed and accounted for in programme design. Shifting the burden of ensuring programme effectiveness from the patient to the programmers will have the added benefit of enabling patients to obtain appropriate treatment whilst retaining their dignity and social and self-respect.

It is time to view TB control within a wider concept of health. Diseases such as tuberculosis are a reflection of underlying societal conditions of inequity and poverty. They are indicators of wider social, environmental and global conditions, and they need to be seen within the broad context of globalisation and intersectoral collaboration. The health and human rights framework enables us to view public health programmes from a perspective that takes these factors into account. If this perspective leads to changes in practice commensurate with improved human rights, then the framework will have achieved its goal.

1 Make a bullet point list of the issues that you think should be taken into account when countenancing such action.
2 Take the role of a public health official and list the arguments that you would use to make a case for isolation and mandatory treatment in the name of public health.
3 Take the role of a social reformer and human rights advocate and list the arguments that you would use to make a case against such approaches.

Feedback

1 The issues that should be taken into account include the following:

- uncertainty
- risk
- the nature of evidence
- how myths become evidential dogma

- perennial tension between individual rights and responsibilities, and public rights and responsibilities
- 'state' control and police powers
- discrimination
- justice.

2 Such an argument could be built as follows:

- Include background on the nature of disease, mode of transmission, potential for transmission, and drug resistance
- Possible justifications for mandatory treatment (see Gostin 2001) include: 1) 'Health preservation' – the threat posed by infectious diseases to the health of those who become infected (this also relates to issues about 'capacity' and mental competence, also to religious reasons to decline treatment); 2) 'Harm prevention' – this relates to the threat posed by infected persons to others (with links to important issues around risk of transmission); 3) 'Preservation of effective therapies' – to prevent development of drug resistant strains (a topical issue in light of MDRTB and drug resistant HIV. One approach to meet this aim has been to detain people until they finish treatment – though not strictly mandatory, release is conditional on treatment, and therefore coercive).
- Discuss the human and economic costs of transmitted disease. The cost to an individual with tuberculosis is increased morbidity (and possibly mortality). Also potential social costs from stigma and so on. Costs may be direct – for example the cost of management of an individual in the UK with drug sensitive tuberculosis is approximately £6000 (for multiple drug resistant tuberculosis the cost rises to £60,000). Indirect costs act through impact on work and possible financial hardship for patient and family.
- Discuss legal and ethical justification such as the European Convention on Human Rights (ECHR). ECHR and other organs of international law allow for detention *to protect public health*. But recourse to coercive measures should not be arbitrary, lawfulness should be judged in a court (which should be timely and impartial), if the reason for a measure such as detention no longer exists then the measure should be removed (for example if detention was for *infectious* tuberculosis and the detainee then becomes *non-infectious*), reviews of the purpose and nature of the measure should occur periodically, the burden to justify the measure should fall on the state not the individual to justify why it should not be applied. But with these provisos, the nature of the public health threat might be argued to be of such magnitude that isolation can be justified – ultimately this is a determination of risk! For mandatory treatment, in some countries this is justified and legal. See Norway public health law.

3 This argument could be built as follows:

- Include background and international legal organs as in question 2
- Focus on uncertainty of scientific understanding of risk, and structural inequities promoting unequal disease burden, and on the need to respond 'upstream'. For example, are there structural impediments to equal health and equal opportunity to health care? Poverty is closely correlated to tuberculosis. Should the focus of control be on ameliorating poverty (through political means) as well as more 'downstream' measures traditionally advocated by TB control programmes?

- Maybe also add something on the lack of evidence to support coercive measures (historically and currently)

Summary

This chapter was concerned with the evolution of infectious diseases and the way we have confronted them over time. You were first introduced to the historical development of our understanding of what infectious diseases are and how they can be contained. You then looked at the importance of infectious disease on the world's health. The nature of the recent changes in infectious diseases and the factors that contribute to them were then discussed. Finally, you were invited to consider the balance between the role of the state and that of individuals to reduce the threat of infectious diseases.

References

Department of Health (2002) *Getting Ahead of the Curve: A Strategy for Combating Infectious Diseases (including other aspects of health protection)*. London: Department of Health.

Farmer P (1996) Social inequalities and emerging infectious diseases. *Emerg Infect Dis* **2**: 259–69.

Gasner MR, Maw KL, Feldman GE, Fujiwara PI and Frieden TR (1999) The use of legal action in New York City to ensure treatment of tuberculosis. *N Engl J Med* **340**: 359–66.

Gostin LO (2001) *Public Health Law: duty, power, restraint* (California/Milbank Series on Health and the Public, 3). Berkeley, CA: University of California Press.

Hurtig AK, Porter JD and Ogden JA (1999) Tuberculosis control and directly observed therapy from the public health/human rights perspective. *Int J Tuberc Lung Dis* **3**: 553–60.

Institute of Medicine (1997) *America's Vital Interest in Global Health: Protecting Our People, Enhancing Our Economy, and Advancing Our International Interests*. Washington, DC: National Academy Press.

McMichael A (1995) The health of persons, populations, and planets: epidemiology comes full circle. *Epidemiology* **6**: 633–6.

Sepkowitz K (1996) How contagious is tuberculosis? *Clin Infect Dis* **23**: 954–62.

World Health Organization (2004) *World Health Report 2004*. Geneva: World Health Organization.

Further reading

Coker R (2000) The law, human rights, and detention of individuals with tuberculosis in England and Wales. *Public Health* **22**: 263–7.

Farmer P (1999) *Infections and Inequalities: The Modern Plagues*. Berkeley, CA: University of California Press. The author provides a critique of economic and health care inequalities.

Garrett L (2000) *Betrayal of Trust: The Collapse of Global Public Health*. New York: Hyperion. This book discusses the impact of globalization of infectious agents and diseases risks throughout the world.

MacLehose L, McKee M and Weinberg J (2002) Responding to the challenge of communicable disease in Europe. *Science* **295**: 2047–50.

Mann JM and Tarantola DJM (eds) (1996) *AIDS in the World II: Global Dimensions, Social Roots, and Responses*. New York, NY: Oxford University Press. This book describes the gap between the pandemic and global response to AIDS.

World Health Organization's Infectious Diseases website (available on http://www.who.int/topics/infectious_diseases/en/, last visited 2 February 2005). This website will provide you with a description of the activities, reports, news and events, as well as contacts and co-operating partners in the various WHO programmes and offices working on infectious diseases.

8 Tobacco: a public health emergency

Overview

Tobacco is unique in being the only product that kills when used as intended. Because about half of all regular cigarette smokers will eventually be killed by their habit, and because the geography of smoking continues to shift from developed to developing countries, tobacco smoking needs to be treated as a major global public health issue. In this chapter you will learn about the health impact of tobacco use and the four-stage model of the smoking epidemic. You will then examine current debates around tobacco control policies and options for these policies. Finally, the chapter discusses how globalization represents a new challenge for tobacco control.

Learning objectives

By the end of this session, you should be able to:

- **describe the health impact of tobacco use and its importance as a public health issue**
- **have a broad understanding of the options for tobacco control**
- **outline the influence that powerful multinationals have in public health policy making**

Key terms

Addiction Dependence on something that is psychologically or physically habit-forming.

Globalization A set of processes that are changing the nature of human interaction by intensifying interactions across certain boundaries that have hitherto served to separate individuals and population groups. These spatial, temporal and cognitive boundaries have been increasingly eroded, resulting in new forms of social organization and interaction across these boundaries (based on Lee 2003).

International Refers to cross-border flows that are, in principle, possible to regulate by national governments.

Tort Legal term used to describe a wrongful act, resulting in harm or loss to another person or their property, on which a civil action for damages may be brought.

Transnational (as opposed to international) Refers to transborder flows that largely circumvent national borders and can thus be beyond the control of national governments alone.

Introduction

Tobacco is causing a major public health disaster; the rising rate of tobacco consumption seen worldwide is set to harm global health on an unprecedented scale. By 2020, tobacco is expected to kill more people than any other single factor, surpassing even the HIV epidemic.

The study of tobacco and the control of its use are therefore warranted simply by virtue of tobacco's huge impact on public health. But tobacco also serves to illustrate many of the issues discussed in previous chapters in this book: it is a major cause of health inequalities and there have been ethical debates around the methods that can be appropriately used to control its use. In addition, tobacco illustrates some of the complex issues facing public health practitioners in the twenty-first century – it highlights the key challenges that globalization poses for public health, the complex relationship between trade and health, the potential conflicts of interest that tobacco control poses for governments and the difficulties of enacting effective public health policies that are opposed by powerful transnational companies.

The history of tobacco use stretches back to the first century AD amongst the Mayan people of Central America. From there, tobacco use spread through America and to the Caribbean islands where leaves were presented to the invading Spaniards at the end of the fifteenth century. A few years later, tobacco was brought back to Spain and Portugal and from there its use gradually spread throughout Europe. Tobacco has subsequently been chewed and smoked in various forms. However, it was not until the late nineteenth century when the introduction of the Bonsack machine led to the mass manufacture of cigarettes that its use really escalated. Since then, cigarette smoking has spread worldwide on a massive scale.

Health effects of smoking

The health impacts of tobacco use are daunting. It has been recognized as the single largest avoidable cause of premature death and the most important known carcinogen to humans. Half of all long-term smokers will eventually be killed by tobacco and of these, half will die during middle age, losing 20–25 years of life. Smoking is also associated with health inequalities by virtue of the social patterning of smoking. For example, international comparisons indicate that overall smoking prevalence is now more common in low- and middle-income countries than in high-income countries (Figure 8.1). In high-income countries smoking is now much less common among the better off, although social-class patterns are less clear in middle-income and low-income countries (Bobak and colleagues 2000).

The direct health effects of tobacco consumption can be considered under two headings, nicotine addiction and health problems.

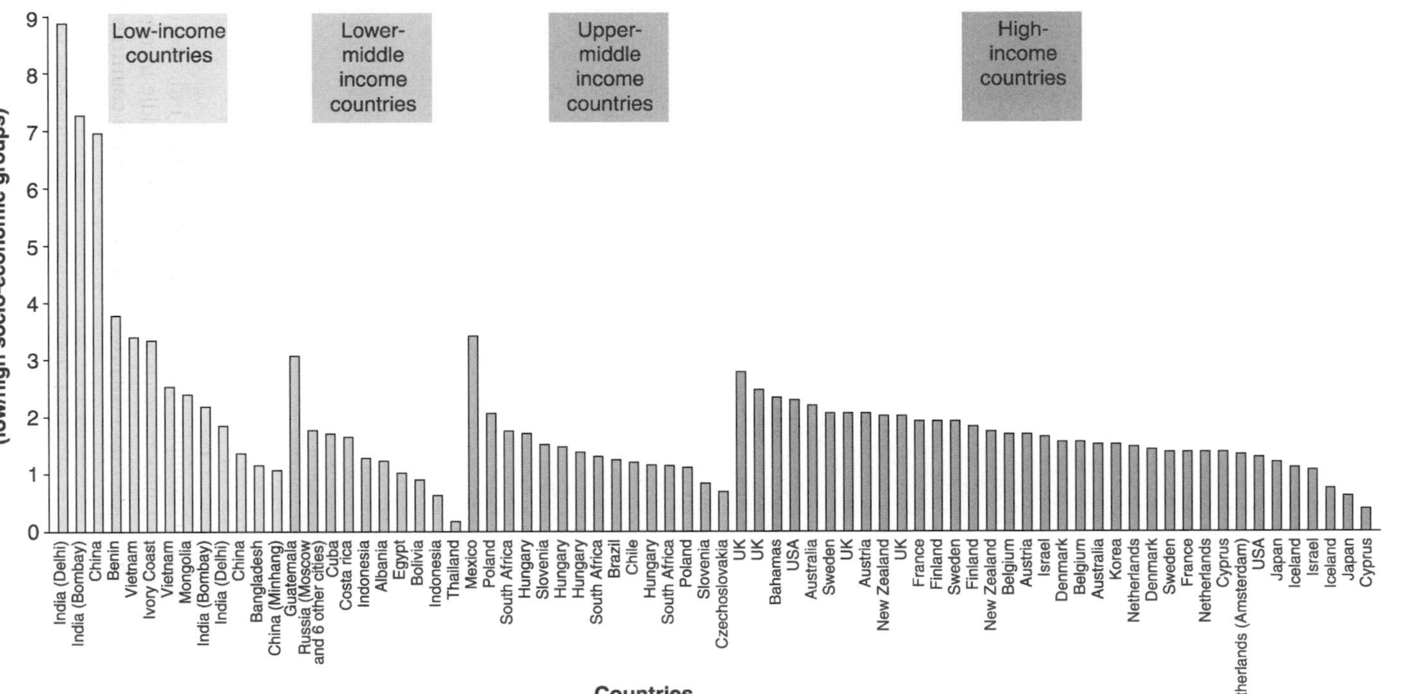

Figure 8.1 Smoking prevalence in the highest and lowest income groups expressed as a ratio

Source: Bobak and collaborators (2000)

Nicotine addiction

Experts conclude that nicotine is as addictive as hard drugs such as heroin and that smoking meets the criteria of substance dependence in both the fourth edition of the Diagnostic and Statistical Manual of Mental Disorders (DSM-IV) and the tenth revision of the International Statistical Classification of Diseases and Related Health Problems (ICD-10). Repeated exposure rapidly leads to physiological and psychological addiction, reinforced by marked withdrawal symptoms. These include irritability, anxiety, restlessness and poor concentration. It is likely therefore that the benefits smokers attribute to nicotine use such as stress relief, improved mood and enhanced cognitive performance are really just the relief of nicotine withdrawal symptoms. Yet the status of nicotine as a seemingly innocuous legal drug and attempts by the tobacco industry to equate addiction to nicotine with addiction to substances such as coffee or chocolate has diverted attention from the highly addictive nature of nicotine in cigarettes.

Health problems

The negative impact of tobacco on health was first reported over 200 years ago in relation to carcinoma of the lip but it was not until the 1950s with the publication of a number of case control studies that the relationship between smoking and lung cancer began to gain credence. Subsequent cohort studies including the pioneering work of Doll and Hill confirmed the enormous health impacts of tobacco and showed that overall mortality is twice as high in smokers as non-smokers and three times as high in middle age.

Activity 8.1 Diseases associated with smoking

Smoking has now been positively associated with over 40 diseases. Try to list as many of these diseases as possible. You can browse through the internet to help you.

Feedback

Smoking has been positively associated with over 40 diseases and negatively associated with eight or nine more. For most diseases the evidence is strong and the associations between smoking and mortality are causal in character. Findings have been confirmed in numerous studies in different populations, biological mechanisms are understood, the association is strong and a dose response relationship is seen. The diseases fall into three main categories, cancer, vascular diseases and chronic lung diseases, as described in Table 8.1, which is taken from the 2004 United States (US) Surgeon General's report on the health effects of smoking.

Table 8.1 Main diseases known to be associated with smoking

Main diseases	
Cancers	Bladder, cervix*, oesophagus, kidney*, larynx, acute myeloid leukaemia*, lung, oral cancer, pancreas*, stomach
Cardiovascular diseases	Abdominal aortic aneurysm*, atherosclerosis, cerebrovascular disease, coronary heart disease
Respiratory diseases	Chronic obstructive pulmonary disease, pneumonia*, respiratory effects in utero, respiratory effects on children and adolescents
Reproductive effects	Fetal deaths and stillbirths, infertility (in women), low birth weight, pregnancy complications
Other effects	Cataract*, diminished health status*, hip fractures, low bone density, periodontitis*, peptic ulcer disease

* Added as being 'causally associated with smoking' in 2004

Source: Adapted from United States Department of Health and Human Services (2004)

Health impacts of involuntary exposure

Tobacco is also a major cause of morbidity and mortality in those involuntarily exposed to second hand smoke or environmental tobacco smoking. Since the 1980s a growing series of high profile reports have drawn attention to its health impact. These include the US National Research Council and the US Surgeon General reports in 1986, the National Health and Medical Research Council of Australia report in 1987 and the United Kingdom (UK) Independent Scientific Committee on Smoking and Health report in 1988. These reports concluded that environmental tobacco smoking can cause lung cancer in adult non-smokers and that children of parents who smoke have increased frequency of respiratory symptoms and lower respiratory tract infections. In 1992, the US Environmental Protection Agency published a review that classified environmental tobacco smoking as a Class A (known human) carcinogen. This is a status afforded to only 15 other carcinogens (including asbestos, benzene and radon) and indicates that there is sufficient evidence that environmental tobacco smoking causes cancer in humans. Moreover, only environmental tobacco smoking has actually been shown to cause cancer at *typical* environmental levels. More recently, the World Health Organization (WHO) and the UK Scientific Committee on Tobacco, amongst others, have published further major reviews. Jointly, these reports indicate that environmental tobacco smoking:

- contains over 4000 toxic chemicals
- is the largest source of particulate indoor air pollution
- has major health impacts that include: 1) in infancy: low birth weight and cot death; 2) in childhood: middle ear infection, bronchitis, pneumonia, induction and exacerbation of asthma; 3) in adulthood: heart disease, stroke, lung cancer, cervical cancer, nasal cancer, increased bronchial responsiveness, miscarriage.

These impacts stand in addition to the irritant effect of environmental tobacco smoking on the eyes and airways and the major damage caused by fires from smoking.

Evidence of the health impacts of environmental tobacco smoking continues to grow. For example a recent study found that just 30 minutes of exposure to environmental tobacco smoking at levels similar to that experienced in venues such as bars compromised the coronary circulation of non-smokers (Otsuka and Watanabe 2001). The most recent work, using improved measures of exposure (measuring cotinine, a nicotine metabolite) has shown that the dangers of passive smoking are substantially greater than was previously thought (Whincup and colleagues 2004).

Despite this overwhelming evidence, European countries have been slower than Australia and the US to implement measures to prevent exposure to environmental tobacco smoking. This lack of action can be attributed to a variety of factors. However, it is clear that the tobacco industry's attempts to distort the scientific debate about the interpretation of second hand smoke studies, thereby delaying pressure for action in this area, has played a role. As early as 1978, the industry identified the health effects of passive smoking as 'the most dangerous development yet to the viability of the tobacco industry'. In the mid-1990s, in an attempt to create unwarranted controversy around the research on passive smoking, the industry arranged a series of advertisements in newspapers across Europe. These compared the risk of lung cancer from passive smoking with a variety of other apparent risks from everyday activities such as eating biscuits or drinking. Reports published in the medical literature also challenged the evidence but it later became apparent that many of these were funded by the tobacco industry. Internal industry documents have revealed that, while publicly denying the evidence – criticizing the methodology of published research and funding its own research to refute the existing evidence – the industry was privately more circumspect, admitting that 'we are constrained because we can't say its safe'. Another attempt by the industry to fuel controversy over environmental tobacco smoking was its effort to undermine the largest European study (by the International Agency for Research on Cancer (IARC)) on the risk of lung cancer in passive smokers (a programme that cost more than twice that spent by IARC on the original study).

The tobacco epidemic

Despite the huge body of evidence on the health impacts of smoking, few realize how hazardous tobacco really is. The industry has sought to subvert the evidence on the health impacts of passive smoking and to undermine public understanding of the health impacts of active smoking. It has denied the negative health impacts, promoted light cigarettes as 'healthier', dissuaded lay journals (via its huge advertising spend) from reporting on health risks, and sponsored biased scientific research. However, the lack of understanding may also arise from the delayed health impact of tobacco, illustrated best in the model of the tobacco epidemic shown in Figure 8.2. This figure shows the smoking epidemic using a four-stage continuum. This model is based on observations of trends in cigarette consumption and tobacco-related diseases in developed countries with the longest history of cigarette use.

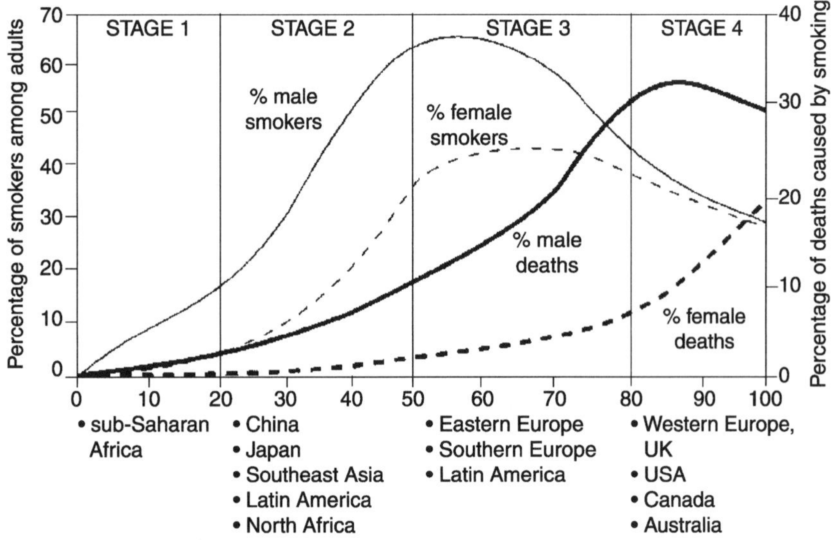

Figure 8.2 Four stages of the tobacco epidemic

Source: Lopez *et al.* (1994)

Activity 8.2 Stages of the smoking epidemic

Examine Figure 8.2 and describe what happens to smoking prevalence and mortality in males and females during each stage of the smoking epidemic.

Feedback

In Stage 1, there is a low prevalence (<20 per cent) of cigarette smoking in the population. Smoking is principally limited to males. There is yet no apparent increase in lung cancer or other chronic diseases caused by smoking. This stage applies to some countries in sub-Saharan Africa that have not yet been drawn fully into the global tobacco epidemic, but that are vulnerable to the growth and changing strategic initiatives of transnational tobacco companies.

In Stage 2, the prevalence of smoking increases to above 50 per cent in men and there is an early increase in women (there is a one to two decade delay between the increase in male and female smoking). There is also a shift towards smoking initiation at younger ages (not shown). The burden of lung cancer and other tobacco-attributable disease is increasing in men. Many countries in Asia (China, Japan, South East Asia), North Africa and Latin America are at this stage of the smoking epidemic. Note that tobacco control activities are generally not well developed during this stage and that health risks of tobacco are not well understood. There is usually relatively low public and political support for the implementation of effective policies to control tobacco use.

In Stage 3, there is a marked downturn in smoking prevalence among men, a more gradual decline in women, and convergence of male and female smoking prevalence. In spite of this, the burden of smoking-attributable disease and death continues to increase. Between 10 and 30 per cent of all deaths are attributable to smoking, and about three quarters of these deaths are found in men. Thus the rise in mortality from tobacco mirrors the rise in smoking prevalence but occurs some three or four decades later. This stage applies to many countries in Eastern and Southern Europe and Latin America. Note that health education about the health problems caused by smoking begins to decrease public acceptance of smoking at this stage of the epidemic, especially among more educated population subgroups. Indeed, there is a shift in the social pattern of smoking as the epidemic advances: smoking is initially more common amongst the upper classes, but as the better educated quit, this pattern reverses accounting for the inequalities in health caused by tobacco.

The last stage of the epidemic is characterized by a marked downturn in smoking prevalence in both men and women. Deaths attributed to smoking among men peak at 30–35 per cent of all deaths (40–45 per cent in middle-aged men (not shown)) and subsequently decrease. In women, smoking-attributable deaths increase to about 20–25 per cent of all deaths. Many industrialized countries in Northern and Western Europe, North America (US, Canada) and the Western Pacific region (Australia) are generally in or approaching this stage. However, there is considerable variation in the progress against tobacco even in these countries and in the ability of the countries to sustain national commitment to reduce tobacco use.

Please note that not all countries in the world follow this four stage model in every detail. In China, for example, the prevalence of smoking among women has remained below 5 per cent despite a high prevalence of smoking among men for several decades. However, the general model does highlight the deadly course of the epidemic in most countries.

The global epidemic

The previous section described the development of the tobacco epidemic within individual countries. Worldwide there have also been shifts in the burden of disease from tobacco. As consumption declines in industrialized countries, the transnational tobacco companies have sought to maintain and expand their profits by seeking favourable markets elsewhere. They entered Latin America in the 1960s, Asia in the 1980s and more recently Africa and the former communist countries of eastern Europe.

As a result of this expansion to formerly closed or new markets, the decline in tobacco consumption in high-income countries has been more than balanced by an increase in low- and middle-income countries (Figure 8.3). This has in turn led both to a global increase in tobacco related diseases and to a shift in the burden of disease from high- to low-income countries. At the beginning of the twenty-first century, tobacco kills one in 10 adults worldwide and accounts for 4.9 million deaths per year. By 2030 or sooner, these figures are predicted to rise to one in six and 10 million deaths per year. Moreover, whilst this epidemic, until recently,

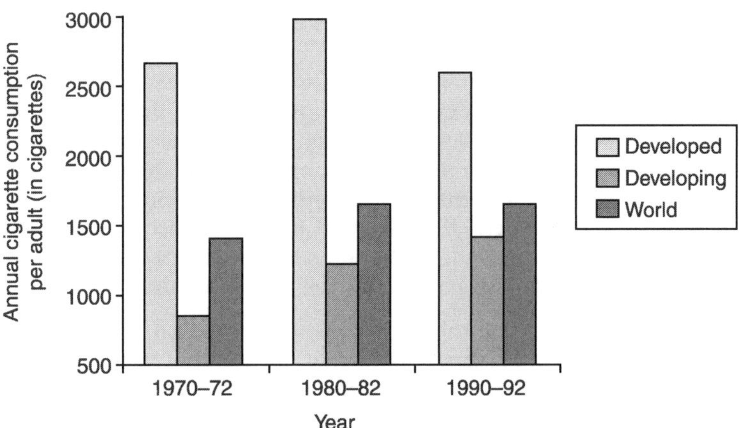

Figure 8.3 Smoking is increasing in the developing world – trends in per capita adult cigarette consumption

Source: World Health Organization (1997)

mainly affected the developed world, by 2030, some 70 per cent of these deaths will be in low- and middle-income countries.

Tobacco control

Given the evidence presented above, it is clear that major action is needed to reduce the appalling impact of tobacco. Tobacco control policies aim to reduce morbidity and mortality from smoking and to reduce inequalities by encouraging quitting, preventing uptake of smoking, reducing exposure to environmental tobacco smoking and reducing consumption amongst continuing smokers. Due to the delayed health impacts of smoking, policies that simply stop young people taking up the habit will not reap benefits for a few decades. To have an impact in the next few decades, policies need to get adult smokers to quit.

There is good evidence of the health benefits of quitting with the chance of survival depending on the age at quitting. Those who stop before 35 years of age have a pattern of survival that does not differ significantly from that of non-smokers. For those who stop later, survival is intermediate between that of non-smokers and continuing smokers but there are still clear benefits. For example, those who stop smoking at age 30 avoid more than 90 per cent of their lung cancer risk, and even stopping at 50 or 60 years avoids most of the subsequent risk. Smoking cessation has a substantial impact on life expectancy. The 50 year follow-up of the landmark British Doctors Study found that stopping at age 60, 50, 40, or 30 led to a gain of about 3, 6, 9, or 10 years of life expectancy respectively (Doll and collaborators 2004). Tailored help, in primary care and health care services, to smokers wanting to quit could thus have major health impacts.

Addiction and the ethics of public health interventions

Tobacco control policies have caused some controversy. This was the case particularly amongst civil libertarians who argue that smoking is a matter for individual choice, not state intervention and that measures that go beyond informing individuals of the risks of smoking are paternalistic. It has similarly been argued that tobacco advertising bans constitute an infringement of commercial speech rights. Interestingly, the release of internal tobacco industry documents as a result of litigation in the US has revealed the extent to which these arguments have been hijacked and exploited by the tobacco industry.

Tobacco control experts oppose this position. They argue that addiction to nicotine means that most smokers do not continue the habit through choice but because they are addicted. Nicotine addiction makes it difficult for smokers to quit. Most smokers start as teenagers and become addicted to nicotine at a young age (when they are more vulnerable to industry advertising and marketing tactics). Later, when they want to quit, only a tiny proportion succeed. In the UK for example, 70 per cent of smokers say they would like to quit, about half tried to quit during the previous five years, yet only about 2 per cent succeed. For these reasons, the population (and some would argue, particularly the young) should be given greater protection via more 'paternalistic' measures.

The growing interest of economists in tobacco control has also served to illustrate the economic arguments for state intervention in the tobacco market. Economic theory assumes that consumer knows best and that privately-determined consumption will most efficiently allocate society's scarce resources. This means that *if* smokers know their risks and internalize all their costs and benefits, there is no justification (in economic terms) for governments to interfere. However, these conditions do not hold for three main reasons:

- inadequate information about the health impacts of tobacco smoking: consumers do not know well the health risks;
- inadequate information about addiction: there is good evidence that the young underestimate the risk of becoming addicted and therefore grossly under estimate the future costs of smoking. In high-income countries about seven in ten adult smokers say they regret their choice to start smoking and two-thirds make serious attempts to quit;
- the external costs of smoking: these include physical externalities (risk of disease and death in non-smokers, nuisance of smell, physical irritation, risk of fire and property damage) and financial externalities which are seen in countries where non-smokers effectively subsidize smokers. This happens for example where there is a taxation based system of health funding and where few have pensions.

For these reasons, economists would argue that state intervention in the tobacco market is justified.

Policy options

Tobacco control policies are generally divided into those impacting on the supply of or demand for tobacco.

Activity 8.3 Examples and effectiveness of tobacco control policies

1 Give examples of control policies that can impact on the supply of tobacco, or on demand for tobacco.

2 Which policies do you think might be more effective at reducing smoking rates in a population? Explain why.

Feedback

1 Examples of policies that can impact on the supply of tobacco include:

- control of tobacco smuggling
- crop substitution
- tobacco subsidies
- youth access restrictions.

Examples of policies that can influence demand include:

- taxation
- workplace and public space smoking bans
- advertising and promotion bans
- counter-marketing campaigns
- information: health education and health promotion programmes (for example, population based media campaigns, school based health promotion campaigns), public reports, research and publication, labelling of tobacco products, bans on misleading descriptors such as 'light' and 'mild'
- smoking cessation services and access to nicotine replacement therapy.

2 There is not one perfect tobacco control policy and in order to have an effect on smoking rates, a comprehensive and sustainable package of measures is needed. However, it is generally agreed that most supply side measures other than the control of smuggling are generally ineffective. There is evidence that restrictions on youth access, if enforced, are effective in reducing teenage smoking rates. However, they are expensive to enforce and other evidence suggests that they may simply delay rather than prevent recruitment into smoking. Indeed, they may even be counter-productive. Some tobacco control experts even argue that such measures, through highlighting that smoking is for adults, may increase the attraction of smoking for adolescents who aspire to be seen as adults and money spent on enforcement is better spent elsewhere. For these reasons, the focus of tobacco control policies is generally on demand side measures. Taxation, and bans on public smoking and on advertising and sponsorship are probably the most effective measures. A 10 per cent price increase reduces demand by approximately 4 per cent in high-income countries and 8 per cent in low or middle-income countries whilst raising revenues by approximately 7 per cent in the short to medium term. Young people and the poor are the most price responsive. Thus, whilst tobacco taxation is regressive (has a greater impact on the poor) tax increases are not, and the overall effect may even be progressive because of the expenditure by the poor is deterred to a greater extent than among the rich.

Evidence from a recent meta-analysis of workplace bans suggests that total bans reduce the prevalence of smoking by approximately 3.8 per cent and reduce consumption amongst continuing smokers by 3.1 cigarettes per day, leading to an overall reduction in consumption of 29 per cent per employee (Fichtenberg and Glantz 2002). At population level, the impact of workplace bans will clearly depend on the number of workplaces that are already smoke free but it seems that such policies are at least as effective as a 10 per cent increase in price. Importantly, total workplace bans are twice as effective as bans that allow smoking in designated areas.

It should be noted however, that enacting smoking bans without public support is fraught with difficulties. Witness the 1976 Loi Veil in France which introduced restrictions on smoking in public places. As anyone who has sat in a Parisian café will know, this law is widely ignored and never enforced largely due to the lack of public support.

Advertising bans are effective in reducing consumption as long as they are comprehensive. Partial bans simply allow a shift of advertising to other media.

The provision of information has been a vital component in tobacco control not least because it influences public opinion and hence the contexts in which policy decisions are made. This is illustrated by the gradual shifts in public understanding of the issues around tobacco: first the recognition that cigarettes were harmful to smokers, then that they were harmful to non-smokers and more recently, through the information released via litigation, that tobacco is an issue of corporate misconduct and fraud.

Many governments have been afraid to discourage smoking, because they fear that the economy might suffer. For example, some policymakers fear that reduced sales of cigarettes would mean the permanent loss of thousands of jobs; that higher tobacco taxes would result in lower government revenues; and that higher prices would encourage massive levels of cigarette smuggling. A wealth of evidence shows that the economic fears that have deterred policymakers from taking action are unfounded. Policies that reduce the demand for tobacco, such as a decision to increase tobacco taxes, would not cause long-term job losses as the savings made by those giving up smoking will be spent on other things. Nor would higher tobacco taxes reduce tax revenues; rather, revenues would climb in the short to medium term as the increase in tax income outweighs the loss from reduced consumption. Such policies could, in sum, bring unprecedented health benefits without harming economies.

Litigation

In the United States litigation against tobacco companies has also become a prominent aspect of tobacco control, albeit a somewhat unpredictable one. Litigation commenced in the mid-1950s but was until recently totally unsuccessful. Fortunes changed in the 1990s for two reasons. First, internal industry documents, initially provided by whistleblowers, started to reveal the extent of corporate misbehaviour and turned public opinion against the industry. Second, litigators started to pursue new paths of action – class action tort suits, state health care reimbursement cases and environmental tobacco smoking cases. The 1990s has seen a mix of successes and defeats. The most positive impacts on tobacco control have probably been indirect, that is, through the release of more highly damaging internal tobacco industry documents.

Tobacco control and globalization

The need for a regional and global response

Tobacco control can be performed at different levels: locally, nationally, regionally and globally. All levels are important. However, as a result of the processes of globalization, it has become clear that even the most comprehensive national control programmes can be undermined without collective regional and global responses (the lessons learned from tobacco control can also be applied to other major public health issues such as obesity and food (see Chapter 9)).

Globalization poses a number of challenges for tobacco control, for example it:

- enhances tobacco industry access to markets worldwide through trade liberalization and specific provisions of multilateral trade agreements;
- increases marketing, advertising and sponsorship opportunities via global communication systems;
- leads to greater economies of scale which arise from the purchase of local cigarette manufacturers, improved access to ever larger markets, and the development and production of global brands;
- enables transnational corporations to undermine the regulatory authority of national governments; and
- facilitates the legal and illegal transfer of tobacco products worldwide and the transfer of tobacco industry policies and strategies from country to country.

As Yach says:

> The tobacco industry acts as a global force. As countries from the former Soviet Union, or in Asia and Africa start to embrace democracy it is often the tobacco companies who are there first selling their products as symbols of new freedoms. Globalization brings with it some very real threats to tobacco control. Tobacco is an issue at the center of contradictions inherent in the evolving process of globalization. It is where the goals of a particular set of multinationals are in conflict with public health and views of most governments.
>
> Source: Yach D (1999)

Thus, not only do weak control policies in some parts of the world affect the capacity to control tobacco consumption elsewhere, highly lucrative operations in new markets enable the industry to remain a thriving concern worldwide despite declining profits elsewhere. As a profitable global industry, tobacco companies can sustain a strong presence and influence in all countries.

The WHO recognized the need for global tobacco control measures and in July 1998 created the Tobacco Free Initiative to focus international attention, resources and action on the tobacco pandemic. The WHO Framework Convention on Tobacco Control, an international tobacco control treaty, forms the cornerstone of Tobacco Free Initiative policy. This world's first public health treaty was adopted unanimously by WHO's 192 member states during the 56th World Health Assembly which took place in May 2003.

Activity 8.4 WHO Framework Convention on Tobacco Control

Go to the WHO Tobacco Free Initiative (http://www.who.int/tobacco/en/, World Health Organization 2005) website and from there select 'WHO FCTC' (left hand side). Browse through this website to learn about the Framework Convention on Tobacco Control. Then answer the following questions:

1 What are the aims of the treaty?

2 How many signatures did the treaty get?

3 How many ratifications were needed to ensure the treaty comes into force?

Feedback

1 The general goal of the Convention is to reduce tobacco-related deaths and disease around the world. In order to achieve this goal, it requires countries to impose restrictions on tobacco advertising, sponsorship and promotion; establish new packaging and labelling using large, clear, visible, legible, and rotating health warnings and messages on tobacco products and its outside packaging; establish clean indoor air controls by the reduction of second-hand smoke in indoor workplaces, public transport, indoor public places and, as appropriate, other public places; and strengthen legislation to clamp down on tobacco smuggling.

2 The Convention was signed by 168 members of the WHO, members of the United Nations, or regional economic integration organizations (for example, the European Union (EU)).

3 The treaty required a minimum of 40 ratifications before it came into force (this number was reached in 2004).

Trade and health

The tobacco industry's penetration of new markets has been facilitated by multilateral trade agreements, which have liberalized trade in many goods including cigarettes. The removal of trade barriers leads to greater competition, lower prices, more advertising and promotion. In turn this leads to increased demand, sales and consumption of tobacco.

In the 1980s, for example, the US government co-operated with the US Cigarette Export Association (USCEA) to threaten trade sanctions against countries in Asia. In these countries, import quotas, high taxes or other restrictions were alleged (by USCEA) to unfairly limit the market to US tobacco products. In the face of US threats, Japan, Taiwan, South Korea and Thailand removed restrictions on tobacco imports. This led to a growth in cigarette trading in these markets, a 75 per cent increase in US cigarette exports to Asia and a rapid rise in smoking rates. The World Bank has estimated that in these four Asian economies, consumption of cigarettes per person was almost 10 per cent higher in 1991 than it would have been if these markets had remained closed. Evidence suggests that the removal of trade barriers has little impact on smoking in high-income countries and greatest impact in low-income countries.

The tobacco industry

In many areas of public health, policies can be enacted without any major opposition. In contrast, tobacco control faces a huge, powerful and politically well organized opposition in the form of the tobacco industry.

A useful comparison has been drawn between the EU response to tobacco and another recent health threat, bovine spongiform encephalopathy. The fear of mad cow disease led to several years of frenzied activity within the EU, producing a range of initiatives designed to minimize risk and protect the health of the public despite the fact that bovine spongiform encephalopathy has caused less than 100 deaths in total. This compares to a yearly total of 500,000 deaths from tobacco. Yet, tobacco has not led to the same degree of activity. Whilst public perceptions of risk from these two health threats (in part based on intrinsic understanding, but perhaps also influenced by industry attempts to confuse risk perception) are quite different, it has been suggested that lack of action on tobacco has resulted mainly for political reasons and, in particular, a failure to tackle the vested interests of farmers, producers, advertisers, distributors, retailers and governments.

In his book the Smoke Ring, Peter Taylor usefully compares the political action taken against cholera in the end of the nineteenth century with the twentieth century scourge of tobacco, reaching similar conclusions:

> The spread of lung cancer in the twentieth century and the subsequent identification of its major cause, is very similar to the history of cholera. But when cigarettes were shown to be the agent responsible, . . . no parallel political action was taken because of the commercial and political interests which cigarettes involved.
>
> Source: Taylor P (1984)

In 2000, the Institute of Policy Studies released a report on corporate power that examined the world's top 200 corporations. It concluded that these corporations are enjoying increasing levels of economic and political clout that are out of balance with the tangible benefits they provide to society. They found that of the largest 100 economies in the world, 51 are corporations and 49 countries. Philip Morris (the largest transnational tobacco company) was identified as the world's 28th largest company, more powerful economically than the governments of Pakistan, Peru, Czech Republic and New Zealand (incidentally, General Motors, Exxon Mobil, Ford Motor, and Daimler Chrysler were all in the top 5, highlighting the difficulty of enacting effective environmental policies).

It will come as no surprise therefore to know that the tobacco industry lobbies extensively and effectively against tobacco control measures. The true nature of industry lobbying did not however become clearly apparent until the recent release of internal industry documents through litigation in the United States. These documents provide fascinating insights into industry behaviour and activities. As indicated above, they have shown how the industry has denied the health impacts of active and passive smoking, sown confusion over the addictive effects of nicotine and promoted civil libertarian debates.

Despite these complexities and the degree of powerful opposition to tobacco control, success is possible! A number of countries have now implemented effective and comprehensive tobacco control policies and seen a decline in tobacco consumption and enormous health benefits as a result. A variety of strategies including legislation, litigation and multi-institutional approaches to tobacco control are needed and great care must be taken to ensure that industry efforts to undermine tobacco control are recognized and counter-acted.

Activity 8.5

Think of the country in which you live. Who are the key stakeholders in relation to tobacco control? How well do you think they understand the issue, and what might be their greatest misunderstandings. Justify your answer.

Feedback

The answer will obviously depend on the country in question but likely candidates include:

- Ministry of Health – likely to support tobacco control. However in some countries they will focus on activities of limited effectiveness, such as youth anti-smoking campaigns (with those funded by the tobacco industry actually increasing the probability of smoking) while failing to take the most effective measures.
- Ministry of Finance – may be concerned about what it wrongly believes to be adverse economic consequences.
- Ministry of Agriculture – especially if tobacco is grown in the country. This ministry is often a key target for the tobacco industry, which can exert a strong influence on it.
- Ministry of Education – often disengaged, even though it can do much to foster an anti-smoking climate.
- Entertainment and hospitality industry (hotels, bars, and so on) – often opposed to a ban on smoking in public places, arguing, wrongly, that it would affect sales. Many industry associations are actually fronts for the tobacco industry. Trade unions representing staff in these countries, once aware of the negative health impacts of second hand smoke are often supportive of bans on smoking in public places.
- Mass media and advertising industry – often opposed to tobacco control, arguing that a ban on advertising would reduce revenue. Many advertising trade associations are fronts for tobacco industry.
- Associations of health professionals (such as medical or nursing associations) – these are often not engaged, focusing their efforts on issues such as pay and working conditions. However where they do take an interest, they can be very powerful.
- Other civil society groups including powerful non-governmental organizations such as, in the UK, the Action on Smoking and Health (ASH UK).

Summary

In this chapter you learnt about smoking as a main public health issue. You read about the major negative health effects of smoking and of involuntary exposure, and examined how the current lack of understanding of these effects can be related to the delayed impact of tobacco, as can be illustrated with the four-stage model of the smoking epidemic. You then looked into the different policy options available to impact on the supply and demand for tobacco, and were invited to consider how globalization (and the influence of multinational companies on public health policy making) represents a challenge for tobacco control.

References

Bobak M, Jha P, Nguyen S, Jarvis M (2000) Poverty and Smoking. In: *Tobacco control in developing countries*. Jha P, Chaloupka FJ (eds). Oxford University Press, pp 41–61.

Doll R, Peto R, Boreham J, Sutherland I (2004) Mortality in relation to smoking: 50 years' observations on male British doctors. *Br Med J* doi: 10.1136/bmj.38142.554479.AE (published 22 June 2004).

Fichtenberg CM, Glantz SA (2002) Effect of smoke-free workplaces on smoking behaviour: systematic review. *Br Med J* **325**, 188–94.

Lee K (2003) *Globalization and health. An introduction*. London: Palgrave Macmillan.

Lopez AD, Collishaw NE, Piha T (1994) A descriptive model of the cigarette epidemic in developed countries. *Tob Control* **3**, 242–7.

Otsuka R, Watanabe H, Hirata K, Tokai K, Muro T, Yoshiyama M, Takeuchi K, Yoshikawa J (2001) Acute effects of passive smoking on the coronary circulation in healthy young adults. *JAMA* **286**, 436–41.

Taylor P (1984) *The smoke ring: tobacco- money- & multinational politics*. New York: Pantheon Books.

United States Department of Health and Human Services (2004) *The health consequences of smoking: A report of the Surgeon General's*. Atlanta: Centre for Disease Control.

Whincup PH, Gilg JA, Emberson JR, Jarvis MJ, Feyerabend C, Bryant A, Walker M, Cook DG (2004). Passive smoking and risk of coronary heart disease and stroke: prospective study with cotinine measurement. *Br Med J* **329**, 200–5.

World Health Organization (1997) *Tobacco and health: a global status report*. Geneva: World Health Organization.

World Health Organization (2005) *Tobacco free initiative (website)*. Geneva: World Health Organization (available on http://www.who.int/tobacco/en/, last visited 2 February 2005).

Yach D (1999) *Nowhere to run, nowhere to hide – world community joins WHO in holding up mirrors to big tobacco. California Tobacco Control Project Director's Meeting Lake Tahoe, California, 1 November 1999*. Geneva: World Health Organization.

Further reading

Gilmore A, Collin J (2002) The World's first international tobacco control treaty: leading nations may thwart this major event. *Br Med J* **325**, 846–7. This provides some background on the political complexities involved in negotiating the WHO Framework Convention on Tobacco Control.

Gilmore A, McKee M (2002) Tobacco control policy: the European dimension. *Clinical Med* **2**, 335–42.

The Action on Smoking and Health (ASH UK) website http://www.ash.org.uk/ (last visited 2 February 2005) This website provides excellent information on tobacco and tobacco control policies and tobacco industry documents. Under the section entitled 'Tobacco industry', you can select 'Documents'. This will take you to a series of reports based on tobacco industry documents. See for example 'ASH's Tobacco Explained', and 'Trust us, We're the tobacco industry'.

9 Food, trade and health

Overview

This chapter will introduce you to the historical development of thinking on nutrition and health. During the past decades, there has been a shift from an emphasis on macro-nutrients and quantity of food to micro-nutrients and non-nutrient components of food – such as contaminants and adulterants. The growing realization of food's complexity has been added to by an appreciation of the human and ecological health consequences of food production. The new health thinking includes concepts such as food miles, environmental degradation, fair trade and sustainable development. This chapter puts such notions into the context of the mechanisms and burdens of disease that are linked to nutrition. It argues that four foci emerge in modern thinking: food safety, nutrition, sustainable development and food security. Finally, the chapter discusses what room for manoeuvre there is within public policy and its levers. It raises the question that, given the evidence base for public health interventions, why is progress so patchy and slow?

Learning objectives

By the end of this chapter you should be able to:

- **describe some key features in the evolution of thinking about the importance of diet on health**
- **assess various social forces affecting changes in dietary behaviour**
- **map the key strengths and weakness of arguments about the impact of social change on nutrition and health**
- **understand that food illustrates the links between human and environmental health**
- **suggest some policy pointers for the future**

Key terms

Food miles Distance that foods travel from where they are grown to where they are ultimately purchased or consumed by the end user.

Food security Physical and economic access for everyone and at all times to enough foods that are nutritious, safe, personally acceptable and culturally appropriate, produced and distributed in ways that are environmentally sound and just.

Nutrition transition Process of change in which populations shift their diet from a restricted diet to one higher in saturated fat, sugar and refined foods, and low in fibre; as a result, diet-related ill health previously associated with affluent Western societies takes root in developing countries.

The debates about diet and health

From the 1950s, evidence mounted from epidemiological studies that dietary composition was a key factor in patterns of disease. As a result, in the last quarter of the twentieth century, food became the subject of heated policy debate in many countries. Arguments raged about what and how much particular factors matter. Was it fats? Which fats? What ratio of fats? Was it micro-nutrients? Was it the overall dietary balance? And latterly, was physical activity a confounding effect or an additional effect? Does genetic inheritance play a role in pre-disposing humans to disease from mal-consumption? Can diet counteract the cards that genetic fate plays us?

Work by a number of diet and disease pioneers suggested that a pattern of eating – characterized by high fat consumption and polyunsaturated / saturated ratios, with high added sugars, low fibre and high salt, low in fruit and vegetables – was coinciding with a rise in the degenerative diseases. The importance of fat was noted by Prof Ancel Keys in the Seven Nations study, where Keys and co-workers showed how Finland and the UK had high coronary heart disease (CHD) rates while Japan and Greece (Crete) had low levels.

The emerging consensus from such studies have been summarized in numerous reports. The 1990 document of the World Health Organization (WHO) entitled *Diet, Nutrition, and the Prevention of Chronic Diseases*, is a good assessment of the consensus towards the turn of the century; an updated version was published in 2003. In 2000, the Sub-Committee on Nutrition of the United Nations (UN) produced another major statement with the *4th Report on the World Nutrition Situation: Nutrition throughout the life cycle*. These reports proposed that trends in global diet – first noted in affluent societies but now emerging in developing societies – are followed by the emergence of clear patterns of chronic disease, particularly: cardiovascular disease (coronary heart disease, high blood pressure, cerebrovascular disease); some cancers (stomach, colorectal, breast, prostate, and so on); diabetes; obesity. They proposed that the world was experiencing these effects as the result of a nutrition transition, a shift from a restricted diet to one with more choices.

While this evidence grew, the application of earlier insights from food science and technology was showing how food controls could reduce the risk of the spread of contaminants, toxins and microbiological threats to human, plant and animal safety. By the 1970s, food technologists felt that they had developed answers to the old policy fears of waste (spoilage), hunger and mal-distribution. Yet within two decades this apparent policy promise had become unravelled. Although progress in raising agricultural output was considerable, the absolute numbers of people experiencing famine remained stubbornly high. Food poverty and the lack of access to an adequate quantity of food had dominated international food and agricultural policy since the 1950s.

By the turn of the new millennium, although global public policy (for example from WHO and the Food and Agriculture Organization (FAO)) was still largely framed by concern about hunger and population growth, the new evidence about the co-existence of under-consumption, over-consumption and mal-consumption required policy responses. The WHO and FAO worked together and in 2004, the WHO produced a new Global Strategy on Diet, Physical Activity and Health, approved at the World Health Assembly in May 2004.

Thus, a new paradigm was emerging for food and health policy, in which thinking was increasingly framed by four distinct discourses on food and health, each giving priority to different aspects of what could better be seen as a whole. These discourses centred on food's role in: ecology and the environment; food safety; nutrition; and food security.

Activity 9.1

Give examples of how population health can be influenced by (1) the environmental conditions of food supply, (2) food safety, (3) the nutritional content of food and its impact, and (4) having adequate food supplies.

Feedback

There are many examples that can be given for all four. A few are listed below:

Ecology and the environment:

- some foods (and water) are contaminated by environmental chemical pollutants such as lead, mercury, polychlorinated biphenyls (PCBs), dioxins and radionuclides with potentially important health effects. Intoxication with lead could for example lead to neurological impairment in children
- globalization and increasing food trades mean that foods travel longer distances before reaching our plates, thus leading to a greater environmental cost (higher use of non-renewable fossil fuels) including higher pollution rates with their associated potential long-term deleterious health effects
- with improved trade routes, populations with limited reach to diverse food supplies can increase their available food. They can move from a diet restricted by local terrain and growing conditions to one where they have access to other land.

Food safety:

- infection with *Listeria monocytogenes* has a mortality rate of 20–30 per cent
- it is estimated that 10 per cent of patients (particularly children) with haemorrhagic colitis caused by verotoxin-producing *Escherichia coli* later develop the life-threatening complication haemolytic uraemic syndrome
- bovine spongiform encephalopathy (BSE) and avian flu have become a new concern among both the public and decision-makers

Nutrition:

- inadequate vitamin A intake leads to high rates of vitamin A deficiency and blindness in many developing countries, particularly in children

- high intake of energy, fat, and sugar have been associated with overweight, cardiovascular disease and some cancers
- sub-clinical deficiency of vitamin D may increase the risk of bone fractures if osteoporosis is already present

Food security:

- the pattern of consumption of fruit and vegetables is known to remain seasonal in many countries (for example, annual cycle of seasonal excesses and out-of-season shortages in the less economically developed countries of the former Soviet Union), with evidence that seasonal shortage may contribute to cardiovascular disease
- poverty is generally associated with reduced access to adequate food supplies
- in 1995/1997, the prevalence of undernourishment was 18 per cent in the developing world (17 per cent in Asia and the Pacific region, 11 per cent in Latin America and the Caribbean, 9 per cent in the Near East and North Africa, and 33 per cent in Sub-Saharan Africa). In comparison it is less than 2.5 per cent in industrialized countries, but it reaches 7 per cent in countries of the former Soviet Union

Some of these issues will be developed further in the next section.

Nutrition, food security, safety and the environment

The greatest burden of disease over the last half century was premature death from hunger and malnutrition. But epidemiological evidence mounted about the toll from inappropriate nutrition, just not under-consumption. Specifically, from the 1950s, the issue of diet-related degenerative diseases emerged. In the European Union (EU), for instance, by the turn of the century the number of deaths due to poor food safety could be measured in the low thousands, while annually 1.5 million people died prematurely due to heart disease. Despite this evidence, even into the 1990s, policy discourse in rich developed countries was largely dominated by the other two concerns – food safety and to a lesser extent the environment – and by food security (that is, under-consumption and poor availability of supplies) in the developing world.

At the end of the twentieth century, although the environmental aspects of food production such as pesticides and genetic modification attracted considerable global attention from the public and from policy makers, it was food safety that had greater impact on the architecture of governance. New food agencies and laws were rushed through the parliaments of many developed nations, under pressure from consumers and industry alike. Developing countries, seeking export markets, had to create parallel institutions or expertise. Consumer confidence in the food supply chain demanded change. Industry introduced risk-based approaches to hazards, particularly by application of the two management approaches; the first being Hazards Analysis Critical Control Point (HACCP), which sought to identify any weak points in the processing system; and the second being new systems of traceability. Both were designed to improve trust and confidence in complex supply chains.

These concerns remind us that the relationship between policy and evidence is not simple. Even though millions may die prematurely from preventable diseases (think of the response to the annual toll from road traffic injuries or smoking), this toll can somehow be accepted as 'normal'. Yet, the return of communicable diseases was not seen in this way. In the 1980s food poisoning figures began to rise in most affluent societies (they were always higher in developing countries). Yet these were the societies with processing industries that prided themselves on being modern, clean and run to high technical standards. The monitoring of food-borne illness suggested that existing controls were not sufficient. Explanations included new varieties of existing diseases (for example new phage types of *salmonella*); new opportunities for diseases due to production changes; changing food handling in the home; poor skills in food service industries; and so on. Outbreaks of comparatively rare diseases such as *E coli* or *listeriosis* became world news, with the emergence of new types, in the case of *E coli 0157*, and new opportunities, in the case of *listeria monocytogenes*. The emergence of food-borne health problems in rich societies followed the emergence of new systems of food handling, associated with changes in women's role. New technologies such as packaging, cook-chill (premade 'TV dinners') and changes in cooking technology (microwaves) gave greater choice to affluent consumers. Cook-chill / TV dinners, for instance, are preserved at 0–3 degrees Celsius, but provided opportunities for *listeria* (which survives in this temperature range) to survive.

After promising that its modern 'clean' products were more wholesome, as well as giving consumers (particularly mothers) greater choice, this evidence was deeply embarrassing to the food industry, particularly the meat sector. Faced with evidence of rising food-borne pathogens, food manufacturers initially tended to put the onus on consumers to protect themselves, blaming consumers for poor handling, particularly in the case of poultry products, which were and are high risk foods. Despite a high percentage of poultry coming to market with detectable levels of contamination (for example *salmonella*), the publicity about food safety suggested that all would be well if only the 'housewife' stored, de-frosted and cooked 'her' bird correctly. Consumer groups argued a public health position, namely that, while consumer management of food post-purchase is of course important, there is little justification for selling food that is contaminated in the first place! Such levels of risk and faulty goods would be unacceptable in cars, for instance. Who would accept that two thirds of car brakes had faults? Yet in the UK, in the early 1980s, the Public Health Laboratory Service suggested that poultry contamination was of that order. It took a decade of scandals and exposés to shake up UK food supply chains, create a new Food Standards Agency and new laws. Similar processes occurred throughout Europe.

If food safety was able to bring public health issues right into everyone's homes, environmental arguments around food and health took longer, perhaps because they seemed initially more distant in their appeal. From the 1960s, a rising tide of evidence emerged about the environmental 'downside' of agricultural and food modernization. Specific questions emerged about residues from pesticides or fertilizer run-off, as well as general policy and philosophical questions about the earth's carrying capacity and cycles of pollution: what sort of lifestyle can the planet sustain? Can populations be healthy if the environment is not? Which social groups are to blame for 'mining' the world's ecology? Such environmental questions raised 'old' questions for public health about equity. The UN Development Programme has calculated that the richest 20 per cent of the world's populations already accounts for:

- 86 per cent of all total private consumption
- 58 per cent of the world's energy
- 45 per cent of all meat and fish
- 84 per cent of all paper
- 87 per cent of all cars
- 74 per cent of all telephones.

Conversely, the poorest 20 per cent of the world consume 5 per cent or less of all of the above goods and services (UNDP 1998).

To promote global human development as though all can aspire to the lifestyle of the presently better-off assumes not just that there are unlimited resources which there are clearly not (Brown 1996), but also that there are not better ways of redistributing those that exist (Dyson 1996). Proponents of maintaining current policies argue that such questions are defeatist or Luddite or anti-progress (a 'luddite' is a person who resists, distrusts or fears the inevitable changes brought about by new technology) or fail to take account of human ingenuity or are immoral in that the poor are being denied opportunities from which the affluent already benefit. There is some validity in this position but there are also some important questions about the earth's carrying capacity (see also Chapter 10) *and* unequal distribution of its output. The critics of the existing system are not arguing a position of 'less for all' but that for health gains to be won for everyone, policies and structures need to be different (McMichael 2001). In fact, there could be a new ecological wealth for all nations.

To meet projected population growth and consumer demand, for example, global food production must double by 2020. The FAO is optimistic that food supplies can and will grow faster than the world population. Even with eight billion people by 2030, the FAO suggests that:

> they can expect to be better fed with more people having an adequate access to food than in earlier times. . . . Growth in agriculture will continue to outstrip world population growth of 1.2 per cent up to 2015 and 0.8 per cent in the period to 2030.
>
> Source: Food and Agriculture Organization (2000)

This optimism is welcome, but a note of caution is due. It is based on total food supplies, and takes little account of distribution or of ecological constraints.

Food security is the phrase used in policy circles to refer to this goal of having countries able to feed themselves or at the household level everyone being confident that they can be fed. In the post World War II period, food security was deemed to be a national concern. Countries aimed for self-reliance, that is, to feed themselves from their own resources. The over-arching policy goal of under-consuming countries was to increase production. By the end of the twentieth century, the goal of food security had been redefined – to mean not necessarily producing food within borders but to produce enough economic output to be able to afford to buy food on world or regional markets. This shift of definition represented the triumph of neo-liberal approaches to managing economies. Global institutions such as the World Bank and also the FAO had encouraged developing countries to build export markets and to abandon the autarkist tendencies of the post-colonial movement for self-reliance. Economic strategies such as Structural Adjustment Programmes enabled this new approach to take root, but ironically, the environmental critique of current 'efficient' food supply systems is re-awakening interest in reducing unnecessary trade. Transporting food long-distance to earn export currencies is a fragile policy; it depends on commodities retaining their value when, as many export-dependent developing countries have found, they may not. Some policy watchers argue that the new public health in the twenty-first century will require more co-ordination between environmental and public health. Notions such as the concept of **food miles** which refers to the distance that food travels before it gets to consumers are increasingly heard in policy critiques of the working of the General Agreement on Tariffs and Trade (GATT) and the World Trade Organization which has managed the GATT since 1994. Although the majority of food is still produced regionally, if not locally, food trade has been encouraged by liberalization measures. An estimated 90 per cent of the world's food consumption occurs where it is produced (McMichael 2001). For food that is traded, food miles are rising between and within countries.

Policy shift?

As political and consumer arguments about food and health such as those that have been summarized above grew in the 1980s and 1990s, the inadequacy of policy to address the new complexities of health and environment in policy areas such as food became ever clearer. It has been argued that, by the end of the twentieth century, the entire post World War II policy framework had begun to unravel. That policy framework had a number of key characteristics and goals:

- intensification of production
- price reduction and cost control
- labour-shedding
- application of food science and technology throughout the supply chain but especially in agriculture
- an emphasis on raising output and quantity (to tackle the spectre of hunger)
- choice as the key driver of consumer behaviour
- concentration and specialization.

This policy package had been successful in all these respects. Yet by the 1990s, its legitimacy/relevance was being questioned and it seemed to be running out of steam. For instance, the rate of increase of crops yields was slowing down. The opposition to environmental consequences of some of the inputs to intensive agriculture (for example pesticides, fertilizers) was growing in credibility. The evidence of externalized ill health costs questioned the claims of capital efficiency. The food sector's value means that it is sensitive to such outside criticism. However it can be also highly resistant to change; there was furious opposition from some large vested interests – for example sugar, soft drinks, dairy – to the proposals in the 2004 WHO Global Strategy on diet, physical activity and health. But by then, there had been over a decade of food crises throughout the world which had heightened political sensitivity, public health commitment and public attention, a combination which perhaps hastened conflict but also change.

The four public health discourses around food – ecology, safety, nutrition, food security – had come together in a politically explosive manner with the emergence of bovine spongiform encephalopathy (BSE), popularly known as mad cow disease.

First noted in cows in the early/mid-1980s, by 1996, this disease was proven to have 'jumped' to humans as variant Creutzfeld-Jakob Disease (vCJD). First occurring in the UK, the impact of BSE went worldwide and altered public concerns about risk, evidence and confidence in decision-makers. The aetiology of BSE is still unclear but it is presumed either to have jumped species or to have spontaneously mutated and to have been spread by human-created cannibalism among cows. Although comparatively few people have died from vCJD in the UK (148 cases by 7 January 2005), the disease rewrote the public policy landscape. The UK was effectively put into quarantine even though it was a member of the European Union which had legally instituted a single market. BSE reminded policy-makers who had for decades prioritized trade liberalization over other policy considerations that public health cannot be assumed. For practitioners in public health, BSE was a reminder that the era of contagious diseases had not yet ended.

The range of potential tactics within public health strategies to reduce food-related ill health is considerable. Tactics include:

- prevention – on an individual and/or population basis
- health education and promotion
- composition regulation
- labelling and product information
- production controls and monitoring
- product traceability
- product development and specification of niche markets such as low-fat spreads, fortification or other technological change
- genetic screening (if and where possible).

In practice, all of these tactics are drawn upon. One reason that food safety crises can be so devastating politically is that they make a nonsense of consumer responsibility. No label warns consumers that food is or may be contaminated. Food is presumed to be safe at source. In the case of nutrition, however, there has been a fierce debate about the level of consumer choice and information. In the case of obesity, for instance, where scientific evidence is strong on the decline of physical activity, are consumers ignoring information about fat contents of processed foods or unable to act on it? Nestle and others have shown how, if agriculture is producing a high level of fat, somehow it will end up down consumers' throats. Producers' invention of 'low fat' products is accompanied by a plethora of other products replete with hidden fats. In 2002, preliminary legal steps were begun in the United States to confront food industry responsibility for hidden fats and the lack of industry warnings about the potential harm from excessive consumption.

Such cases might alter the intellectual landscape of food and health, and de-emphasize policy attention on food safety. With regard to the impact of poor nutrition on health, most strategic emphasis is given to health education and to appeals for individuals to take responsibility for behavioural change. Table 9.1 draws out some distinctions between individualist and population approaches to food and health.

Two exceptions to the general domination of individualism in modern food and health policy shine out of the policy literature: Thailand and Finland. Both are strongly recommended by the UN Sub-Committee on Nutrition (SCN). Indeed,

Table 9.1 Individualist and population approaches to food and health

Policy focus	*Individualist public health approach*	*Population public health approach*
Relationship to general economy	Trickle down theory; primacy of market solutions; inequality is inevitable	Health as economic determinant; public-private partnerships; inequalities require societal action
Economic direction for health policy	Individual risk; personal insurance; reliance on charity	Social insurance including primary care, welfare and public health services
Morality	Individual responsibility; self-protection; consumerism	Societal responsibility based on a citizenship model
Health accountancy/costs	Costs of ill health not included in price of goods	Costs internalized where possible
Role of the State	Minimal involvement; avoid 'nanny state' action; resources are best left to market forces	Sets common framework; provider of resources; corrective lever on the imbalance between individual and social forces
Consultation with the end user	As consumer; dependent on willingness to pay	Citizenship rights; authentic stakeholder
Approach to food and health	The right to be unhealthy; a medical problem; individual choice is key driver; demand will affect supply; niche markets	The right to be well; entire food supply geared to deliver health

Source: Adapted from Lang and Caraher (2001)

Finland saw major changes in mortality from coronary heart diseases, accounted for mainly by dietary changes (operating through lowering plasma cholesterol and blood pressure levels) that were achieved through community action and the pressure of the consumer demand on the food market. In Thailand, since the mid-1970s nutrition is an integral element of primary health care and community development, each seeking to improve food and nutrition security within households; this provides an infrastructure that has extended beyond government services to include community participation.

The core message is that degenerative disease can be tackled even in developing countries, but there has to be concerted action, for which the precondition is political will. If a country wishes to reduce its toll of diet-related disease, a population approach rather than just individualism or technology is essential. The policy challenge is to meet health objectives not just through choice but by generating a health-enhancing culture, where the reflex is health.

Despite these laudable population-based approaches and interventions, the drift in policy attempts to tackle diet-related ill health is at the individual level. There are good reasons for this. Governments and companies are more comfortable offering a combination of exhortation, advice and individual appeals than in setting out to re-frame food culture. They are frightened of accusations of 'nanny state-ism', an ethic set by the neo-liberal consensus in the face of public health evidence. There has been rapid market concentration (domination by fewer giant companies). They vie for market share and compete in the tough market where tens of thousands of food products jostle for consumer attention; they are uncomfortable with a population approach. The prevailing logic is to appeal to consumers to choose particular products and to take responsibility for themselves. In the corporate world, health is a matter of appealing to people to change diet to make themselves more beautiful, to be culturally positive, to seek sexual advantage, to follow role models, to fit social marketing norms, to respond to advertising, to be targeted by advice leaflets, and so on.

The prognosis

An audit of progress on the four policy fronts outlined here provides a mixed picture. Food safety is poor, particularly in the developing world. Environmental externalities are only just being appreciated. Hunger is proportionately declining but static in absolute numbers. In all countries, obesity and diabetes are rocketing. In many affluent societies the incidence of heart disease is gently declining even though it is high in developing ones. The worry is that with the rapid rise in child obesity, a new second wave of diet-related ill health associated with affluence may be expected. CHD may be contained by statins (a class of drugs that lowers the level of blood cholesterol by reducing the production of cholesterol by the liver), but can such a strategy be honed for diabetes?

The new integrated approach to food and health proposed here is threatening and awesome in its implications. Some sections of the food processing and farming industries – particularly those producing fats, using salts and sugars and making/selling refined foods – are troubled by the new analysis and evidence. Tactics familiar to the tobacco and health discourse have emerged. These range from denial to stonewalling defensive tactics. This has led some people to wonder if the spread of obesity worldwide means that diet and food are the new 'tobacco'? (Daynard 2003). In 2002, financial analysts (for example JPMorgan and UBS-Warburg) began to audit food companies to assess how exposed their product ranges were to accusations that they contributed to obesity.

Activity 9.2

List tactics that some food processing and farming industries can use to reject any integrated approach to food and health.

Feedback

There are several tactics used. They include:

- denial that there is an issue
- refusal to accept evidence
- employment of dissident scientists to cast doubt
- *ad hominem* and personalized attacks on opponents
- strategic company and political alliances

- appeals to Government to consider the economic consequences of constraint
- advertising to 'drown' health messages
- revised marketing
- development of niche products that can offer 'choice'
- preparation of 'escape routes' (diversification of whole industries)
- and so on

The food sector is famously powerful but it went through a period of remarkable change in the late twentieth century creating considerable internal tensions. The interests of farming, processing, retailing, food service, advertising, and so on are rarely identical. In many countries, a number of major companies emerged dominating each sectors. There was also considerable cross-border activity in mergers and acquisitions. Food manufacturing internationalized first but food retailing (supermarkets), food service (restaurants and hotels) and cultural industries (advertising and marketing) followed. This adds complexity to the public health challenge. Diet-related problems may be manifest at the national or local level but significantly framed by powerful forces at the regional or global level.

Food – where science and politics mix

When considering the new public health agenda on food, it can be helpful to recognize that arguments about food are not new. Modern food policy might have to juggle quality, production efficiencies, prices, ownership, education, public health, food security, cultural messages, and more, but these also have their equivalents in governmental debates in earlier centuries. Nevertheless, we can note some important policy shifts over the last century. For instance, the mid twentieth century concern with quantity has now shifted to quality; similarly, attention has moved from macronutrients to micronutrients. Unravelling this history can be illuminating and reminds us how public health is socially constructed. The roots of nutritional science are just such an example.

Dr James Lind, although not the first to note the connection between diet and ill health, is often credited with beginning to put it on a scientific basis in the eighteenth century (although his results were ignored for several decades). With the viability of European/British trade routes dependent upon maintaining the health of ships' crews, the problem of scurvy was a major threat to European expansionism. Scurvy could devastate ships' efficiency by wiping out sailors. In 1753, Lind published the results of the first controlled study showing conclusively that scurvy could be prevented and cured by eating citrus fruit (such as oranges and lemons). This was an early demonstration of how the science of nutrition could contribute to economic and even military well-being, although in this case the main driver was to facilitate trade. State interest in nutrition tends to rise in times of war. Napoleon Bonaparte is famously stated to have said that an army marches on its stomach; he initiated in the late eighteenth century the search that delivered canning, the means to perfect, portable and long-lasting food (and also the French sugar beet industry!). But war is not the only occasion which threatens state interests in relation to nutrition. One reason for policy concern about obesity is its cost even to advanced economies, even more so to economies with less well resourced health care systems.

Two and a half centuries on from Lind, nutrition now covers a vast field ranging from social nutrition (for example studying at risk social groups), nutritional epidemiology (plotting the contribution of diet to diseases), biochemistry (the study of the biochemical interaction of nutrients and the body), sports nutrition (optimizing physiological performance), animal nutrition (ditto) and psychophysiology (including the study of attitudes and food choice).

Partly fuelled by huge pharmaceutical and food industry research funds, it is biochemistry that dominates nutrition today, with researchers seeking the holy grail of a discovery that can be turned into a profitable food ingredient, technology or product. This pursuit began with Sir Gowland Hopkins' discovery in 1901 that human bodies could not make the amino-acid *tryptophan,* an essential part of protein, and later established that it could only be derived from the diet. He demonstrated a principle that without a proper diet, bodily function could be impaired or deficient. Hopkins proved the existence of what he called food hormones or 'vitamines' (sic). The 'e' got dropped and they are now called vitamins. Most were discovered by the end of the 1930s.

Despite increasing scientific sophistication, nutrition – like any subject based on the study of humans – is inevitably framed by social assumptions. Is the pursuit of better nutrition a social duty and right? Or a tool for national efficiency? Throughout the twentieth century, nutrition was a battleground with some forces seeing and using nutrition as an opportunity for social control and others arguing that it could either constrain or liberate human potential. This tension between social control and democracy – 'top down' science versus people-oriented science – still characterizes the world of food.

Although the recent history of public health and food policy has been stormy, it seems reasonable to hope that a new integrated policy approach might emerge. The success or otherwise of the WHO's 2004 Global Strategy and of moves to develop and implement solutions which integrate food policy with other policy areas such as environment and social justice will be important to watch in coming years.

Activity 9.3

'A burger with fries and a packet of cigarettes please' – industry, corporate responsibility and health

A news item in The Lancet (10 August 2002) reported that a group of New Yorkers had filed a lawsuit against four large fast food chains, alleging that their restaurants had knowingly served meals that cause obesity and other diseases. One of the plaintiffs claimed that the marketing efforts by the restaurants misled him into thinking the meals were good for him. In contrast, the representative of the National Restaurant Association said that the claims were 'senseless, baseless and ridiculous'.

In a paper published in the same issue, Ebbeling and collaborators (2002) mount a serious criticism of the role that the food industry has played in the rise of childhood obesity. Read the following extract from their paper and perform the following task.

You are a special adviser on nutrition policy to a health minister in a country of your choice in which childhood obesity is increasingly recognized as a problem. Your minister has a distinguished record of effective action against the tobacco industry and has asked you to prepare a brief setting out the lessons that might be learned from anti-smoking campaigners in their actions against the tobacco industry in tackling the issue of fast food. Describe the arguments that you would include in such a document.

Childhood obesity: public health crisis, common sense cure

Prevention and treatment

Prevention and treatment of obesity ultimately involves eating less and being more physically active. Though this sounds simple, long-term weight loss has proven exceedingly difficult to achieve. The relative intellectual and psychological immaturity of children compared to adults, and their susceptibility to peer pressure, present additional practical obstacles to the successful treatment of childhood obesity. For this reason, most efforts to reduce obesity in children have used either family-based or school-based approaches, though pharmacological and surgical treatments are also available.

Limitations of current approaches

Although a few family-based studies produced significant long-term weight loss in motivated individuals, the overall success of non-surgical approaches has been disappointing, leading some specialists to conclude that treatment of obese children, which aims to establish a normal bodyweight, is unrealistically optimistic. Why is substantial long-term weight loss so difficult to achieve? One explanation is that the dietary and physical activity prescriptions used in family-based and school-based programmes might not be particularly efficacious. Indeed, most dietary interventions focus on reduction of fat intake, even though dietary fat might not be an important cause of obesity. Remarkably few paediatric obesity studies have sought to ascertain the effect of dietary composition on bodyweight, controlling for treatment intensity, physical activity, and behavioural modification techniques. With respect to physical activity, many studies have used conventional programmed exercise prescriptions, although increasing lifestyle activity or reducing sedentary behaviours might be better for long-term weight control. A second explanation for the difficulty in obtaining long-term weight loss is that adverse environmental factors overwhelm behavioural and educational techniques designed to reduce energy intake and augment physical activity.

The toxic environment

Battle and Brownell (1996) wrote, 'it is hard to envision an environment more effective than ours [in the USA] for producing . . . obesity'. This statement probably applies to much of the developed world and, increasingly, to some developing countries. Several pervasive environmental factors promote energy intake and limit energy expenditure in children, undermining individual efforts to maintain a healthy bodyweight.

Food quality, policy, and advertising

In the late 1970s, children in the USA ate 17 per cent of their meals away from home, and fast foods accounted for 2 per cent of total energy intake. By the mid-1990s to late-1990s, the proportion of meals eaten away from home nearly doubled to 30 per cent, and fast food consumption increased five-fold, to 10 per cent of total energy intake. From 1965 to 1996, per capita daily soft drink consumption among 11–18-year old children rose from 179 g to 520 g for boys and from 148 g to 337 g for girls. There are 170 000 fast food restaurants in the USA alone. These trends have been driven, in part, by enormous advertising and marketing expenditures by the food industry, including an estimated US$12·7 billion directed at children and their parents. Marketing campaigns specifically target children, linking brand names with toys, games, movies, clothing, collectibles, educational tools, and even baby bottles. By contrast, the advertising budget for the US National Cancer Institute's '5-A-Day' programme to promote consumption of fruits and vegetables was $1·1 million in 1999. Large meals, often containing a child's total daily energy requirements, can be purchased for little additional cost over smaller portions, whereas fresh fruits and vegetables tend to be less readily available and comparatively more expensive. Furthermore, fast-food and soft-drink vending machines pervade schools. That US children overconsume added sugar and saturated fat, and underconsume fruits, non-starchy vegetables, fibre, and some micronutrients, is therefore not surprising.

Sedentary lifestyle

Availability of sedentary pursuits, including television, video games, computers, and the internet, has risen greatly. Children in the USA spend 75 per cent of their waking hours being inactive, compared with remarkably little time in vigorous physical activity; estimated at only 12 min per day. Opportunities for physical activity have decreased for various reasons. Physical education, typically considered less important than academic disciplines, has been eliminated in some school districts. In schools that do offer physical education, large class size and lack of equipment present barriers to successful programme implementation. After-school participation in unstructured activities can be limited, because of absence of pavements (sidewalks), bike paths, safe playgrounds, and parks in many neighbourhoods. Moreover, our culture places a premium on convenience: the car is preferred to walking, the lift to stairs, and the remote control to manual adjustment. These cultural forces arguably culminate in the drive-through window of fast-food restaurants, where a maximum of energy can be obtained with a minimum of exertion.

Barriers to change

Many special interests contribute to this problem of obesity, actively or passively, for financial reasons. The food industry, which generated almost $1 trillion in sales in 2000, spends enormous amounts of money to promote consumption of high calorie processed foods of poor nutritional quality. Underfunded school districts make money by establishing pouring rights contracts with soft drink companies, allowing them to place vending machines on school property and to sell beverages at school events. To save money, schools have subcontracted lunch programmes to corporate food services, encouraging the sale of high profit, low quality foods, including fast food. At the same time, budgetary pressures have led to reduction or elimination of physical education classes. Many communities do not adequately invest in urban environments that encourage physical activity, and instead pursue policies that favour real estate development to open space. Parents, for various socioeconomic reasons, work excessively long hours, leaving little time to prepare home-cooked meals and supervise non-sedentary activities. Professional nutritional societies maintain lucrative relations through sponsorships and endorsement with the food industry, creating a potential conflict of interest. According to the Center for Responsive Politics, candidates for the US Congress and presidency received more than $12 million between 1989 and 2000 from the sugar industry. Might these political contributions have a corrosive effect on regulatory efforts to revise national nutritional policy? Finally, the US health insurance industry reimburses poorly, if at all, for medical treatment of childhood obesity. However, all these short-term financial incentives are trivial when compared with the long-term costs to individuals and society. Annual hospital costs alone related to paediatric obesity in the USA approximate $127 million, and the effect of obesity on individuals is incalculable. Sadly, 10 per cent of children with type 2 diabetes develop renal failure, requiring dialysis or resulting in death by young adulthood, according to a preliminary report.

Conclusion

Almost three decades ago, an editorial in *The Lancet* called for efforts to prevent obesity in childhood. Since then, the worldwide prevalence of childhood obesity has risen several-fold. Obese children develop serious medical and psychosocial complications, and are at greatly increased risk of adult morbidity and mortality. The increasing prevalence and severity of obesity in children, together with its most serious complication, type 2 diabetes, raise the spectre of myocardial infarction becoming a paediatric disease. This public health crisis demands increased funding for research into new dietary, physical activity, behavioural, environmental, and pharmacological approaches for prevention and treatment of obesity, and improved reimbursement for effective family-based and school-based programmes. However, because this epidemic was not caused by inherent biological defects, increased funding for research and health care, focusing on new treatments, will probably not solve the problem of paediatric obesity without fundamental measures to effectively detoxify the environment (Figure 9.1).

A common sense approach to prevention and treatment of childhood obesity

Home	Set aside time for Health meals Physical activity Limit television viewing
School	Fund mandatory physical education Establish stricter standards for school lunch programmmes Eliminate unhealthy foods – eg, soft drinks and candy from vending machines Provide healthy snacks through concession stands and vending machines
Urban design	Protect open spaces Build pavements (sidewalks), bike paths, parks, playgrounds, and pedestrian zones
Health care	Improve insurance coverage for effective obesity treatment
Marketing and media	Consider a tax on fast food and soft drinks Subsidise nutritious foods – eg, fruits and vegetables Require nutrition labels on fast-food packaging Prohibit food advertisement and marketing directed at children Increase funding for public health campaigns for obesity prevention
Politics	Regulate political contributions from the food industry

Figure 9.1 Suggested approach to prevention and treatment of childhood obesity

Source: Ebbeling and collaborators (2002)

Although these measures require substantial political will and financial investment, they should yield a rich dividend to society in the long term.

Feedback

Possible points include:

- The importance of tackling head on the issue of individual responsibility versus collective/environmental action – 'healthy choices need to be the easy choices'
- Evidence of harm is necessary but not sufficient to motivate policy change – we already have sufficient knowledge to act now on fast foods, rather then using the call for research as a means of delaying action. Some countries, correctly, took action to control tobacco when we still had much to learn about the harm it caused. However it was clear that we had enough evidence that it was dangerous to justify action.
- Decisions to act need not wait for evidence of the effectiveness of interventions – Initial tobacco control interventions were not evidence based but represented sound judgment at the time: we know now what has worked for tobacco and can adapt some elements immediately.
- We need to look at the wider issues involved in food production, for example concerns of farmers. For tobacco control, this meant addressing all forms of tobacco use and not just cigarettes; and considering the concerns of tobacco farmers and providing convincing evidence that their livelihoods were not under threat in the mid-term. For the diet/nutrition area this will be more complex and require that close interaction be sought between those working to address hunger, micronutrient deficiencies and under-nutrition in general and those working to develop policies for overweight and chronic disease prevention. The goal should be to promote the optimal diet for all.
- We have learned from tobacco that the more comprehensive the package of measures considered, the greater the impact.
- Media-savvy individual and institutional leadership is extremely important.
- Change in support for tobacco control took decades of dedicated effort by all, so we should not expect immediate results.
- Modest, well-spent funds can have a massive impact. But without clear goals they may not be sustainable.
- Rules of engagement with the tobacco and food industries may need to be different but there is scope for those involved in promoting healthy lifestyles in both areas to learn from each other.

These points draw on a report on lessons from tobacco control compiled for Oxford Vision 2020, a movement dedicated to tackling the growing tide of chronic diseases globally. We should also note continuing efforts at national levels to produce comprehensive multi-sectoral approaches to obesity, a symbol of the challenges facing food and health practitioners (see for example the report by Nesle and Jacobson (2000) for an American example).

Summary

In this chapter you learnt about the development of thinking on nutrition and health and the need for a new integrated approach to improve dietary intake and health. The chapter described the key features in the evolution of thinking about the importance of diet on health and the four foci in modern thinking (food safety, nutrition, sustainable development and food security). It discussed the social forces affecting changes in dietary behaviour, and the key strengths and weakness of current arguments about the impact of social change on nutrition and health. Finally, it examined how food illustrates the links between human and environmental health and suggested some public policy pointers for the future.

References

Battle EK and Brownell KD (1996) Confronting a rising tide of eating disorders and obesity: treatment vs prevention and policy. *Addict Behav* **21**, 755–65.

Brown LR (1996) *Tough choices: facing the challenge of food scarcity*. London: Earthscan.

Daynard RA (2003) Lessons from tobacco for the Obesity Control Movement. *J Public Health Policy* **24**, 291–4.

Dyson T (1996) *Population and food: global trends and future prospects*. London, Routledge.

Ebbeling CB, Dorota DT, Ludwig DS (2002) Childhood obesity: public health crisis, common sense cure. *The Lancet* **360**, 473–82.

Food and Agriculture Organization (2000) *Agriculture: Towards 2015/2030 technical interim report April 2000*. Rome: Food and Agriculture Organization Economic & Social Department.

Lang T, Caraher M (2001) International Public Health. In Pencheon D, Melzer D (eds.) *Oxford Handbook of Public Health*. Oxford, Oxford University Press, pp.168–76.

McMichael P (2001) The impact of globalisation, free trade and technology on food and nutrition in the new millennium. *Proc Nutr Soc* **60**, 215–20.

Nesle M, Jacobson MF (2000) Halting the obesity epidemic: a public health approach. *Public Health Rep* **115**, 12–24.

UNDP (1998) World Development Report, quoted in UNEP (2002) *Global Environment Outlook 3*. London: Earthscan / UNEP p. 35.

Further reading

Lang T, Heasman M (2004) *Food Wars: the global battle for mouths, minds and markets*. London: Earthscan. This book discusses the impact of the growth of a single global market on what we eat, with corresponding implications for public health.

Nestle M (2002) *Food Politics*. Berkley CA: University of California Press. This book offers a critique of the role of the food industry in shaping our diets, and by extension our health.

Puska P, Tuomilehto J, Nissinen A, Vartiainen E (eds.) (1995) *The North Karelia project: 20 year results and experiences*. Helsinki: National Public Health Institute of Finland. [This book will introduce you to the different measures used in Finland to help improve population health.

The Commission on the Nutrition Challenges of the 21st Century (2000) Ending Malnutrition by 2020: An Agenda for Change in the Millennium. *Food and Nutrition Bulletin (United Nations)* 21 (3, Suppl). This report proposes major new initiatives to speed up the aid process to eradicate malnutrition.

World Health Organization (2003) Diet, nutrition and the prevention of chronic diseases. WHO Technical Report Series No. 916. Geneva: World Health Organization. This report examines the science base of the relationship between diet and physical activity patterns, and the major nutrition-related chronic diseases.

10 Drains, dustbins and diseases

Overview

Environmental issues, in particular the potential health effects of pollution, are a growing cause of concern among populations around the world. For many years people have pointed an accusing finger at motor vehicles and fuel combustion in residential, commercial and industrial heating and cooling and coal-burning power plants. However, the potential health hazard of commonly adopted waste disposal systems such as landfill and incineration are also examined more closely nowadays. In addition, indoor air pollution is now recognized as a major contributor to disease burden with major impacts particularly in developing countries. Health protection being a key element of public health, the protection of the populations from toxic chemical substances coming from all sources of pollution need to be closely examined as it links with other aspects of public health practice. This chapter will discuss the environmental and health aspects of waste disposal systems. You will also be introduced to the health impacts of indoor and outdoor air pollution. Other examples such as water management would also be relevant but are not discussed here.

Learning objectives

After completing this session you will be able to:

- **describe local health impacts of landfill and incineration**
- **describe global ecological impacts of waste disposal activities**
- **discuss the health impacts of outdoor and indoor air pollution for different groups of people in developed and developing countries**

Key terms

Ecological footprint Accounting tool for ecological resources developed by the Task Force on Healthy and Sustainable Communities at the University of British Columbia (Canada). It corresponds to the area of productive land and aquatic ecosystems required to produce the resources used, and to assimilate the wastes produced, by a defined population at a specified material standard of living, wherever on Earth that land may be located.

Environmental or occupational exposure Any contact between a substance in an environmental medium (for example water, air, soil) and the surface of the human body (for example skin, respiratory tract); after uptake into the body it is referred to as dose.

Exposure assessment Is the study of distribution and determinants of substances or factors affecting human health (Nieuwenhuijsen 2003).

Precautionary principle This principle states that when there is reasonable suspicion of harm, lack of scientific uncertainty or consensus must not be used to postpone preventative action to avoid serious or irreversible harm.

Waste and health: an overview

The composition of goods is very complex. Think for example of a computer, microwave oven, or television set. You can easily imagine that each of these goods is made of a vast number of components, each in turn made of a vast number of substances. In order to have a better idea of how these products could affect the health of a population, you could decide to analyse their specific chemical composition and the health aspects of their production and disposal, taking into account the accompanying environmental and social impacts.

Activity 10.1

Let's take a specific example. Think about two different consumer goods: a Ferrari and a personal computer. List some hazardous materials coming from them.

Feedback

A car is a heap of waste. Raw materials for a Ferrari come from all continents, are packaged in Italy, and get dispersed in the environment usually, but not always, in the country where it has been purchased. Many hazardous materials come from cars and are dispersed in the environment. These include for example:

- headlight bulbs and anti-lock braking systems which contain mercury
- anti-corrosion coating which contains some hexavalent chromium and cadmium
- the battery which contains lead
- the catalytic converter, which contains platinum

Other substances include arsenic, polyvinyl chloride, and polychlorinated biphenyls.

A particular problem is posed by compound substances, such as tyres and plastics included in cars: they are more difficult to recycle than the steel and metals.

Electronic and electrical equipment is responsible for an increasing proportion of all hazardous waste produced in developed societies. Examples of hazardous materials in a personal computer include:

- plastic which contains brominated flame retardants (they produce dioxins when burned)
- cathode ray tubes (in the monitor) which contain lead
- the switches and gas discharge lamps which contain mercury.

The United Kingdom (UK) has agreed in principle with European member states that new legislation will compel industry to 'take-back' old electronic and electrical equipment and become responsible for its disposal. This is aimed at reducing the dispersal of valuable materials such as metals and plastics in the environment, where they represent a health hazard.

Local health impacts of landfill and incineration

Landfill and incineration are the most commonly adopted waste disposal options. Unfortunately, both options result in the dispersal in the environment of materials hazardous to health.

Landfill

Activity 10.2

Figure 10.1 shows a schematic representation of a landfill, with its sources, pathways and receptors. Describe the fate of the waste materials disposed in it.

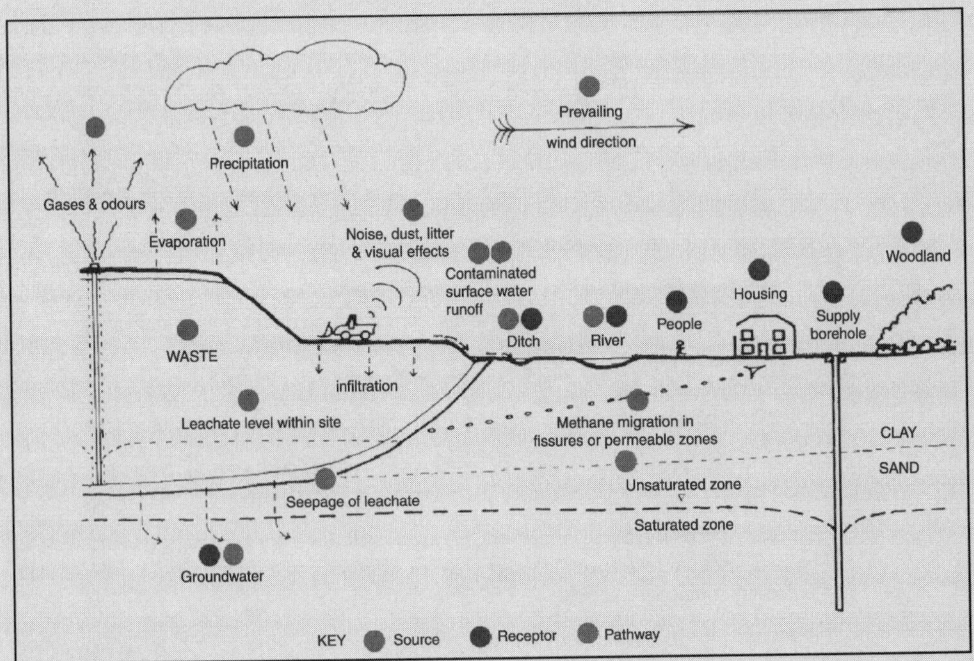

Figure 10.1 Schematic representation of a landfill

Source: Vrijheid (2001)

Feedback

We can see that gases and odours are emitted from the surface, going into the air. Contaminated rainwater infiltrates the landfill and leachate (water seeping from the waste) is produced. Unfortunately it contains a mixture of the landfill materials and can amount to thousands litres per day. Rainwater also leads to the production of contaminated surface water which runs off from the landfill to contaminate ditch and river water. The leachate and seepage in the landfill site infiltrates groundwater and migrates in the soil in unsaturated zones with the potential of affecting the quality of the water supplied by the borehole. Methane is also produced by the landfill; it migrates through fissure or permeable zones.

In the UK, as in many other countries, landfill has been the most popular option for waste disposal. A study by the Small Area Health Statistics Unit (SAHSU) (Elliott and colleagues 2001) found that over 80 per cent of the UK population lives within 2 km of a landfill. In the past, highly hazardous materials have often been disposed of in the same sites as municipal solid waste, in so called co-disposal sites, however this practice is being phased out.

Indeed, due to concerns across Europe, a case-control study – the EUROHAZCON STUDY – was conducted to look at the risk of birth defects in the vicinity of hazardous waste sites (Dolk *et al.* 1998). The study showed an increasing risk of congenital malformations with increasing vicinity to a site, having controlled for socio-economic status. The public concern from these results persuaded the UK government ministry responsible for the environment to review research priorities in relation to waste disposal and to consider funding a national case-control study of landfills and malformations. In addition, the UK Department of Health decided to commission further research on this topic. One of the outputs was a review on the potential teratogenicity (potential to cause birth abnormalities) of substances emanating from landfill published in 2001 (Sullivan and colleagues 2001). This review classified substances according to their potential teratogenicity. The substances for which animal and/or human data demonstrate clear teratogenic potential (or potential for other important reproductive effects) at relatively low doses/exposures (thus being the most likely candidates for teratogenic effects of landfill waste) include:

- Benzene
- 1,3 Butadiene
- Carbon disulphide
- Chloroform
- 1,2-Dichloroethylene
- Ethylbenzene
- Formaldehyde
- Methyl chloride
- Tetrachloroethylene
- Trichloroethylene
- Vinyl chloride

Cancer is the other health concern of people resident near landfills. Evidence is weak but cannot be entirely dismissed. Mutagenicity (potential to cause cancer) tests conducted on leachate show a higher mutagenic activity of leachate than various types of surface water. However much more work is needed before anything conclusive can be said about the risk of cancer in the vicinity of municipal landfill sites.

Incineration

Though cancer has also been a concern in the vicinity of incinerators, dioxin and its dispersal via the food chain has been more prominent among the concerns of local residents. Another aspect, which public health authorities have been asked to comment on, is the potential health hazard represented by incinerator ash. This has a very high concentration of metals and dioxins. A group of experts on incinerator ash reviewed different types of disposal practice. The preferred disposal practices are either leachate containment and collection, or controlled contaminant release. The latter option means that disposal should be supported by a monitoring programme to allow control of the disposal of the hazardous components of the material.

In summary, direct impacts from landfill and incineration have not been demonstrated clearly by epidemiological studies, however there are many potential areas where health impacts are plausible and community concerns cannot be ignored based on the little evidence currently available.

Ecological impacts of waste

We depend on nature for the supply of our food and energy, the absorption of our waste products, and for other life-support services. But in order to preserve this situation, we must ensure that nature's productivity isn't used more quickly than it can be renewed, and that waste isn't discharged more quickly than nature can absorb it. The impacts of waste production on the ecosystem are indeed very hazardous and they are considered by some to be more worrying than the direct health impacts of waste.

In order to find out whether nature provides enough resources to secure good living conditions, the Task Force on Healthy and Sustainable Communities at the University of British Columbia has developed an accounting tool for ecological resources: the ecological footprint. It is a measure of how sustainable our lifestyles are and is calculated as the area of productive land and aquatic ecosystems required to produce the resources used, and to assimilate the wastes produced, by a defined population at a specified material standard of living, wherever on Earth that land may be located.

An example of the application of the concept of ecological footprint is offered by a study in Liverpool, England (Barrett and Scott 2001). This study examined the ecological sustainability of the city and concluded that:

- The average Liverpool resident requires 4.15 hectares of land (compared with 4.9 hectares for the UK average) to supply him or her with all the necessary resources, transportation needs, and use and disposal of those resources. In comparison, 80.3 per cent of the world's population has an ecological footprint less than 4 hectares, and their total share of the world's footprint is 38.3 per cent, with an average footprint of 1.36 hectare.
- For the city of Liverpool, waste had the highest impact (1.6 hectare/person), followed by the provision of resources (1.1 hectare/person), transport of passengers and freight (0.7 hectare/person), utilities (0.63 hectare/person), biodiversity protection (0.3 hectare/person), and buildings and land (0.1 hectare/person).
- A sustainable ecological footprint is 2 hectares/per capita. This could be

achieved by working on three key areas: energy (reduction of energy consumption, domestic waste, and water (reduction of leakage and domestic use consumption)). With regards to domestic waste, recycling alone would not be sufficient (the city will need to recycle 93 per cent of domestic waste by 2021) and waste minimization schemes are essential.

A similar study but applied to the whole planet (Wackernagel and colleagues 2002) suggested that the Earth as a whole has used more than the total capacity of its ecological services (water, soil capacity) for a few years already, and that we run the risk that the capacity of soil and water systems to regenerate may be overcome. This conclusion was based on several assumptions, including the fact that it is possible to keep track of most of the resources we use and the wastes we generate, that most of the resource and waste flows can be measured according to the biologically productive area needed to maintain them, that the planet can be assessed in terms of 'global hectares' (representing the average productive hectare on Earth for that particular year), that natural supply of ecological services can be measured in the same way, and that area demand can exceed area supply, a phenomenon called ecological overshoot. The ecological overshoot described in this study could have public health as well as environmental impacts.

A waste management hierarchy thus conveys the idea that waste reduction and minimization should be considered a higher priority than recycling, and recycling a higher priority than either landfill or incineration. This appears justified based on consideration of both (local) health and ecological effects of waste production and disposal. However, recycling rates in Europe remain relatively low, particularly in the UK (Figure 10.2). However one could argue that waste minimization has not been pursued with the desirable vigour across all of Europe, and perhaps the UK with its peculiar flexibility of approach to industrial development can seize the waste minimization challenge more effectively than most.

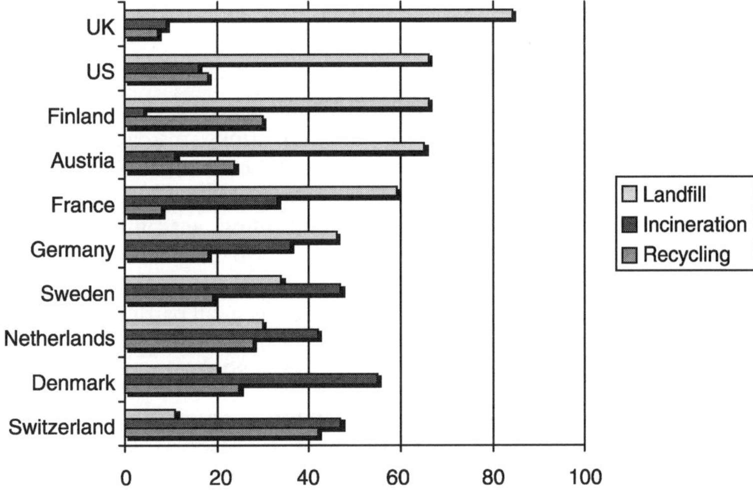

Figure 10.2 Waste disposal (%) in selected European countries and in the United States

Source: Vrijheid (2001)

From the local public health point of view, waste is an issue that is not going to go away, with many communities dissatisfied with the passive approach of many official agencies. There are examples in the UK of new housing having received planning permission right next to the edge of landfills, inevitably leading to complaints about odour and health effects.

The possible contributions that public health professionals can make to waste management, locally, nationally and internationally, involve policy change and local action. They include:

- surveys and models of exposure in vicinity to landfills
- meetings with communities and health protection teams
- health surveys
- advice on the health impacts of proposed waste management activities (landfill and incineration) under Integrated Pollution Prevention and Control (IPPC) legislation of the European Union
- contribution to regional and local waste strategies, including health impact assessments (see Chapter 6).

Public health professionals who would like to contribute to waste management can also collaborate with several agencies outside the health system, including the Environment Agency, academic units, and others, to develop their work in this difficult area.

Indoor and outdoor pollution

Air pollution, both indoor and outdoor, is a major environmental health problem affecting developed and developing countries alike. It comes from sources of dust, gases and smoke, and is generated mainly by human activities. Air pollution has numerous adverse health effects starting from modest transient changes in the respiratory tract and impaired lung function, continuing to restricted activity and reduced performance, emergency room visits and hospital admissions, and to mortality (World Health Organization Regional Office for Europe 2004).

During the last decades, attention has focused mainly on pollutants in outdoor air (for example particulate matters, ozone, nitrogen dioxide) or on indoor hazards such as asbestos or environmental tobacco smoke. However, it is often forgotten that more than two billion people worldwide continue to depend on solid fuels, including biomass fuels (wood, dung, agricultural residues) and coal, for their energy needs. Using these on open fires or traditional stoves (for cooking or heating) results in high levels of indoor air pollution that contains a variety of health-damaging pollutants such as small particles and carbon monoxide. Overall, indoor air pollution would be responsible for 2.7 per cent of the global burden of disease (World Health Organization 2002).

Our dependence on solid fuels for energy can also have a major negative impact on the environment, for example if it leads to deforestation (for example in areas where wood fuel is scarce and the demand for wood outweighs nature re-growth) which can be associated with soil erosion and serious mud slides (such as those observed in Haiti in the summer of 2004 following tropical storm Jeanne) or to greenhouse gas emissions (for example because biomass stoves used in developing country homes typically have a low efficiency, thus leading to the lost of a large percentage of the fuel energy as products of incomplete combustion with an important greenhouse effect).

Activity 10.3

A non-governmental organization working in the developing world has argued that international agencies are paying too much attention to outdoor air pollution at a time when many millions of people in poorer countries are exposed to high levels of indoor air pollution. They argue that indoor air pollution may be more easily addressed in the short term than some of the problems of outdoor pollution. You have been invited by the United Nations Environment Programme to prepare a short briefing paper setting out the arguments that might be used to give priority to each of the two sources of pollution. What would be the key points that you would consider? As a guide you can use the papers from Bruce and collaborators (2000) and from McMichael (2000), as well as documents from the World Health Organization (2005) (all are available from the internet).

Feedback

- Burden of disease attributable to each type of exposure
- Understanding of causal pathways leading from exposure to disease
- Availability of effective interventions
- Feasibility of interventions
- Impact on for health of each type of exposure
- Potential to intervene
- Unequal burden of pollution by social class/ environmental equity/ justice
- Unequal burden of outdoor/indoor pollution by development stage of country
- Precautionary principle and approach, what influence on setting standards
- Process of setting standards for air quality, influence of scientific, policy, public/ societal factors in framing the question and the solutions

Summary

In this chapter we discussed the health and environmental aspects of waste, as well as air pollution. We examined the local health impacts of landfill and incineration as well as the global ecological impacts of waste disposal activities. We also discussed the health impacts of outdoor and indoor air pollution for different groups of people in developed and developing countries.

References

Barrett J, Scott A (2001) *An ecological footprint of Liverpool: developing sustainable scenarios. A detailed examination of ecological sustainability*. Stockholm: Stockholm Environment Institute.

Bruce N, Perez-Padilla R, Albalak R (2000) Indoor air pollution in developing countries: a major environmental and public health challenge. *Bull World Health Organ* **78**, 1078–92. (available on http://whqlibdoc.who.int/bulletin/2000/Number%209/78(9)1078–1092.pdf, last visited 2 February 2005).

Dolk H, Vrijheid M, Armstrong B, Abramsky L, Bianchi F, Garne E, Nelen V, Robert E, Scott JE, Stone D, Tenconi R (1998) Risk of congenital anomalies near hazardous-waste landfill sites in Europe: the EUROHAZCON study. *The Lancet* **352**, 423–7.

Elliott *et al.* (2001) Risk of adverse birth outcomes in populations living near landfill sites. *Br Med J* **323**, 363–8.

McMichael AJ (2000) The urban environment and health in a world of increasing globalization: issues for developing countries. *Bull World Health Organ* **78**, 1117–26 (available on http://whqlibdoc.who.int/bulletin/2000/Number%209/78(9)1117–1126.pdf, last visited 2 February 2005).

Nieuwenhuijsen M (ed) (2003) *Exposure assessment in occupational and environmental epidemiology*. New York: Oxford University Press.

Sullivan FM, Barlow SM, McElhatton PR (2001) A review of the potential teratogenicity of substances emanating from landfill sites. London: Department of Health.

Vrijheid M (2001) *Risk of congenital anomalies in the vicinity of hazardous waste landfill sites (thesis)*. London: University of London.

Wackernagel M, Schulz NB, Deumling D, Callenas Linares A, Jenkins M, Kapos V, Monfreda C, Loh J, Myers N, Norgaard R, Randers J (2002) Tracking the ecological overshoot of the human economy. *Proc Natl Acad Sci* 99: 9266–71.

World Health Organization (2002). *World Health Report 2002*. Geneva: World Health Organization.

World Health Organization (2005) *Global burden of disease due to indoor air pollution*. Geneva: World Health Organization (available on http://www.who.int/indoorair/health_impacts/burden_global/en/, last visited 2 February 2005).

World Health Organization Regional Office for Europe (2004) *Health aspects of air pollution. Results from the WHO project 'Systematic review of health aspects of air pollution in Europe'*. Copenhagen: World Health Organization Regional Office for Europe.

Further reading

McMichael T (2001) *Human frontiers, environments and disease. Past patterns, uncertain futures*. Cambridge: Cambridge University Press.

National Research Council (2000) *Waste incineration and public health. National Research Council, Committee on Health Effects of Waste Incineration, Board on Environmental Studies and Toxicology, Commission on Life Sciences*. Washington, DC: National Academy Press.

Vrijheid M (2000) Health effects of residence near hazardous waste landfill sites: A review of epidemiologic literature. *Environ Health Perspect* **108(Suppl 1)**, 101–12.

Glossary

Addiction Dependence on something that is psychologically or physically habit-forming.

Age-standardization Way of controlling for age so that we can compare rates of deaths or disease in populations with different age structures.

Avoidable mortality Premature deaths that should not occur in the presence of timely and effective health care.

Burden of disease A measure of the physical, emotional, social and financial impact that a particular disease has on the health and functioning of the population.

Discrimination Direct discrimination occurs where one person is treated less favourably than another is, has been, or would be treated in a comparable situation on grounds of race, ethnic origin or other factor; indirect discrimination occurs where an apparently neutral provision, criterion or practice would put persons with a given trait (for example racial or ethnic origin) at a particular disadvantage compared with other persons, unless that provision, criterion or practice is objectively justified by a legitimate aim and the means of achieving that aim are appropriate and necessary.

Ecological footprint Accounting tool for ecological resources developed by the Task Force on Healthy and Sustainable Communities at the University of British Columbia (Canada). It corresponds to the area of productive land and aquatic ecosystems required to produce the resources used, and to assimilate the wastes produced, by a defined population at a specified material standard of living, wherever on Earth that land may be located.

Environmental or occupational exposure Any contact between a substance in an environmental medium (for example water, air, soil) and the surface of the human body (for example skin, respiratory tract); after uptake into the body it is referred to as dose.

Exposure assessment Is the study of distribution and determinants of substances or factors affecting human health.

Food miles Distance that foods travel from where they are grown to where they are ultimately purchased or consumed by the end user.

Food security Physical and economic access for everyone and at all times to enough foods that are nutritious, safe, personally acceptable and culturally appropriate, produced and distributed in ways that are environmentally sound and just.

Germ theory The theory that all contagious diseases are caused by micro-organisms.

Globalization A set of processes that are changing the nature of human interaction by intensifying interactions across certain boundaries that have hitherto served to separate individuals and population groups. These spatial, temporal and cognitive boundaries have been increasingly eroded, resulting in new forms of social organization and interaction across these boundaries.

Health expectancy Summary measure of population health that estimates the expectation of years of life lived in various health states.

Health gap Summary measure of population health that estimates the gap between the current population health and a normative goal for population health.

Health inequalities Differences in health experience and health status between countries, regions and socioeconomic groups.

Health system A health system includes all the activities whose primary purpose is to promote, restore or maintain health.

Health system goals Improving the health of the population they serve, responding to people's expectations, providing financial protection against the cost of ill health.

International Refers to cross-border flows that are, in principle, possible to regulate by national governments.

Intersectoral action for health The promotion of health through the involvement of actors in other sectors, such as transport, housing, or education.

Libertarianism Philosophical approach that favours individualism, with a free-market economic policy and non-intervention by government.

Life course epidemiology Study of the long-term effects on later health or disease risk of physical or social exposures during gestation, childhood, adolescence, young adulthood or later adult life.

Life expectancy The average number of years a person can expect to live on average in a given population.

Nutrition transition Process of change in which populations shift their diet from a restricted diet to one higher in saturated fat, sugar and refined foods, and low in fibre; as a result, diet-related ill health previously associated with affluent Western societies takes root in developing countries.

Precautionary principle This principle states that when there is reasonable suspicion of harm, lack of scientific uncertainty or consensus must not be used to postpone preventative action to avoid serious or irreversible harm.

Public health The science and art of promoting health and preventing disease through the organized efforts of society.

Regeneration Reviving run-down or deprived areas, for example by providing employment and training schemes, improving housing, developing transport links, offering local health services, landscaping and creating green spaces from derelict areas etc.

Summary measures of population health Indicators that combine information about mortality and health states to summarize the health of a population into a single number.

Tort Legal term used to describe a wrongful act, resulting in harm or loss to another person or their property, on which a civil action for damages may be brought.

Transnational (as opposed to international) Refers to transborder flows that largely circumvent national borders and can thus be beyond the control of national governments alone.

Index